Packin' It in Wisconsin

WEST
SIDE
PUBLISHING

Contributors: Nan Bialek, Brian D'Ambrosio, Linda Godfrey, Jonathan Kelley, Nina Konrad, Joan Loshek, Christy Nadalin, Jay Rath, Mike Sandrolini, Sue Sveum, Lynda Twardowski, Amanda Wegner, Jennifer Plattner Wilkinson

Factual Verification: Kathryn Holcomb

Cover Illustration: Simon Fenton

Interior Illustrations: Art Explosion, Linda Howard Bittner, Jupiter Images, Robert Schoolcraft

Contents

Welcome to Wisconsin!............7

Laura Ingalls Wilder: From
   Little House to Big Success.....8

Everybody Loves the Circus!...10

Lager Looms Largest...............12

Taste of Wisconsin:
   Cranberry Quiz.....................13

Fast Facts..............................15

America's Only King................16

Wisconsin Symbols Say it All ...19

A Culinary Tradition:
   The Wisconsin Fish Fry.........22

Talkin' Wisconsin.....................24

Holy Hill, Batman!...................25

Bucky Badger's Winning Ways...27

Fast Facts..............................30

Quiz......................................31

Crazy Legs Propelled Elroy Hirsh
   to the End Zone...and Fame 32

Medieval Milwaukee................34

Timeline................................36

Taste of Wisconsin: Foie Gras 37

Milwaukee's "Mr. Showman"...38

Ski Wisconsin: The American
   Birkebeiner............................40

Taste of Wisconsin:
   Maple Syrup.........................42

Viva la Bubbler!.......................44

Fast Facts..............................45

Aldo Leopold: Friend of
   the Environment...................46

You Can Thank Wisconsin.......48

Legendary Lake Mills.............49

Fast Facts..............................52

Bay View Tragedy...................53

It's All Political: Quiz...............56

Long Live the
   Crime-Fighting King.............59

Cheeseheads Unite.................60

Wisconsin's Three
   UFO Capitals.......................62

Talkin' Wisconsin.....................63

TV Shows Feel at
   Home in Wisconsin...............64

Wisconsin Cow Chip
   Throwing Fun.......................67

Wisconsin's Federal
   Fearmonger...........................68

Fast Facts..............................70

Waters of Wisconsin.................71

Clinton's "Mad Man" 74

From the Badger State
   to Tinsel Town 76

Pettit Center Keeps Fast Pace....77

Wisconsin Olympic
   Athletes Are Golden 79

Taste of Wisconsin: Pasties 80

Baseball's Rodney Dangerfield...82

Bragging Rights 84

The Beasts Are Back 85

Peshtigo Fire Sparks
   Devastation............................88

Fast Facts.................................91

The Wright Stuff 92

You Can Thank Wisconsin 95

Hammerin' Hank's
   Last Hurrah 96

White Buffalo Miracle..............98

Monster Moo-vies: Wisconsin-
   related Fright Flicks.............101

Quiz...104

Grand Old Party
   Begins in Ripon....................105

Braves, Bears, and Minor League
   Brewers Meant Baseball in
   Milwaukee 107

Houdini Escapes Obscurity
   in Appleton 109

Fast Facts............................... 111

Eden in Wisconsin................. 112

Lawrencia Bembenek:
   Run, Bambi, Run! 115

Gangster's Paradise..............117

Talkin' Wisconsin...................120

Timeline.................................121

Lady Liberty Emerges from
   Lake Mendota 122

Fast Facts..............................124

Exploring Cave of the
   Mounds...............................125

A Game of Bridge.................128

Local Legends: The Hodag....130

Fast Facts..............................132

Butter Battles in the
   Dairy State..........................132

Legendary Wisconsinite:
   John Muir 136

Between a Rock and a Weird Place:
   The House on the Rock 140

From the Badger State
   to Tinsel Town 143

Packers Make Ice Bowl
   History 144

Timeline.................................146

Dairy Farming: An Industry
   on the Mooove 147

Fast Facts..................149

Taste of Wisconsin: Extra
Cheddar, Please: More
Cheese Facts 150

Big A and Big O Invade
Bucktown...............................151

You Can Thank Wisconsin 153

Fast Facts..................154

Taste of Wisconsin:
Unusual Eateries.................155

The Biggest *M* of Them All ...157

Wisconsin Olympic
Athletes Are Golden 158

Jeffrey Dahmer:
"The Milwaukee Monster" ..159

Talkin' Wisconsin...................162

A Superior Tragedy:
The *Edmund Fitzgerald*.......163

The Sacred Altar of the
Angler 166

Taste of Wisconsin:
The Sundae 167

Fast Facts..................169

Wisconsin's Cartoon Heritage ..170

A Staggering Spectacle...........173

Odd and Unusual
Wisconsin Laws...................174

Timeline..................176

Wisconsin Dells Has
Ducks in a Row 177

On, Wisconsin! 179

Taste of Wisconsin: Morels 182

Fast Facts..................184

Groundhog Day: Badger
State Edition..........................185

Home Sweet Home:
Miller Park...........................187

Fast Facts..................190

Wisconsin Capitol Stands Above
the Rest..................................191

Timeline..................194

Vince Lombardi:
Football Hero........................195

Talkin' Wisconsin...................197

Notable Wisconsin Scalawags...198

Vorsicht! Fliegende Kraut!
(Beware! Flying Cabbage!)..200

Quiz..201

Taste of Wisconsin:
International Cuisine 202

Baraboo's Space-Time
Blast-pad...............................205

From the Badger State
to Tinsel Town 206

You Can Thank Wisconsin:
The Typewriter......................207

Welcome, Extraterrestrials 209

Brewing Great Ideas:
  Beer in Wisconsin 210

Fast Facts.................................213

Ludicrous Laws 214

Summerwind: Wisconsin's
  Most Haunted House 216

Wisconsin Olympic
  Athletes Are Golden 219

'Sconsin Scandals...................220

You Can Thank Wisconsin 222

Aztalan: A Prehistoric Puzzle.223

A Striking Pastime: The Badger
  Bowling Obsession 226

Fast Facts.................................229

How to Talk Wisconsin...........230

Taste of Wisconsin:
  Cheese Quiz 233

Taste of Wisconsin: Extra
  Cheddar, Please: More
  Cheese Facts 235

Timeline...................................236

Badger Legacies: University of
  Wisconsin Traditions............237

Fast Facts.................................240

Wisconsin's Subterranean
  Secrets 241

Talkin' Wisconsin....................244

It's a Logger's Life for Me 245

The Clairvoyant
  Crime-Buster........................248

From the Badger State
  to Tinsel Town 250

Badger Ingenuity: Damming the
  Red River..............................251

Backwoods Butcher:
  Ed Gein 254

Fast Facts.................................255

Major Richard I. Bong: America's
  "Ace of Aces".......................256

Wisconsin Olympic
  Athletes Are Golden 258

Taste of Wisconsin:
  Bratwurst..............................259

Werewolves in Wisconsin?.....262

A Tangy Tourist Attraction:
  The Mustard Museum 263

Fast Facts.................................265

Quiz...266

The Real Indiana Jones..........267

You Can Thank Wisconsin 270

Timeline...................................271

A Tale of Two Cinemas 272

Index.......................................275

Contributing Writers..............286

Welcome to Wisconsin!

❊ ❊ ❊ ❊

 The name "Wisconsin" comes from the Native American words for "gathering of the waters," and in keeping with that sentiment, we've gathered together a variety of exciting stories and intriguing information for *Packin' It in Wisconsin*. While there may not be as many facts in this book as there are lakes in Wisconsin (there are nearly 15,000 lakes, after all), we still think you'll find lots to ponder or chuckle about in these pages.

What is there to learn about in the Dairy State besides milk and cheese? In this book you'll take a winding journey to discover Wisconsin's unique history, amazing attractions, spellbinding sites, and the unstoppable spirit of its residents—both past and present. And yes, you'll learn why the state was, and still is, an unbeatable force in the dairy industry.

So, let's begin our trek into this great and important state. Here's a small taste of what you'll find:

• Taliesin, the home and studio of Frank Lloyd Wright

• The flesh-and-blood inspiration for Indiana Jones

• A mysterious and elusive creature known as the Hodag

• Flying cabbages and cow chips

• A pickup truck perched in a tree

• And much, much more

Once you begin your trip through Wisconsin, it will be hard to stop. Without further delay, go ahead and get going to learn about some of the great things the state has to offer.

Sit back, relax, and enjoy your visit to Wisconsin.

Laura Ingalls Wilder: From Little House to Big Success

✳ ✳ ✳ ✳

It seems that everyone wants to claim a piece of author Laura Ingalls Wilder. Anyone who watched the Little House on the Prairie *TV series knows that Walnut Grove is in Minnesota and there's a bust of Laura on display in Missouri where she settled in her later years. Laura also lived in Kansas, Iowa, South Dakota, Florida, and New York. Near the tiny village of Pepin, Wisconsin, is where it all began.*

Little House in the Big Woods

Caroline and Charles Ingalls were living near Pepin in a small log cabin when their second daughter was born on February 7, 1867. They named her Laura Elizabeth. Little did they know that 100 years later Laura Ingalls Wilder, their little "Half Pint," as she was known on the TV show, would become a household name around the world.

Charles Ingalls was an explorer at heart and dreamed of settling in unknown territories out west. (Wanderlust may have come naturally to Laura's pa—he was a descendant of Richard Warren, who traveled to the New World aboard the *Mayflower.*) The Ingalls family lived in Pepin for just two years before they moved to Kansas. But times were hard on the prairie, and in another two years, they were back in the big woods of Wisconsin where Laura and her sister Mary attended the Barry Corner School.

Book It

It was those early years that became the inspiration for *Little House in the Big Woods,* the first of eight books written by Laura Ingalls Wilder. Although she didn't keep a diary as a young girl, Laura often wrote down her thoughts on scraps of paper and saved them. When Laura's sister Mary lost her sight, her father told Laura that she would need to be Mary's eyes—describing the people, places, and things that Mary could not see for herself. That attention to detail served Laura well when she finally sat down to write about her life in 1932, at the age of 65.

Little House in the Big Woods tells the story of Laura's childhood and describes pioneer life in Wisconsin's vast woods in the 19th century. Even vacationers who come to enjoy the Wisconsin wilderness today would have a hard time picturing the northwoods of Laura's day. In her book, she tells readers there were no houses, no roads, and no people—just trees and the wild animals who made their homes there.

She tells of hunting and cooking over a fire and describes how they used to smoke venison, weave rugs, tap trees to get real maple syrup, and even make bullets. Laura's original intention was to write a single book called *When Grandma Was a Little Girl*, but her editors at Harper Brothers suggested she turn it into a series. Her books were hugely successful and remain so today.

Although it's based on her life, certain creative embellishments made their way into the text. For instance, fans may be surprised to find out that the character of Nellie Oleson, Laura's nemesis, is not actually based on one individual, but rather a combination of three people.

Time Travel

If you didn't get enough of Laura in her books or on TV's *Little House on the Prairie*, which aired from 1974 to 1983—and is still shown in syndication and is available on DVD—take a drive to Pepin, Wisconsin. You'll find a replica of her log cabin at the Little House Wayside and an historical marker in Pepin Park. And if you happen to be in town in mid-September, be sure to catch Laura Ingalls Wilder Days. You'll be swept back in time to life in the Big Woods.

Everybody Loves the Circus!

❋ ❋ ❋ ❋

Can you imagine life in the 19th century with no TV, no computers, and no MP3 players? What did people do for entertainment? Well, if you were lucky, maybe once a year a circus came to town. And if you lived in Baraboo you were lucky all year round.

They Called It Ringlingville

Wisconsin got the nickname "The Mother of Circuses" thanks to five young men by the name of Ringling. Even as boys, the brothers—Al, Otto, Charles, John, and Alf T.—had a love for the circus. They put on small shows complete with juggling, dancing, and animal acts. Little did they know what their passion had in store for them in the years to come.

The Ringling Brothers Circus began in Baraboo in 1884. It started out fairly small and traveled around the region just like other circuses of the time. By the end of the decade, however, the Ringling Brothers Circus had grown to be one of the largest circuses in the country. More importantly, the brothers were known for their honesty and integrity in a business that, well, wasn't always associated with those qualities. The brothers outlawed shell games and the three-card monte acts popular with other carnivals. They also didn't allow their customers to be shortchanged by ticket sellers. As their reputation for fair play grew, so did their circus and their profits.

The circus grew even more in 1889 when the Ringling Brothers bought some railroad cars. That may not sound like a big deal, but its impact was huge in the days when the primary mode of transportation was horse-pulled wagons—a slow and laborious way to travel. With the rails in front of it, the circus had no limits. The circus could travel farther away

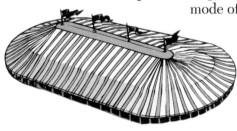

to larger cities where the demand for a circus—and the pay—was greater. It became the largest traveling circus of the day. Trains played an integral part in later years, as well, when the circus traveled across Wisconsin on a two-day trip from Baraboo to Milwaukee, as part of the Great Circus Parade.

The Greatest Show on Earth

When the Ringling Brothers started their circus, they set up winter quarters in Baraboo. Buildings were erected along the north bank of the Baraboo River, and many of them still stand today—the largest group of original circus buildings still around. The Ringling Brothers wintered there until 1918. In 1919, they merged with the Barnum & Bailey Circus, from Delavan and moved the winter quarters to Bridgeport, Connecticut.

In the 1930s, the Ringling Brothers and Barnum & Bailey Circus saw business suffer due to the Depression. While prosperity grew after World War II, the circus never regained its previous status. Suddenly, the country was bursting with a new love of technology— radio shows, movie theaters, and eventually television won American hearts. The circus lost its luster.

The Ringling Brothers and Barnum & Bailey Circus still exists today, and it travels the country with two circus trains, representing two different shows. Consisting of 60 cars each, they bring the traditional three-ring circus to life in large cities along the way.

And the Rest Is History

Back in Baraboo, the circus—and its storied history—is alive and well all year round. Circus World Museum spans 64 acres of land and features 30 buildings—as well as the original train complex. A National Historic Landmark, Circus World Museum houses one of the largest collections of circus artifacts in the world—from photos to wagons to posters. Everything is there—except the peanuts.

Lager Looms Largest

✿ ✿ ✿ ✿

If 7,340,796 cans of beer could be popped open and drained into one container, they would yield exactly enough to fill the massive storage tanks that make up the World's Largest Six-Pack display, which towers over City Brewery on Third Street in La Crosse. And amazingly, that is just what City Brewery has done.

Even good King Gambrinus, the patron saint of beer whose statue guards the humongous six-pack, could not have concocted a more spectacular tribute to one of mankind's most ancient and revered beverages. Built in 1969, the giant storage tanks were originally painted to depict G. Heileman Brewing Company's Old Style beer cans. But when Heileman sold its business in the 1990s, the working tanks were painted over and remained a boring blank space for several years.

The new owners of City Brewery eventually decided they were missing the advertising boat by leaving the gargantuan six-pack's tanks neutral, and they placed vinyl facades over the three streetside cans to imitate the packaging of their LaCrosse Lager. The refurbished cans are now complete with artwork showing the firm's trademark: sparkling artesian water.

An informative sign at the base of the cans cites the six-pack's amazing stats, which include the fact that the 22,200 barrels of beer held in these working storage tanks would be enough to provide one thirsty person with a six-pack a day for 3,351 years. (However, the sign does not speculate on the size of the beer belly the guzzler would accumulate in that time.)

City Brewery claims other titanic achievements as well. It is one of the largest beverage producers in the United States, as it also produces soft drinks, energy drinks, and teas. It brews around seven million barrels of 40 kinds of beer every year and makes as many as 24,800 gallons per batch. That's enough to fill a lot of giant six-packs!

Taste of Wisconsin

No Thanksgiving table is complete without cranberries—that gelatinous, deep-hued, tin-can-shape mass thrown in a fancy crystal dish. Thanksgiving purists might labor over a hot stove, boiling down whole berries into sauces and chutneys, but in Wisconsin, that cylindrical blob is a welcome sight, as there's a good chance the potent berries are another batch of "Something Special from Wisconsin." Thought Wisconsin was all beer and cheese? Take a crack at this cranberry quiz.

1. Wisconsin produces enough cranberries to feed _____
   a) an army.
   b) the world's population.
   c) the equivalent of Wisconsin's cow population, doubled.
   d) All of the above.

2. Cranberries grow _____
   a) in water! Haven't you seen the juice commercial?
   b) on bushes.
   c) on vines.
   d) All of the above.

3. Cranberries are a necessary part of a smart diet because _____
   a) they contain high levels of antioxidants, including proanthocyandins, which promote a healthy immune system.
   b) they are cholesterol-free, fat-free, and low in sodium.
   c) they are good for bladder health.
   d) All of the above.

4. In 2004, in honor of the cranberry's impact on the state's economy, the Wisconsin Legislature _____
   a) enacted a law requiring all state citizens to consume their requisite 26 berries.
   b) named the cranberry the official state fruit.
   c) issued a proclamation declaring Wisconsin's new nickname the "Cranberry State" and offering the old nickname, the "Dairy State," to California.
   d) All of the above.

5. The "Cranberry Highway" is ____

a) a 50-mile stretch of road traversing Wisconsin's oldest cranberry beds in north-central Wisconsin.

b) a swath of highway that is often littered with renegade cranberries that have jumped the truck—and subsequently been smashed to color the roadway red—at harvest time.

c) the record album produced in honor of the state's cranberry industry.

d) All of the above.

6. True or False: All of Wisconsin's berries make it to the Thanks-giving table, either as whole berries or formed into can shapes.

Answers:

1. B. *Wisconsin's cranberry growers produce enough berries so that every person on the planet, young and old, could have 26.*

2. C. *If you said A, you're sort of right. Cranberries grow on low-trailing vines in marshes. These marshes are flooded at harvest time, as cranberries contain small pockets of air that allow them to float to the surface. Floating on the surface of the water, they are easier for the harvesting machines to collect.*

3. D. *Research proves all these facts, even the bladder one, especially in the prevention of urinary tract infections. Your mother and the* British Medical Journal *say so.*

4. B. *Wisconsin produces almost 60 percent of the nation's cranberries. In 2008, 4.3 million barrels of cranberries were grown and sold, making it the best year ever for state growers. Interesting caveat: Cranberries aren't shipped in barrels. They were long ago, the standard stuck, and each of today's "barrels" equals 100 pounds.*

5. A. *The Cranberry Highway is a self-guided drive that stretches from Wisconsin Rapids to Warrens and between Pittsville and Nekoosa. There is also the 29-mile Cranberry Biking Trail that runs through marshes and cranberry beds.*

6. False. *Only five percent of Wisconsin's cranberries are sold as whole berries. The other 95 percent are used in food and beverage products, including cranberry-infused brats, beers, wines and juices, salsas, chips, rice and stuffing mixes, and wiggly molded cranberry masses, straight from the can.*

Fast Facts

- When the USS Arizona *was bombed and destroyed at Pearl Harbor, its captain was Franklin Van Valkenburgh of Milwaukee. Refusing to go to a safer command location, Van Valkenburgh directed* Arizona's *fight until he died. He was posthumously awarded the Medal of Honor.*

- *Most pitchers don't hit well, but Milwaukee Braves pitcher Bob Buhl was in a sad league of his own. In 1962, he went 0–70 for a batting average of exactly .000. Still, it was only a slight downtick for Buhl, whose career average was .089.*

- *The artificial insemination of cattle brought new dilemmas, since the fertility cycles of cows are measured in hours. Before liquid nitrogen freezing, prize bull semen was highly perishable. The 1940s Wisconsin solution? Drop fresh bull semen to farmers by parachute. Look out below!*

- *Door County has the most shoreline of any county in the United States: more than 250 miles of it spanning the shores of Green Bay and Lake Michigan.*

- *Hank Blumer, a farmer from New Glarus, used to make a healing unguent from skunk grease back in the 1920s. The idea was that it helped alleviate respiratory complaints.*

- *Mrs. Margarethe Schurz, a German immigrant from Hamburg, founded the United States' first kindergarten in her Watertown home in 1856. The racket drove her husband nuts, so she soon moved the kindergarten to a nearby frame building.*

- *Milwaukee pioneered a sustainable solution to the problem of human waste disposal well before many places. Since 1925, the Milwaukee Metropolitan Sludge District has sold sewage sludge as a fertilizer called Milorganite.*

- *If you win the Iron Cross at UW-Madison, it's certainly not for your great skill as a World War I or World War II German soldier. The Iron Cross Society inducts 20 to 30 juniors and seniors each year, chosen for their leadership and service.*

America's Only King

❊ ❊ ❊ ❊

Few people would believe that a separate empire with its own full-fledged king once existed within the borders of the United States of America. But James Jesse Strang was indeed crowned ruler of a Lake Michigan island kingdom in the mid-1800s. His bizarre road to royalty, though, began in southeastern Wisconsin.

Growing the Garden

Strang was born in 1813 in Scipio, New York. He moved to Wisconsin in 1843 with his wife, Mary, to a large parcel of land just west of what would become the city of Burlington.

The red-haired, 5′3″ Strang set up a law practice and, thanks to family connections, met the Mormon prophet Joseph Smith on a trip to Nauvoo, Illinois. Strang's rise to fame began, as Smith immediately appointed him an elder in the faith and authorized him to start a Mormon "stake" in Wisconsin named Voree, which meant "Garden of Peace."

Mormons from around the country flocked to Voree to build homes on the rolling, forested tract along the White River. A few months after Strang became a Mormon, Joseph Smith was killed. To everyone's amazement, Strang produced a letter that appeared to have been written and signed by Joseph Smith, which named Strang as the church's next Prophet.

Another leader named Brigham Young, whom you may have heard of, also claimed that title, and Young eventually won. As a result, Strang broke away to form his own branch of Mormonism.

Secrets from the Soil

In September 1845, Strang made a stunning announcement. He said that a divine revelation had told him to dig under an oak tree in Voree located on a low rise called the "Hill of Promise." Four followers armed with shovels dug under the tree and unearthed a box containing some small brass plates, each only a few inches tall.

The plates were covered with hieroglyphics, crude drawings of the White River settlement area, and a vaguely Native American human figure holding a scepter. Strang said he was able to translate them using special stones, like the ones Joseph Smith had used to translate similar buried plates in New York. The writing, Strang said, was from a lost tribe of Israel that had somehow made it to North America. He managed to show the plates to hundreds of people before they mysteriously disappeared.

As his number of followers grew, he created sub-groups among them. There was the commune-style Order of Enoch, and the secretive Illuminati, who pledged their allegiance to Strang as "sovereign Lord and King on earth." Infighting developed within the ranks, and area non-Mormons also raised objections to the community. Some Burlington residents even went so far as to try to persuade wagonloads of Voree-bound emigrants not to join Strang.

In 1849, Strang received a second set of divine messages, called the Plates of Laban. He said they had originally been carried in the Ark of the Covenant. They contained instructions called *The Book of the Law of the Lord,* which Strang again translated with his helpful stones. The plates were not shown to the group at that time, but they did eventually yield support, some would say rather conveniently, for the controversial practice of polygamy.

Polygamy Problems

Strang had personal reasons for getting divine approval to have multiple wives. In July 1849, a 19-year-old woman named Elvira Field secretly became Strang's second wife. Just one problem—he hadn't divorced his first one. Soon, Field traveled with him posing as a young man named Charlie Douglas, with her hair cut short and wearing a man's black suit. Yet, the "clever" disguise did little to hide Field's ample figure.

At about that time, Strang claimed another angel visited to tell him it was time to get out of Voree. Strang was to lead his people to a land surrounded by water and covered in timber. This land, according to Strang, was Beaver Island, the largest of a group of islands in the Beaver Archipelago north of Charlevoix, Michigan. It had recently been opened to settlement, and the Strangites moved there in the late 1840s.

The Promised Island

On July 8, 1950, Strang donned a crown and red cape as his followers officially dubbed him King of Beaver Island. Falling short of becoming King of the United States, he was later elected to Michigan's state legislature, thanks to strong voter turnout among his followers. Perhaps reveling in his new power, eventually, he took three more young wives, for a total of five.

On the island, Strang's divine revelations dictated every aspect of daily life. He mandated that women wear bloomers and that their skirts measure a certain length, required severe lashings for adultery, and forbade cigarettes and alcohol. Under this strict rule, some followers began to rebel. In addition, relations with local fishermen soured as the colony's businesses prospered.

On June 16, 1856, a colony member named Thomas Bedford, who had previously been publicly whipped, recruited an accomplice and then shot Strang. The king survived for several weeks and was taken back to Voree by his young wives. He died in his parents' stone house—which still stands near Mormon Road on State Highway 11. At the time, all four of his young wives were pregnant. And back in Michigan, it wasn't long before local enemies and mobs of vigilantes from the mainland forcibly removed his followers from Beaver Island.

James Jesse Strang was buried in Voree, but his remains were later moved to a cemetery in Burlington. A marker, which has a map of the old community, stands just south of Highway 11 where it crosses the White River, and several of the old cobblestone houses used by group members are preserved and bear historical markers. Strang's memory also lives on in a religious group formed by several of his followers, the Reorganized Church of Jesus Christ of Latter-Day Saints.

Wisconsin Symbols Say It All

❋ ❋ ❋ ❋

What makes Wisconsin unique? What sets it apart? Cheese, cows, and lakes are some things that come to mind. But more importantly, what does Wisconsin want people to remember? Well, just like every other state, Wisconsin has a long list of state symbols and emblems—things that Wisconsinites think represent the state best. Do Wisconsinites know there is a state soil? Did anyone know there is a state soil? Read on.

- **State Animal:** You wouldn't be a Badger fan if you get this one wrong. Yup, it's the badger, and there are plenty of them throughout the state, although you don't often see them. These nocturnal creatures are a bit shy, hiding in their dens during the day and hunting at night.

- **State Nickname:** Wisconsin is "The Badger State." This wasn't a trick question, although you might get the second part of the question wrong. Does the nickname come from the state animal? Nope. In fact, the state animal probably came about after the nickname. Wisconsin has been known as the Badger State since the 1830s, when miners dug tunnels into the hillsides to search for lead and stay warm in the cold Wisconsin winters—just like the animals.

- **State Wildlife Animal:** How many state animals can one state have? The Wisconsin wildlife animal is the white-tailed deer. You've probably seen them along the side of the road.

- **State Domesticated Animal:** In America's Dairyland, what else could it be? The dairy cow, of course. Officially named in 1971, this animal represents the importance of the dairy industry to Wisconsin's economy.

- **Name for Wisconsin Residents:** Wisconsinites

- **State Mineral:** Illinois might have a quaint little town called Galena, but Wisconsin has an abundance of the mineral of the same name, also known as lead sulphite.

- **State Grain:** Knee-high by the Fourth of July, the favorite grain is corn. It is used for livestock feed and ethanol fuel—and who can resist a good Sweet Corn Festival in early August?

- **State Nickname(s):** Oops. Didn't we already have this one? Over the years, Wisconsin has also been known as the Cheese State, the Dairy State, America's Dairyland, and the Copper State.

- **State Dog:** Named in 1985, the American Water Spaniel represents hunting and water sports in Wisconsin. But does anyone know someone who actually has one?

- **State Tree:** An 1893 vote among the children of Wisconsin made the sugar maple the official tree. A second vote was held in 1948, but the sugar maple prevailed once again and it was made official once more in 1949. Maybe the beautiful red-orange autumn leaves and the delicious syrup made from its sap have something to do with this tree's popularity among residents and tourists alike.

- **State Soil:** What? There's a state soil? Yes, it's Antigo Silt Loam. If you forget the name—which you probably will—just remember that this silty soil was created by the glaciers that once covered much of the state. It's good for dairy farming, growing potatoes, and raising timber.

- **State Fish:** Its official name is the muskellunge, but most anglers know it as the musky—a large fish found in the lakes of northern Wisconsin.

- **State Motto:** Adopted in 1851, the motto, "Forward," represents Wisconsin's drive to be a national leader.

- **State Bird:** The robin won the title by a margin of 2–1 over the nearest competitor in a vote of schoolchildren in 1927. The robin usually leaves for warmer climates in October, and its familiar red breast marks the unofficial start of spring when it returns.

- **State Symbol of Peace:** Losing out to the robin for state bird, the mourning dove got its own designation in 1971.

- **State Dance:** It's the polka! This one was honored in 1993, representing the state's German, Czech, and Polish heritage. Even if you've never taken a whirl around the dance floor, you'll probably recognize "The Beer Barrel Polka," a popular tune in Milwaukee.

- **State Beverage:** Some may guess beer, but in keeping with the title of America's Dairyland, the real state beverage is milk.

- **State Song:** "On, Wisconsin!" What else could it be?

- **State Flower:** The wood violet got the nod from Wisconsin's schoolchildren in 1909. In 1948, it was discovered that the designation had never been made official and it was put to the legislature, who sealed the deal in 1949.

- **The State Seal:** In an attempt to include everything Wisconsin, the state seal is a bit complicated. Industry is represented by a pick and shovel, arm and hammer, and anchor. Thirteen vertical stripes and the motto "E Pluribus Unum" show Wisconsin's dedication to the Union. A sailor and yeoman symbolize the state's land- and water-based workforce. Lead ingots and a cornucopia highlight state resources. The seal is rounded out by a badger over the shield and the state motto: "Forward."

- **The Wisconsin State Flag:** When soldiers wanted a state flag to fly during the Civil War, legislators created one by highlighting the state seal on a blue background. In 1979, the word "Wisconsin" was added in white letters across the top to make it more easily recognizable.

- **The State Quarter:** With so many symbols to choose from, it was almost impossible to decide which one should grace Wisconsin's contribution to the 50 State Quarters Program. Six concepts were chosen from a pool of almost 10,000 entries. A statewide vote narrowed it to three, and residents ultimately picked the Agriculture Dairy Barns theme to represent Wisconsin's quarter, issued in 2004. A cow, cheese, and an ear of corn are featured along with the word "Forward" and the year Wisconsin became a state—1848.

A Culinary Tradition:
The Wisconsin Fish Fry

❋ ❋ ❋ ❋

Every Friday night around Wisconsin, it's traditional to turn out for a shared meal. This weekly Thanksgiving is served in the trendiest restaurants, but also at lodges, churches, friendly neighborhood taverns, and the lowest dive bars—and usually it's all you can eat.

Let's Fry Some Fish!

The traditional Wisconsin fish fry features battered, deep-fried fish, french fries, coleslaw, and a roll. Still, within the state, the types of fish served vary by region. Battered, deep-fried Icelandic cod is the most common. "Some of that has to do with the fact that by the time native fish stocks were declining, the Norwegians in Wisconsin already had these connections to get cod for lutefisk," a traditional delicacy from their homeland, says University of Wisconsin professor Janet Gilmore.

Around Green Bay, Yellow Perch is favored. In northern resort areas, walleye is often the fish of choice. Beyond the choice of fish, tradition can even extend to the meal's bread; for some purists, rye is best served alongside.

A Tasty History

The roots of Wisconsin's fish diet can be traced all the way back to Native American Ojibwa (Chippewa) peoples. Later, during Prohibition, when business at Badger taverns fell off, the weekly fish fry attracted customers and built a tradition that is far less prevalent outside of Wisconsin.

"In a lot of other parts of the country, fish fries are seen as associated with Lent in Catholic areas, or they're events: church picnics or during periods when fish are really abundant. Preparing fried fish is something that people don't really like to do at home, but it's an easy way to prepare a lot of fish very quickly," says Gilmore.

If you really want to study the origins of the fish fry, however, you have to go to Great Britain, where the traditional British meal of fish and chips itself owes its origins to Judaism. A study of British multicultural cuisine traced deep-fried fish to 16th-century Jewish immigrants. It was called *pescado frito* and was usually cod deep-fried in vegetable oil. It was brought to England by Portuguese Jews fleeing persecution. They also spread it to the Netherlands, Japan, and France, where it's known as *goujonettes*.

The meal was not complete, however, until 1860, when the very first fish and chip shop opened in London's East End. There, Joseph Malin, a Jewish immigrant, was the first to marry deep-fried fish with deep-fried "chipped potatoes," which were previously offered only in Irish potato shops. The Industrial Revolution, with steam-powered fishing fleets and mechanical icing, let fried fish become a popular treat. Fifty years after the first East End shop opened, there were 25,000 fish and chip shops in England.

Bringing the Tradition Home

But wait a minute—down-home Wisconsin fish fries come from Portuguese Jews at the time of Shakespeare? Given the documented history, that much seems obvious. However, perhaps this is only half the story. Ultimately, it's what Wisconsin has made of the fish fry that makes it truly significant—at least to Wisconsinites.

"When we think about the fish fry, we focus on the food," Gilmore says. "But what I find interesting is that people who are fish fry attendees—they tend to go to the same places again and again. It's very neighborly. It's a public environment but it has a private feeling. It makes it feel like the end of the week. You're satisfying the social mandate that everything is all right."

"It's like having a family celebration in a public place."

Talkin' Wisconsin

"If you want to be a Badger, Just come along with me, By the bright shining light of the moon."

—Professor Julian Olson, 1919 UW Band's Traditional Closer for Each Pre-game Performance

"Speak to a cow as you would a lady."

—William D. Hoard, 19th-century Wisconsin governor and "Father of American Dairying"

"The state of Wisconsin presents to the farmer a combination of advantages which are scarcely to be met within any other country. The occupier of a farm, whether large or small, is almost invariably the owner, and the land he cultivates he can, therefore, turn to what purpose he considers it the most fitted for. In Wisconsin, there is not a single laborer on a farm who will receive less than from six shillings to a dollar per day; at the same time enjoying the advantages of excellent schools for the education of his children, gratuitously. The consequence is that the farm laborers and their families are well fed, well dressed, well educated in all the ordinary elements of knowledge, intelligent in conversation, and very superior to the same class in most parts of the old country."

—Samuel Freeman, The Emigrant's Hand Book, and Guide to Wisconsin, *1851*

"Wisconsin is rarely flashy. Tradition matters, and steady marks its course. The state is sophisticated yet naturally wild, ruggedly individualistic but socially involved, and reverent towards antiquity but open to new people and ideas—all at the same time."

—From Wisconsin: A Photographic Tour *by Carol M. Highsmith and Ted Landphair*

"Minnesotans and Wisconsinites are pretty similar....They claim 10,000 lakes, but we have at least that many that we don't even talk about because in Wisconsin, we think things speak for themselves, so we don't have to."

—From Wisconsin Curiosities *by Michael Feldman*

Holy Hill, Batman!

❊ ❊ ❊ ❊

At about 1,300 feet above sea level, amidst the hills and valleys of Washington County's Kettle Moraine, is the highest peak in southeastern Wisconsin. It is a holy hill called . . . well, Holy Hill. What is it about this area, other than glorious scenery, that attracts more than 500,000 visitors a year? Most come to visit the National Shrine of Mary, Help of Christians. The extensive shrine and the Holy Hill grounds in the town of Erin have a long history of inspiring spiritual quests.

In the Beginning

The Potawatomi and Menomonee peoples told tales of a Jesuit missionary clad in a black robe with a cross and rosary on his belt appearing in about 1673. Lore claimed that this mysterious figure planted a primitive cross on the point of Holy Hill and built its first altar with stone. For centuries, legend said that this Holy Hill pioneer was none other than esteemed holy man and explorer Father Jacques Marquette. While this story is probably inaccurate, people still associate Father Marquette with Holy Hill.

One Shrine Day

Holy Hill's first shrine was a simple log cabin called the Shrine of Mary, Help of Christians, as designated by Father George Strickner on May 24, 1863. Around that same time, an eccentric French hermit named Francois Soubrio took up solitary residence on Holy Hill. One account claims that he ostracized himself from society as penance for his murder of a loved one. But Soubrio's notoriety persists largely because many believe that his partial paralysis was cured after a night vigil of intense prayer atop Holy Hill. Since then, Holy Hill has been believed to possess miraculous powers of healing.

In Good Hands

Over time, Holy Hill became an increasingly popular pilgrimage destination. In 1905, Archbishop Messmer invited a group of Discalced Carmelites from Bavaria to officially assume control of the Shrine of Mary. This was an appropriate choice because the Carmelites had been steadfastly devoted to the Blessed Mary since the 13th century.

The Discalced Carmelite presence remains prominent today as their order pays tribute to its founders, St. Teresa of Jesus and St. John of the Cross. Inside the upper church, mosaics depict St. Teresa being interrupted by a little boy while at prayer in the cloister courtyard. In the story the scene depicts, the child asked, "Who are you?" She replied, "I am Teresa of Jesus, and who are you?" The child then responded, "I am Jesus of Teresa." Then he disappeared.

A Minor Basilica and a Major Deal

About 30 miles northwest of Holy Hill, Milwaukee's Basilica of St. Josaphat was the third church in the United States to be declared a minor basilica when Pope Pius XI deemed it so in 1929. In 2006, Holy Hill earned the same distinction by joining its neighbor's illustrious ranks. Pope Benedict XVI officially designated Holy Hill to be Wisconsin's second minor basilica church.

Modern Times

The Shrine of Mary experienced an unfortunate act of vandalism on June 6, 2006 (or 6/6/06), when two spray-paint-wielding cousins desecrated walls, statues, and crosses. They wrote "Hail Satin" and other pro-devil (or pro-fabric) messages. Clearly, there will be no spelling bee championships in their futures. In addition to their typos, they now have hate crime convictions on their criminal records.

Today, Holy Hill welcomes hikers, tourists, and visitors of all religions. According to Father Don Brick, shrine minister, "This is a place of solitude and solace. It's so quiet and peaceful. You get away from everything. It's a spiritual treasure." Today, people come for many reasons, from enjoying its beauty to seeking its healing powers.

Bucky Badger's Winning Ways

❊ ❊ ❊ ❊

Bucky Badger, the University of Wisconsin's lovable mascot, has long been the face of Wisconsin. Furry and friendly, Bucky never fails to delight the crowd, whether it's rabid Badger fans at a football game, or the littlest patient at the UW Children's Hospital. Dressed in a red and white striped sweater with a large "motion W," Bucky has cheered and danced his way into our hearts at sporting events and special appearances since the 1940s.

The First Badger Wasn't Fuzzy, Was He?

Way before Wisconsin had a "Bucky," the university's sports teams adopted the nickname "Badgers." Oddly, the name wasn't in honor of the furry little critters found around the state. Instead, it came from the lead miners of the 1820s who had to burrow into hillside tunnels to keep warm in the winter—just like badgers.

The name may have originated from an occupation, but the mascot has always existed in animal form. In fact, the first badger mascots were live animals that were more ferocious than funny. Several escaped their handlers, and the critters were eventually retired to the Vilas Zoo.

Bucky's Background

The first badger costume came to life in November 1949 after Connie Conrad, of the university's art department, was asked to create a papier-mâché badger head. It debuted at homecoming, with cheerleader Bill Sagal of Plymouth wearing it first. The furry fellow was such a hit that a contest was initiated to name him. Several names, including Benny, Bouncy, Bobby, Bernie, and Buddy, were all tried, but none really seemed to suit him. The winning name, of course, was Buckingham U. Badger—or Bucky to his friends.

Thankfully, Bucky gained a following and managed to withstand a threat of extinction from assistant attorney general Howard Koop in the 1970s. The ill-advised politician got little support when he suggested replacing Bucky with Henrietta Holstein. What a cheesy idea.

If You Want to Be a Badger

Nowadays, Bucky's familiar face is portrayed by not one, but seven students. With more than 600 appearances a year, it takes a lot of dedication—and schedule juggling—to make it all work. Tryouts are held each April for the job, which is, by the way, a year-round commitment. Candidates are warned that Bucky may need to be available over Thanksgiving, winter break, and even summer vacation.

That doesn't seem to deter those who want the job, however. They come to tryouts prepared to show their stuff in the areas of role-playing and body language, handling props, and rhythm. And anyone who's seen a Badger football game in person knows that Bucky needs one more skill—doing push-ups for every Badger point, repeated each time they score.

In most years, the seven mascots are all men. Yet this isn't a sexist decision. In fact, there were two female Buckys in the 1990s. There are two main problems facing female badgers, however. One is height. Bucky needs to look the same wherever he goes. Heights of the seven mascots typically range from 5′10″ to 6′2″ and the crowd doesn't seem to notice the difference. Yet, showing up with a 5′2″ Bucky might raise a few eyebrows. The other problem is weight. Not the weight of the student playing the part. No, the weight in question is Bucky's head, which tips the scales at an astonishing 35 pounds. That's a lot for a mascot to shoulder.

It Takes (More Than) Two

The chosen mascots divvy up a schedule that includes all home and away football games, both men's and women's basketball, wrestling, men's and women's soccer, volleyball, and softball games. Other UW sports may get an occasional visit by Bucky, and he attends all postseason tournament appearances. And did we mention hockey? Bucky also needs to be available to skate in front of the crowd at UW hockey games.

And that's not all. The mascot world isn't all about sports, and Bucky knows that better than anyone. He attends other university-sponsored functions, including parades, pep rallies, community events, and even some private functions (for a price).

The 2009 fee schedule offers Bucky appearances ranging from $25 per half-hour for UW student organizations and up to $100 per half-hour for Madison area nonprofit groups. Private and out-of-town events cost a bit more. But wouldn't it be worth it to have Bucky at your wedding? The most unusual event Bucky has attended, according to Spirit Squad Director Josette Scheer, is the funeral of a die-hard fan.

Claim to Fame

Bucky usually just cheers for his teams and brings smiles to the faces of Badger fans everywhere, but he also gets an opportunity to gain a little glory for himself. Along with the rest of the UW Spirit Squad, Bucky has the chance to compete to be top dog, er, Badger at the UCA College Mascot National Championship held every January at Disney World. Each school submits a video clip of its mascot in action, and finalists are judged on their video along with their use of props, a short skit, and crowd interaction. In 2008, Bucky was awarded with his best finish ever—2nd place.

And even though he's still alive and going strong, Bucky got his biggest honor yet in 2006. Along with Aubie, Auburn's Tiger and YoUDee, the Blue Hen Chicken of Delaware, Bucky was inducted as a charter member of the Mascot Hall of Fame's College Division.

Go, Bucky!

Fast Facts

- If you were born in or before the Vietnam era, you probably remember the yo-yo fad. It was cool to have a Duncan Yo-Yo. They were manufactured in Luck, Wisconsin, for Duncan by Flambeau Products. Today, they're made in Indiana.

- Like any well-raised Green Bay native, Tony Shalhoub is a Packer fan. He's also one of the nation's most prominent Arab American actors, known for playing the titular neurotic detective on Monk.

- One of the Brew Crew's great clowns was 1970s pitcher Jim Colborn. A capable hurler, in the last game of 1976 he masqueraded as a plate umpire (with the umps' connivance) and went out for the lineup exchange. The Brewers' manager Alex Grammas didn't notice until Colborn said something.

- The dreaded Spanish flu epidemic of 1918–1919 hit Wisconsin hard. More than 102,000 Wisconsinites fell ill with the disease and 8,549 of them died. It could have been far worse, but Wisconsin launched effective quarantine programs to limit the onslaught.

- Two Wisconsin National Guard regiments (the 2nd and 3rd Wisconsin Volunteer Infantry) helped invade Puerto Rico during the Spanish-American War in 1898. When the 3rd marched in to liberate Ponce, it turned out the town had already surrendered... to a reporter.

- With Wisconsin's large German population, it was perhaps inevitable that some would join the Nazi-sympathizing German American Bund in the 1930s. At the time they named their retreat campground "Camp Hindenburg." Of course, no one could have known then how that would sound to later generations.

- Curly Lambeau got lost under the Polo Grounds stands at halftime of the 1938 NFL championship against the Giants. He wound up on the street, locked out of the stadium. The security guards wouldn't let Curly back in until he made a huge scene. After the ordeal, Lambeau's troops lost, 23–17.

Quiz

So you think you know all about the Badger State?
Then try the Wisconsin Cultural Literacy Quiz!

1. True or false: There were once slaves in Wisconsin.

a) True
b) False

2. Milwaukee's first brewery was opened in 1840 by three men from what country?

a) Germany
b) Austria
c) Belgium
d) Great Britain

3. Humans have lived in Wisconsin for how many years?

a) About 200
b) About 400
c) At least 1,000
d) At least 12,000

4. PETA may not like it, but Wisconsin leads the nation in production of _____.

a) steaks
b) lucky rabbit's feet
c) mink pelts
d) ham

5. For how many years was Wisconsin territory part of Great Britain?

a) Less than 50
b) Between 50 and 100
c) More than 100
d) More than 200

6. How is the state of Wisconsin much larger than you may think?

a) The state boundary extends to the center of Lake Superior
b) The state boundary extends to the center of Lake Michigan
c) The state boundary extends to the center of the Mississippi River
d) All of the above

7. Which Beaver Dam native starred in such classic films as *Double Indemnity* and *The Caine Mutiny*?

a) Kirk Douglas
b) Fred MacMurray
c) Errol Flynn
d) James Cagney

Answers: 1. a, 2. d, 3. d, 4. c, 5. a, 6. d, 7. b

Crazy Legs Propelled Elroy Hirsch to the End Zone ... and Fame

✳ ✳ ✳ ✳

His jersey was retired, and his name and number 40 are one of only a handful emblazoned along the edge of the upper deck at Camp Randall Stadium in Madison. Elroy Hirsch played football for only one season at UW-Madison, but to Wisconsin fans, he is as beloved as Bucky Badger himself.

Born a Badger

Hirsch was born in Wausau in 1923 and made his mark in both high school football and basketball before moving on to the University of Wisconsin. He played halfback in 1942 on a team that went 8–1–1. The most memorable game of his UW career was a 17–7 win over a number-one-ranked Ohio State team. Hirsch threw a touchdown pass and accumulated more than 200 yards of total offense. Excelling in all aspects of the game, he finished the season with 786 yards rushing, 390 yards receiving, and 226 yards passing.

Who knows what heights Hirsch would have reached as a Badger if it had not been for World War II. He joined the Marine Corps and had to transfer to the University of Michigan where he completed his college career as a Wolverine. In fact, Hirsch is still the only athlete in U of M school history to letter in four sports—football, basketball, baseball, and track. On one remarkable day in 1944, Hirsch took part in the broad jump at an outdoor track meet (where he placed third), and then hopped into his car and drove 150 miles to Bloomington, Indiana, where he pitched a four-hitter in the second game of a double-header.

The Birth of Crazylegs

Although he spent more time as a Wolverine, Hirsch would never forget his Badger roots. During a 1942 Wisconsin game against Great Lakes he ran 61 yards for a touchdown with a wobbly style. This prompted sportswriter Francis Powers to say Hirsch ran like a demented duck, adding, "His crazy legs were gyrating in six different directions all at the same time." "Crazylegs" was born.

A first-round draft choice in 1945, Hirsh joined the Chicago Rockets in the All-America Conference. In 1949, he became an L.A. Ram and rode the bench much of his first season before finding his place on the team as an end. As part of the Rams' three-end offense, Hirsch exploded on the professional football scene.

Undeniably, his best season was 1951, when he tore up the field for 1,495 receiving yards on 66 catches and scored a league-high 17 touchdowns—10 of them on plays covering more than 34 yards. The longest touchdown was a 91-yard play in a big game against the Chicago Bears. Backed up to their own goal line, the Rams tossed the ball to Hirsh, who caught the pass and never looked back. He simply outran the Bears defenders.

Back to Badger Land

In 1969, with his playing days behind him, Hirsch took on another role working with the sports he loved. He became the Director of Athletics at the University of Wisconsin, giving the struggling program the boost it needed. He expanded varsity sports from only 12 programs for men to 25 men's and women's sports and raised average football game attendance from 43,000 in 1968 to 70,000 just four years later.

In addition to netting himself All-American Honors in 1942 and 1943, those crazy legs got Hirsch inducted into the National High School Hall of Fame, the Wisconsin Athletic Hall of Fame, the Madison Sports Hall of Fame, and the NFL Hall of Fame. Not one to lay about, he also starred in three movies, including *Crazylegs,* a film about himself. And don't forget the Crazylegs Classic—an annual run to raise money for UW athletic scholarships.

Medieval Milwaukee

❋ ❋ ❋ ❋

Wisconsin's connection to France could be said to go back even earlier than the 17th-century explorations of the French Jesuit priest Jacques Marquette. The St. Joan of Arc chapel, now on the campus of Marquette University, was originally built in the French countryside 200 years before Marquette was even born.

A Storied Past

The story of how a medieval building made its way from a French village to the campus of Marquette University begins long ago. The chapel, built in the French village of Chasse in about 1400, was originally known as the Chapelle de St. Martin de Sayssuel. According to village lore, Joan of Arc stopped at the chapel to pray during one of her trips through the Rhone Valley in the 1420s.

After the French revolution at the end of the 18th century, it fell into disrepair and probably would have become a nondescript pile of rubble. Fortunately, a young French architect, Jacques Couëlle, took it upon himself to start rebuilding the chapel after World War I. The architect's efforts caught the attention of Gertrude Hill Gavin, a wealthy American railroad heiress. A devout Catholic, she felt the best way to help preserve the building would be to buy it. In 1927, she arranged with the French government to ship the entire building, stone by stone, across the Atlantic to her Long Island, New York, estate.

Under the guidance of one of America's most renowned architects of the time, John Russell Pope, the chapel was reconstructed alongside Gertrude Hill Gavin's chateau—which she had also brought from France. Money was no object for the project. New stained-glass windows were added, and it was furnished with Christian antiquities, which Gavin had collected during her European travels. The most famous of these treasures was the Joan of Arc

Stone. Legend has it that Joan of Arc had prayed to a statue of the Virgin Mary. Afterward, she kissed the stone where the statue was placed, and ever since, the stone has been said to be colder than the other stones surrounding it.

On the Road Again

The Gavin family sold the 50-acre estate in 1962. Just five days before the new owners were to move in, a fire broke out in the chateau and burned for 16 hours, nearly destroying the entire building. Miraculously, the chapel was untouched. Because they could not move into the now uninhabitable chateau, the new owners, Marc and Lillian Rojtman—former residents of Milwaukee—decided to donate the chapel to Marquette University. Workers spent months taking the chapel apart once again. The original terra-cotta roof tiles were dismantled, and all of the stones were carefully labeled so that each one would be put back in its original place. Next, everything was loaded onto trucks, and the little French chapel headed for the Milwaukee university named for the great French explorer.

It took more than a year to put the tremendous number of stones back together again. At Marquette, the chapel was also lengthened and modernized. In 1966, after it was reconstructed, the chapel was dedicated to Joan of Arc. According to Marquette University, it remains "the only medieval structure in the entire Western hemisphere dedicated to its original purpose: *Ad Majorem Dei Gloriam.*" This Latin term means "For the greater glory of God."

Today, visitors to the chapel can marvel at this architectural landmark's gothic altar and vaulted ceiling. They can even touch the fabled Joan of Arc Stone and decide for themselves if they feel the legendary coolness of the stone. One can only imagine how surprised the French explorer Jacques Marquette would have been to see a chapel from the French countryside sitting on the campus of a college named in his honor!

Timeline

450,000,000 BCE
The Rock Elm crater is formed when a massive meteorite slams into Earth about 70 miles east of Minneapolis.

11,000 BCE
Paleolithic peoples inhabiting what is now the state of Wisconsin are known to have hunted and butchered wooly mammoths around this time.

1000 CE
Native peoples create charcoal drawings in a cave near present-day La Crosse.

1675
Father Jacques Marquette, the Jesuit missionary and explorer, makes his final journey through what is now Wisconsin. Sick with typhus, he later dies in what is now the state of Michigan.

July 1814
The Battle of Prairie du Chien during the War of 1812 ends with the British capturing the city. The U.S. will not regain possession until the conclusion of the war.

1828
Army Surgeon William Beaumont is transferred to Prairie du Chien. While there, he will conduct a series of experiments on human digestion, earning himself the sobriquet "Father of Gastric Physiology."

August 2, 1832
Illinois militia massacre a band of Black Hawk peoples along Wisconsin's Bad Axe River. The Black Hawk War will end three weeks later with the surrender of Chief Black Hawk.

April 20, 1836
The U.S. Congress establishes the Territory of Wisconsin.

September 14, 1837
Roseline Peck gives birth to a baby girl. She is the first child born to settlers in Madison. Roseline names her daughter Wisconsiana.

February 11, 1842
Representatives Charles Arndt and James Vineyard of the Wisconsin Territorial Legislature get into a brawl on the house floor that ends with Vineyard fatally shooting Arndt in the chest.

1846
Solomon Laurent Juneau, a Canadian-born fur trader who laid out portions of the city of Milwaukee in 1835, is elected the city's first mayor.

May 29, 1848
Wisconsin becomes the 30th state to join the United States of America.

August 21, 1851
Irish immigrant John McCaffary, convicted of drowning his wife, becomes the first and last person to be executed by the state of Wisconsin. A botched hanging leaves McCaffary to slowly strangle at the end of his noose. The gruesome spectacle leads state leaders to abolish the death penalty.

(Continued on p. 121)

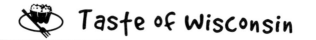# Taste of Wisconsin

Animal rights activists don't like it. Neither does famed chef Wolfgang Puck. But the fact remains that foie gras played a big role in catapulting the little town of Watertown, situated about halfway between Madison and Milwaukee, into high society.

Foie gras is one of the most popular and well-known French food delicacies. It is made from duck or goose livers and has become quite controversial. Its rich yet delicate taste is achieved by force-feeding the birds. Puck has banned foie gras from his food empire, and the city of Chicago banned its sale in restaurants for a few years. But as far back as the 1850s, Watertown, with its strong German tradition, was the culinary center stage for an interesting process for fattening geese.

The process, which passed down through the generations, was called goose noodling and was long considered an art. Local farmers would raise geese through the spring and summer and, starting in early November, would force-feed the birds noodles made from a paste of barley, wheat, and rye every four hours, day and night. Within three weeks, the geese were ready for market.

Noodling resulted in rapid weight gain, especially of the liver, and the heavier the bird, the higher the price. As the birds were prepared for market, the prized livers were quickly removed and prepared for shipment, destined to become *pate de foie gras.* The rest of the bird became famous as the "Watertown Stuffed Goose."

Wealthy families out East, especially in New York, Boston, and Philadelphia, prized Watertown geese. Many maintained standing orders for the birds from year to year for their Christmas feasts. At the height of Watertown's noodling business, more than 150,000 pounds of stuffed geese were sold annually. The local industry fizzled in the late 1970s. Today, the only vestige of Watertown's poultry industry is the Gosling, the city's high school mascot.

Milwaukee's "Mr. Showman"

✻ ✻ ✻ ✻

Why does the Wisconsin Historical Society's collection include a silver jacket, embroidered with birds of paradise and six pounds of sequins? It once belonged to a famous Wisconsinite: Liberace.

A Product of His Environment?

Liberace, the flamboyant pianist, is one of Wisconsin's most surprising exports. How could Las Vegas's most outlandish, jewelry-laden, candelabra-collecting icon have grown up in Wisconsin?

Wladziu Valentino Liberace was born in the Milwaukee suburb of West Allis in 1919. His father, Salvatore Liberace, an Italian immigrant, was a classically trained musician who had resigned himself to earning a sporadic living playing in movie theater orchestras. As a toddler, Liberace would accompany his father while he worked— gaining exposure not only to music but also to the opulence of Milwaukee's grandest movie houses. Liberace's mother, raised in a Polish community in rural Wisconsin, was the more practical of his parents. She often ended up supporting the family through her grocery store business—that she ran in the living room of their house.

Salvatore was intent that his children be musically trained, regardless of the cost. Despite the family's meager income, the Liberaces had the best piano on the block. Lessons were given to the children from the time they could reach the keyboard. Wally (as he was known) took to the instrument immediately. At the age of four he was able to play the music from his older sister's lessons, and soon he could play any piece he heard.

A Rise to Fame

His reputation as a child prodigy grew. He received a prestigious scholarship to the Wisconsin College of Music, and he even played for a time on Milwaukee's WTMJ radio station. With the onset of the Depression, work for the elder Liberace dried up, and everyone in the family pitched in. Wally found that he could make extra money playing at dances and parties and eventually in nightclubs. In fact, he would perform in some of Milwaukee's less savory venues when he was as young as 16, yet he kept with it—as long as it paid.

After graduating from West Milwaukee High School, Liberace toured with a community orchestra. He was singled out as "having every quality that a virtuoso should possess." On the strength of these reviews he was invited to audition for the Chicago Symphony Orchestra and eventually appeared with the group. So why is it that Wladziu Liberace did not pursue a career as a concert pianist? It all came down to a concert in La Crosse, Wisconsin, in 1939. At the end of a traditional classical program, someone in the audience called out for an encore. Liberace chose to play "Three Little Fishies," which was a popular song at the time, in the style of Bach. The audience loved it. Liberace had found his niche, combining glitz and humor with classical music pieces.

Fame, Fortune, and Philanthropy

Liberace developed his singular style of showmanship playing Wisconsin clubs and cocktail lounges. Eventually, he reached a point where he had, in his words, "gone has far as he could in his hometown." New York beckoned, and at the age of 21 he left Wisconsin for good. Ultimately he settled in Las Vegas where, over the years, the costumes became more flamboyant, the candelabras multiplied, and the audiences (along with his bank account) exploded. He remained one of America's most successful and beloved performers up to his death in 1987.

While he spent most of his life outside of Wisconsin, Liberace was a Midwesterner at heart. He was conservative in his politics and domestic in his daily life. He was also famously kind, especially to those who worked for him. To this day, Liberace's legacy lives on in Milwaukee through the generous scholarships that his estate provides to the Wisconsin Conservatory of Music. When Milwaukee's next piano prodigy emerges, he or she may have Liberace to thank!

Ski Wisconsin: The American Birkebeiner

❋ ❋ ❋ ❋

Northern Wisconsin's annual cross-country ski race had very humble beginnings—and a very grand vision. Back in 1973, one woman and 34 men waited at the starting line for their signal to begin the 50-kilometer race from Hayward to Cable. Little did they—or founder Tony Wise—know the American Birkebeiner would still be going strong in the next millennium.

Welcome to America

The idea for the race actually came from an event that took place 800 years ago in Norway—but it wasn't a ski race. Much like the marathon, the origin of this sporting event had major historic roots. In 1206, Birkebeiner skiers, who got their name from the birch bark leggings they wore, skied through the mountains and forests of Norway during the Norwegian Civil War. They were entrusted with the task of moving an infant prince to safety. This event inspired the first Birkebeiner ski race, which was held in Norway, in 1932.

Tony Wise, founder of the American Birkebeiner, envisioned a similar event running right through northern Wisconsin. When the first race got its start in 1973, there were only 30,000 pairs of cross-country skis in the entire United States. But skiers are an enthusiastic bunch and their enthusiasm proved contagious. Those who came to the first Birkebeiner loved the event and the trail through the beautiful Wisconsin woods and hills. Some of them returned the following year, others told their friends, and some did both.

As the race grew in popularity, the event was refined and improved. For the first year, a temporary course was created using snowmobile trails and logging roads. It was adequate, but when it became obvious that the event would be a recurring thing, a new trail was designed and built for the American Birkebeiner. By the 1979 race, 4,459 skiers took part, and it became clear that it was time for more improvements. Specifically, the trail needed to be widened to accommodate the large number of athletes. A new trail was created in 1980, and it has remained about the same since then.

They Come from Far and Wide

Since it began, more than 195,000 skiers have participated in the Birkebeiner and its sister event, the Kortelopet (which is about half the distance). Annually, more than 9,500 skiers take part in the race and another 15,000 spectators come to watch and have fun in the Wisconsin winter. As part of the Worldloppet, a circuit of 15 ski races that take place on four continents, the American Birkebeiner is truly an international affair. The 3-day event has attracted skiers from 21 countries and 48 states. Amazingly, there are three people who have skied in every race since it began, and more than 800 skiers have competed for 20 years or more. Some participants are elite skiers hoping to actually win the race and are able to complete the Birkie, as it's fondly known, in about two hours. There are many others who do it for recreation and to enjoy the challenge of making it to the finish line.

As cross-country skiing has become more popular, Birkebeiner organizers have added other events to appeal to the more casual athletes and families. In addition to the original Birkie, there is now a Birkie trail for skate-style skiers and one for classic skiers. There is the 23K Kortelopet, a kids trail, other shorter races, demonstrations, a torch lighting ceremony, and a couple of carb-laden breakfasts.

When Tony Wise founded the race, he chose the Birkebeiner name as a symbol of courage and perseverance. Wise passed away in 1995, but his vision—and the race—lives on.

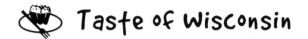

Taste of Wisconsin

A Badger Obsession

For centuries, Wisconsinites have tapped trees, collected sap, and boiled it over a roaring fire to concentrate it into "liquid gold."

America's Dairyland ranks fourth in U.S. production of maple syrup. The official state tree is, of course, the Sugar Maple, and there is even an annual Maple Queen. Enthusiasts speak a secret language of the "syruping" or "sugaring" that goes on in "sugar camps."

In fact, tapping maple trees—as well as birch and box elders—goes back to prehistory. Eastern pioneers learned it from the Native Americans living there. In Wisconsin, the Ho-Chunk, Ojibwa, and other peoples tapped trees with reeds or hollowed twigs. They'd let the sap freeze and then lift off the ice, leaving behind increasing concentrations of sugar. They also boiled down the sweet sap to use as a soft drink and to make syrup, candy, and money—maple sugar and syrup were valuable trade items.

Even today, pure maple syrup is expensive, costing as much as $13 a pint. It should be noted that typical grocery-store maple syrup contains only a fraction of the real thing. Pure syrup is valuable because it's rare, and it's rare because it takes so much time and trouble to obtain. Typically, six trees must be tapped to get about 35 to 40 gallons of sap, which must then be boiled for five days. All of this yields one gallon of pure maple syrup. There's a good reason for all the boiling. As sap is boiled, the water that it contains naturally turns to steam and evaporates. Once the water is taken out, sweet, concentrated maple syrup is left behind.

Getting It Right

An average maple must grow for about 40 years and be more than 12 inches in diameter before it can be tapped. Otherwise, there is a risk of hitting the heart of the tree and doing great damage. Temperature adds another complication. For the sap to flow up from the roots, the weather should be freezing cold at night and warm and sunny during the day. Ideal weather consists of 20- to 25-degree Fahrenheit nights and temperatures in the high 40s during the daytime.

Those late winter and early spring temperatures also offer the possibility of another, uniquely seasonal way of enjoying maple syrup, though it's sadly gone out of fashion. In her youth in the 1870s, Laura Ingalls Wilder recalled eating fresh syrup that was ladled onto plates of snow. "It cooled into soft candy, and as fast as it cooled they ate it," she wrote in *Little House in the Big Woods*.

In describing this winter treat, Wilder also offered some words to live by for maple syrup lovers: "They could eat all they wanted, for maple sugar never hurt anybody."

❉ ❉ ❉ ❉

- *Once they reach the proper age, maple trees can produce sap for 100 years.*

- *Why don't people collect sap in the late spring and summer? Once a tree buds, the sap becomes bitter—not the best flavor for pancakes!*

- *Among maple producing states, Wisconsin ranks fourth behind Vermont, New York, and Maine.*

- *Who said health food has to taste bad? Maple syrup has the same amount of calcium as whole milk.*

- *In maple syrup, the main variety of sugar is sucrose—which is the same as table sugar.*

Viva la Bubbler!

❋ ❋ ❋ ❋

Some say "drinking fountain," Wisconsinites say "bubbler." Others even say "water fountain." They're all synonyms, and the Wisconsin word is just as good as the others, whether you like it or not.

Bubbler is the name for a device from which one can obtain fresh water for drinking (this apparatus is also called "water fountain" or "drinking fountain," if you insist), designed by Harlan Huckleby back in 1888. Huckleby was an employee of Wisconsin's Kohler Water Works, now the Kohler Company, one of the world's leading manufacturers of plumbing products, which trademarked the Bubbler name. The original Bubbler had just a one-inch stream, making the flow of water appear, well, bubbly. Over the years, the Bubbler's trajectory was improved, creating the easy-to-drink water arc we know today. In the meantime, other companies brought their own versions of the Bubbler to market, but with the name taken, they had to fall back on less-desirable terms like the "Gusher" and the "Gurgler." Kohler still makes its Bubbler today.

The word "bubbler" is an eponym, or an everyday word derived from a formal name, much like "Kleenex" for facial tissue and "Jell-O" for gelatin. The capital B was dropped long ago, and "bubbler" is a formal entry in most complete dictionaries. "Drinking fountain" is there too for "bubbler" detractors, but, sorry, "water fountain," Merriam-Webster doesn't like you.

Use of the term "bubbler" extends throughout Wisconsin, save for the northwest corner. There, for shame, they prefer "drinking fountain," much like neighboring Minnesotans. Bubbler-speak is particularly strong throughout southeastern Wisconsin, especially Milwaukee and its suburbs. Perhaps it's no coincidence that the village of Kohler is due north of Milwaukee, near Sheboygan. True Wisconsinites in Madison, where working bubblers can be found in the state capitol, use the term. So let's lift our glasses to this home-grown word . . . after we fill them at the bubbler.

Fast Facts

- When the U.S. Navy's aircraft carriers took the fight toward Japan in World War II, one key admiral was Marc "Pete" Mitscher of Hillsboro. His pilots decimated the best remaining Japanese air contingent in the June 1944 Marianas Turkey shoot, destroying hundreds of Japanese planes and three carriers.

- Kato Kaelin, the houseguest of O. J. Simpson who got all the media and stand-up comedy attention during O. J.'s murder trial, was born in Milwaukee and graduated from Nicolet High in Glendale.

- If you missed the golden age of strategy board gaming, you also missed the Roberts Award-winning, Greg Costikyan-designed The Creature That Ate Sheboygan. One player designs and plays as the monster; the other uses police and military forces to defend the good citizens and property of Sheboygan.

- In 1971, artist Marjorie Engelman of Green Bay decided that women's political advances deserved representation in a U.S. flag—made partly from bras. The stars were arranged like birth control pills, and the bras provided the white horizontal stripes. The Wisconsin Historical Society now has the flag.

- The Ho-Chunk people chose Ho-Poe-Kaw (which means "Glory of the Morning") as their chief in 1727 when she was 18. Many of her descendants became chiefs, and she seems to have lived to be at least 105. She is also the last female chief of the Ho-Chunk.

- In 1897, the Badgers robbed the University of Chicago Maroons of a football conference title in a very odd way. The Maroons' star halfback, Clarence Herschberger, challenged a teammate to an eating contest. As a result, Herschberger was so sick he couldn't play, and Wisconsin won 23–8.

- Major Charles Whittlesey of Florence commanded the "Lost Battalion" of the 77th Infantry Division during its World War I agony. During the 1917 Meuse-Argonne Offensive, his battalion advanced and became isolated, suffering over 50 percent casualties from heavy German counterattacks before it could be relieved.

Aldo Leopold: Friend of the Environment

❀ ❀ ❀ ❀

This wildlife ecology wunderkind made Wisconsin's lands his laboratory.

Inspired by Nature

It might be a stretch to call Aldo Leopold a god—or a poet, for that matter. But there's no denying that the man who is now considered the father of wildlife ecology was a creator. And as anyone can tell you who has been moved by the poetic musings of his book *A Sand County Almanac,* his opus about the changing land around his Wisconsin farm, what Leopold created—a national transformation in thinking about the relationship between man and nature—was nothing short of poetic.

Rand Aldo Leopold, born in 1887, grew up in Iowa and—ironically perhaps—was a hunter. With an aim to ensure that wildlife remained wild (and likewise, fruitful for hunters), Leopold joined the U.S. Forest Service shortly after graduating from Yale. His first assignment? Managing the Arizona territories, including its timber and what he then called "varmints"—wolves, coyotes, and other predatory animals that preyed on valuable livestock and game. His attitude was in line with the common thinking of the time: Wildlife had to be controlled in order to protect the interests of man.

A Major Attitude Adjustment

It's possible that a long bout of nephritis—which struck Leopold after being caught in a flood and blizzard in 1913—gave him time to reflect. Perhaps the crisis of World War I broadened his view. Whatever the impetus, Leopold, who had married and become a father, recovered his health, and resumed his work with the Forest Service, began to see conservation as more than a matter of economics.

It was in Wisconsin that the seeds of Leopold's brave new thinking took root and blossomed. As a professor of game management at the University of Wisconsin-Madison, Leopold penned the revolutionary book *Game Management* which was published in 1933. Part philosophy and part how-to manual of skill and technique, Leopold's book began shaping the conservation ethic—the notion that humans and wilderness exist in a state of mutual interdependence and that it is a privilege, not an obligation, to bend the earth to people's will.

But was it too late? Could humans undo what damage had already been done? In 1935, Leopold was determined to find out. He purchased a small square of worn-out former farmland alongside the Wisconsin River near Baraboo. On the grounds were the remains of a dilapidated old chicken coop, where Leopold, his wife, Estella, and their five children would stay during their visits. Though the family fixed it up, the coop's nickname—"The Shack"—remained. The family retreated to the land on weekends and school vacations to relax, explore, and, in typical Leopold fashion, to experiment.

Working in the World's Biggest Laboratory

Leopold saw the exhausted land as an outdoor laboratory, a living workshop in which he could test his ideas about restoring health to the depleted earth. He and his family enriched the soil, built a garden, cut firewood, fought drought, and planted prairie grasses, flowers, hardwoods, and conifers—nearly 40,000 pines alone.

This life-size, and lifelong, test of Leopold's land proved fruitful. He eventually transformed the farm into a healthy, thriving landscape and in the process helped shape many of the environmental restoration techniques used today. Sadly, Leopold didn't live to see all that his little plot of land on the Wisconsin River would come to mean to the world; he died of a heart attack while struggling to fight a brush fire that was encroaching on his land in 1948.

You Can Thank Wisconsin

A lot of big corporations have company cars, but Madison's Oscar Mayer has taken that to the extreme with the Oscar Mayer Weinermobile, a 27-foot-long hot dog on wheels.

Meal on Wheels

The first Weinermobile (a mere 13 feet long) was created in 1936 by Oscar Mayer's nephew Karl, as a way to promote the company's products at grocery stores throughout the Midwest. It caught on, and Oscar Mayer's staff steered the sausage around the country. There are currently seven in use—each assigned to a different part of the country.

About ten versions have been made over the years. In 1969, a prototype was actually designed and built by Oscar Mayer mechanics right at the Madison headquarters. This was the first Weinermobile to be showcased in a foreign country. The same design was used, this time by Plastic Products in Milwaukee, to create another Weinermobile in 1975. The newest addition to the Weinermobile family is more of a smoky link. It's a smaller replica of its big brother—just 15 feet long, on top of a Mini Cooper chassis.

A Recipe for Success

Today the full-sized Weinermobiles weigh as much as 150,000 hot dogs. They put 1,000 miles on their buns per week and clock about 50,000 miles a year. The interior sports a hot dog-shape instrument panel, catsup-and-mustard-colored seats, and a removable bun roof.

So who drives such a thing? Well, the hot doggers, of course—recent college graduates who attend Hot Dog High at the Oscar Mayer plant in Madison. They bulk up their knowledge of the company's history and products and hit the road for a year. The competition for hot doggers is tough, and hundreds apply each year. Essentially a public relations job, the new hot doggers are ambassadors for the company—and all of them relish their jobs.

Legendary Lake Mills

❋ ❋ ❋ ❋

Along the interstate between Madison and Milwaukee is the small town that dubbed itself "Legendary Lake Mills." It's legendary, indeed, and controversial too.

An Underwater Mystery

Since the 1840s, locals have buzzed about "stone tepees" standing at the bottom of Rock Lake. The idea seems plausible. Less than three miles due east is Aztalan State Park, an archeological site where the ancient remains of a Middle-Mississippian village, temple mounds, and ceremonial complex have been restored.

But Native American legend and local folklore, combined with years of third-party research, have not been enough to persuade top scientists that there are pyramids beneath Rock Lake's waters. In fact, the phenomena has been dubbed "North America's most controversial underwater archeological discovery of the 20th century."

One theory holds that Ancient Aztecs believed that their ancestors hailed from a land far north of Mexico, called Aztalan. The legend goes that in 1066, the Aztalans of Lake Mills appealed to the gods for relief from a long drought by building sacrificial pyramids. Rain came down, creating a beautiful lake and submerging the pyramids. They named the lake *Tyranena,* meaning "sparkling waters."

Fast-forward 800 years. When the first white settlers set up camp along Tyranena's banks in the 1830s, the resident Winnebago people shared the story of Tyranena with them. But even the Winnebago didn't quite understand the story, as it came from a "foreign tribe." The lore remained as elusive as the small islands that settlers reported as floating above the water.

Soon after the settlers arrived, a sawmill and a gristmill were built on the lake's edge, subsequently raising the water level. What little was left to see of the supposed pyramids was submerged.

Doubt and Circumstance

Over the next 200 years, the lake would be caught up in a continuous cycle of sensationalism and doubt, false starts, and circumstance. In the early 1900s, two brothers, Claude and Lee Wilson, went out duck hunting one hot, clear day during a drought and were able to reach down and touch the so-called pyramid's apex with an oar. Local residents would find the pyramid again the next day, but by the time a reporter got onto the lake a week later rain had fallen, ending the drought and raising the water level. Through the decades, anglers would declare their belief in the structures when they snagged their lines and nets, but interest waned.

The lore was rekindled in the 1930s when a local schoolteacher, Victor Taylor, took it upon himself to canvass residents and dive over the pyramids, without diving equipment. He described four conical underwater structures. With this "evidence," state and national agencies threw money into the effort, even hiring professional divers to explore the underwater structures. But these divers were literally mired by the lake's deteriorating, muddy bottom, mucking up belief in the pyramids once again.

Eventually the controversy would reach an MIT engineer, Max Nohl, the man who invented the first scuba-type device. A master excavator, Nohl made it his personal mission to uncover the truth beneath the lake. He rekindled the town's pyramid fever with his extensive dives and written accounts with detailed measurements.

Debunked?

While Nohl successfully made his case, the curious fact remained that no professional archeologist wanted to be associated with Rock Lake. The establishment theory contends that the lake bottom anomalies are merely glacial castoffs from the last Ice Age. In an article in the September 1962 issue of *The Wisconsin Archeologist,* the pyramids were wholly debunked by the state's academes, who alleged that Native Americans didn't work in stone and that mound-building only began 2,000 years prior, whereas Rock Lake was at least 10,000 years old. Case closed. Or not.

In July 1967, Jack Kennedy, a professional diver from Illinois, was sport diving with friends on Rock Lake. Near the end of the day, after all of his comrades had run out of air, Kennedy took one last dive... over a pyramid. Shocked at his discovery, he removed three rocks from its wall. Further analysis revealed the rocks were made of quartzite from a riverbed. The first concrete evidence was now in hand.

Kennedy continued to dive at Rock Lake, eventually making a sketch of a structure 70 feet long, 30 feet wide, and 15 feet tall, which appeared in *Skin Diver* magazine. His discovery led to a resurgence in the exploration of Rock Lake, a summer haven for leisure boaters and beachgoers. Explorers have documented stone rings, tombs, curiously long rock bars, and pyramidal structures in dives, sonic sonar, and aerial photography. In 1998, two Rock Lake enthusiasts, Archie Eschborn and Jack LeTourneau, formed Rock Lake Research Society to "document and help preserve these archeological treasures that could rewrite North American history... and persuade state officials to declare Rock Lake a historical site."

History Still Unwritten

Does the Aztalan connection hold water? How does glacial activity fit in the picture?

To date, Rock Lake remains just that, a lake, which is still unprotected as a historical site. But locals continue to believe, if not for the archeological and anthropological truth, then for the opportunities the lore and legend provide. In Lake Mills, you can stay at the Pyramid Motel or throw back a Stone Tepee Pale Ale, made by the city's resident Tyranena Brewing Company. Or perhaps you can head to one of the city's three beaches and try your hand at uncovering the mysteries of the "sparkling waters" yourself.

Fast Facts

- Want to watch Air Force bombing practice? Squadrons from across the Midwest go to Hardwood Range (near Finley in Juneau County) to pound 12 square miles of Wisconsin with dummy ordnance. The public is invited to watch, if it stays out of the way.

- Of those who spoke out against slavery in pre-Civil War Wisconsin, Jonathan Walker had perhaps the most credibility. He had been captured in Florida helping slaves escape and was branded on the right palm with S S, for "slave stealer." The scar spoke silent volumes to all who saw it.

- In 1972, Cornucopia resident Ryan O'Malley founded a yacht club for people with yachts—and those without. The Cornucopia Yacht Club didn't even host any aquatic events. Anyone could join, and hundreds did, including President Gerald Ford. Applicants had to answer only one question: "What is the name of your boat, and if you don't have one, what would you call it?" Had O'Malley not passed away in 1991, the Club might still be afloat.

- John Heisman—yes, as in the trophy—is buried in Rhinelander. He wasn't a native Wisconsinite, but his wife was.

- Madison attorney Edward Ben Elson was slightly odd. In 1973, citing information obtained from aliens visiting his yard, he decided that Comet Kohoutek was an alien spaceship that would rescue the righteous from a sinful Earth—and sold tickets for ten dollars. No refunds! Sadly, Elson committed suicide ten years later.

- A branch of the family tree resulting from the relationship between Thomas Jefferson and his slave Sally Hemings took root in Wisconsin. One of Tom and Sally's sons wound up in Madison, where the family used the Jefferson surname and lived prominently as whites, which they were able to do thanks to their fair complexions.

- Today, obviously, you can't drag home part of the Great Wall of China. However, in the 1920s, Chinese leader Sun Yat-sen gave some Great Wall bricks to a well-liked American executive. They're now part of a little wall in Clintonville.

Bay View Tragedy

❋ ❋ ❋ ❋

*"Eight hours for work, Eight hours for rest,
Eight hours for what we will."*

*Those were the words emblazoned across a banner carried during
a parade of some 3,000 Milwaukee industrial workers on Sunday,
May 2, 1886. They demanded that their workdays be reduced to
eight hours. Just a few days later, organized labor's "Eight Hours"
campaign would shut down the city's bustling factories and
culminate in a bloody showdown near the shores of Lake Michigan.*

All Work and No Play

Although Milwaukee laborers had staged several strikes before and
after the Civil War, they preferred to use the ballot box to elect politicians sympathetic to their cause. By the late 1880s, however, the
entire country was buzzing about labor's demand for an eight-hour
workday, and Milwaukee workers were eager to join the fight. Conditions were ripe for reform. The city's industrial laborers typically
toiled for ten hours a day, six days a week, earning little more than a
dollar per day. In machine shops and mills, workers endured dangerous conditions that threatened their lives and their health.

About half of the city's blue-collar workers were members of the
Knights of Labor, led by German immigrant Robert Schilling. As a
union organizer and editor of the *Volksblatt,* a daily labor newspaper,
Schilling was a prominent voice arguing locally for the adoption of
the eight-hour day. A more strident voice was that of the Central
Labor Union's Paul Grottkau, a Socialist and editor of another
German-language labor newspaper, *Arbeiter Zeitung.*

When the unions called for a May 1, 1886, deadline for adoption of the eight-hour day in Milwaukee, the city's industrial workers were ready to drop their tools and strike until their employers
agreed to the demand. Julius Perry, a machinist who joined the

Knights of Labor in 1884, recalled the mood of the workers at the time in a 1930 interview with the *Milwaukee Leader* newspaper's Jessie Stephen.

"The eight-hour day strike of 1886 was a time of great excitement," Perry said, "not only in Milwaukee, but all over the country."

The Big Day

When Saturday, May 1, dawned, about 7,000 people were either on strike or locked out of Milwaukee businesses. They included tailors, bakers, carpenters, joiners, cabinetmakers, slaughterhouse hands, clothing cutters, broom-makers, mill hands, laborers, and brewers. In the following days, about 16,000 blue-collar workers would be idled.

Grottkau's Central Labor Union organized a parade on Sunday morning, May 2, to bang the drum for the cause. About 2,500 laborers, six buses full of tailors, and a series of marching bands paraded through the streets of Milwaukee. About 20,000 spectators were urged to join the march, which ended with a picnic at the Milwaukee Garden beer garden.

The festive atmosphere took a serious turn on Monday, May 3, when about 14,000 workers either walked off their jobs or were locked out by their employers. Eight of the nine Milwaukee breweries were all but deserted. Strikes broke out across the city, and laborers marched on businesses that were still open, urging those workers to join the protest.

Milwaukee Mayor Emil Wallber and law enforcement officials were becoming increasingly anxious as Governor Jeremiah "Uncle Jerry" Rusk arrived in Milwaukee and called out the militia. On Tuesday, May 4, a crowd of about 3,000 men marched on the only factory still open, the North Chicago Rolling Mill in Bay View, calling for workers inside the plant to come out and join them. When the Kosciusko Guards militia detachment arrived to repel the crowd, the soldiers were met with a shower of sticks, stones, and insults. The militia fired warning shots into the air, and the crowd dispersed.

Frightening Turn of Events

Meanwhile, a crowd of strikers in Chicago was gathering in Haymarket Square to demonstrate against the shootings of several protesters the day before. At the end of the rally, a bomb was hurled into a group of police officers, killing eight. The news of this event escalated an already hair-trigger situation in Milwaukee.

About 1,000 strikers regrouped at St. Stanislaus church on Milwaukee's south side on Wednesday morning, May 5. With a banner demanding an eight-hour workday waving before them, the crowd began to march toward the Bay View rolling mill. Major George P. Trauemer, in command of the militia, ordered the strikers to halt, but the workers pressed ahead. This time, the soldiers' volleys would be aimed squarely at the strikers. Trauemer had orders from the governor to fire directly at them.

Perry, the Knights of Labor machinist, remembered the next terrifying moments: "I was in the front rank of the parade carrying the American flag as we started our march. Just before we got to the mills, I handed the flag to the man next to me to carry for a while and it was only a few minutes later that he was shot down right next to me."

When the shots rang out, the strikers scattered in chaos, leaving the dead and dying behind. Some say five strikers died, others insist nine people lay dead, and the historical records are unclear. Among the victims were two uninvolved bystanders—a 12-year-old boy and a retiree who was watching the confrontation from his backyard.

Rusk became a hero, hailed as the man who saved Milwaukee from anarchists. But on the first Sunday in May, the city's labor leaders commemorate the "Bay View Tragedy" as they gather near a historical marker on a bluff overlooking Lake Michigan. There, on the site of the old rolling mill, they raise a banner in support of the eight-hour workday.

It's All Political

❋ ❋ ❋ ❋

Many politicians, military top guns, and other illustrious leaders have ties to Wisconsin. Test your knowledge of eminent Wisconsin-related figures. Match each name to the appropriate biographical description.

Wisconsin War Heroes

a. Richard Bong
b. Douglas MacArthur
c. Billy Mitchell

1. This headstrong son of a Wisconsin Senator served as a Lieutenant Colonel in the U.S. Navy during World War I. After earning the Distinguished Service Cross, the Distinguished Service Medal, and several foreign decorations, this flyboy returned from France a war hero. Yet after the war, his outspoken ways caught up to him. He was eventually court-martialed and convicted of insubordination. Still, five years after his 1936 death, a major Wisconsin airport was named for him.

2. This smokin' brave fighter pilot was known as World War II's "Ace of Aces." Flying P-38s in the Pacific, this young firecracker shot down 40 enemy planes. Tragically, he was killed at age 24 while test piloting the first Lockheed jet fighter plane. He is buried in his hometown of Poplar.

3. This life-long army man became the most famous of his prominent Wisconsin clan. His grandfather, Arthur served on the state's second judicial circuit bench before President Grant appointed him associate justice of the Supreme Court in 1870. Arthur's son, also named Arthur, was a Congressional Medal of Honor recipient during the Civil War. But this offspring exceeded both with his service during World Wars I and II. He is perhaps the most famous U.S. General of the 20th century.

Answers: 1. c, 2. a, 3. b

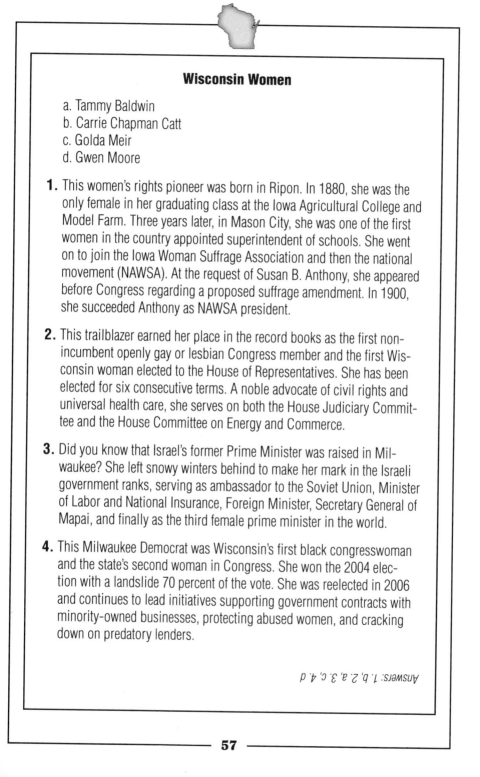

Wisconsin Women

a. Tammy Baldwin
b. Carrie Chapman Catt
c. Golda Meir
d. Gwen Moore

1. This women's rights pioneer was born in Ripon. In 1880, she was the only female in her graduating class at the Iowa Agricultural College and Model Farm. Three years later, in Mason City, she was one of the first women in the country appointed superintendent of schools. She went on to join the Iowa Woman Suffrage Association and then the national movement (NAWSA). At the request of Susan B. Anthony, she appeared before Congress regarding a proposed suffrage amendment. In 1900, she succeeded Anthony as NAWSA president.

2. This trailblazer earned her place in the record books as the first non-incumbent openly gay or lesbian Congress member and the first Wisconsin woman elected to the House of Representatives. She has been elected for six consecutive terms. A noble advocate of civil rights and universal health care, she serves on both the House Judiciary Committee and the House Committee on Energy and Commerce.

3. Did you know that Israel's former Prime Minister was raised in Milwaukee? She left snowy winters behind to make her mark in the Israeli government ranks, serving as ambassador to the Soviet Union, Minister of Labor and National Insurance, Foreign Minister, Secretary General of Mapai, and finally as the third female prime minister in the world.

4. This Milwaukee Democrat was Wisconsin's first black congresswoman and the state's second woman in Congress. She won the 2004 election with a landslide 70 percent of the vote. She was reelected in 2006 and continues to lead initiatives supporting government contracts with minority-owned businesses, protecting abused women, and cracking down on predatory lenders.

Answers: 1. b, 2. a, 3. c, 4. d

Politicos

a. Joseph McCarthy
b. Robert La Follette
c. William Rehnquist
d. William Proxmire

1. This three-term governor of Wisconsin was the engineer behind the "Wisconsin Idea," a proposal to reform corporate taxation and set stricter railroad regulations. He later became a senator in order to share his ideas at a national level. In 1957, the U.S. Senate named this forward thinker one of the five greatest senators of all time.

2. Several Wisconsin politicians have been notable; this one was notorious. At the age 30, he held the distinction of being the youngest circuit judge ever elected in the U.S. He went on to become the youngest member of the U.S. Senate. Not bad, right? Sadly, he abused his power and initiated a widespread Communist witch-hunt, starting with the State Department. During the early 1950s, hundreds of political, military, and entertainment figures were smeared by his campaign.

3. The hardest working man in government? Look up the word "lazy" and you will find no reference to this five-time Wisconsin senator. Perhaps check under "frugal" or "opinionated." Beginning in 1975, he devised the annual Golden Fleece Awards to not just recognize, but to ridicule, the most egregious and outlandish displays of wasteful government spending. On a separate note, this thrifty watchdog holds the record for casting the most consecutive U.S. Senate votes: more than 10,000!

4. This Supreme Court Justice knew his fate even as a lad in a suburban Milwaukee elementary school. During the FDR era, his teacher asked him what he wanted to do when he grew up. His response? "I'm going to change the government." This adamant right-winger first warmed the bench as an associate justice under President Nixon. When the seat of Chief Justice of the Supreme Court opened up in 1986, President Reagan appointed this stickler for small government to the post.

Answers: 1. b, 2. a, 3. d, 4. c

Long Live the Crime-Fighting King

✳ ✳ ✳ ✳

If a chubby, jumpsuit-wearing Elvis came karate-kicking out of a limo, what would you do?

Back in 1977, shortly before Elvis ended his reign as the King of Rock and Roll, you would run, which is just what two trouble-making teens did when Presley gave them the scare of their lives.

Around midnight on June 23, The King arrived in Madison for a show. En route to his hotel from the airport, Presley's limousine, a 1964 Cadillac, hit a red light at the intersection of Stoughton Road and East Washington Avenue. Peering out the window to the right, Presley was watching a young man reading the gas meters at the corner Skyland Service Station, when two teenage misfits charged at the employee and began beating him up.

With a penchant for helping others, Presley, wearing his trademark aviator sunglasses and a dark blue Drug Enforcement Agency jumpsuit over his sequined outfit, busted out of the limousine, despite his bodyguards' requests. He ran toward the scene, kicking karate-style and saying, "I'll take you on."

The hoodlums ran off. As it turned out, the young attendant's father owned the service station and one of the attackers had recently been fired. Getting back in the limousine, Presley reportedly laughed and said, "Did you see the looks on their faces?"

With a caravan of fans in pursuit having just witnessed Presley's crime-prevention skills, the King's entourage continued on to the hotel. The next day, Presley gave a lackluster concert, prompting one local reviewer to write: "So, long live the King. His reign is over. But that is no reason for us not to remember him fondly."

Presley died 51 days later, on August 16, 1977, yet as the reviewer said, many remember his Madison exploits fondly. While Skyland closed years ago, the lot was most recently the site of a used car store, which paid homage to Elvis and Madison's famed gas station altercation with a marble plaque.

Cheeseheads Unite

❊ ❊ ❊ ❊

Of course, the term "Cheesehead" is used to describe the big, soft, triangular headwear seen at sporting events. However, "Cheesehead" also refers to the big, soft, diehard fans that wear them.

Eat Cheese, You Flatlanders!

It's hard to believe that the wildly popular hats actually originated as an insult from the fine citizens of Illinois. Exhilarated by their 1986 Super Bowl victory, Chicago Bears fans began making fun of their northern neighbors by referring to residents of the Dairy State as "Cheeseheads." But Wisconsinites didn't seem to take it personally, and they didn't take it lying down.

The rivalry escalated during baseball season, when Chicago White Sox fans mocked Brewers fans, chanting "Cheeseheads." Ralph Bruno of Milwaukee decided to take action. A cheese-lover himself, Bruno wanted to show the Illinois bullies, and his Wisconsin brethren, that there's really nothing wrong with being a Cheesehead.

A Business Was Born

In 1987, Bruno wore the first wedge-shape cheesehead to a Milwaukee Brewers game. It was fashioned from his mother's sofa cushion. The score of the game is irrelevant to the history that was made that day—the hat was a hit. Bruno got such a positive reaction from other fans that he started developing the idea immediately. In fact, by the next day, he was carving the master mold out of Styrofoam.

Combining elements of several cheese varieties, the Cheesehead is distinctive in its appearance. It has holes for Swiss cheese, the triangular shape associated with Gouda, and, of course, the yellow of Wisconsin cheddar. Bruno himself produced the original hats in his spare time. A pattern-maker for mechanical and industrial machinery, Bruno created his own equipment and begged help from family and friends.

Today, the headgear is so closely associated with football that it may surprise some to learn that the hats were originally produced primarily for baseball fans at County Stadium. That actually led to the first hybrid Cheesehead hat—shaped like a baseball cap. This came about after Brewers owner Bud Selig complained that the larger triangle-shape version obstructed the view for other fans.

A Cheesy Idea

At first, it was hard to get financial support for the business. The idea was intriguing to bankers but hardly a sure thing. In fact, most thought the headwear would only be a short-lived fad. Using credit cards, Bruno got the business up and running—just in time for the Packers' Super Bowl years.

Suddenly, the Cheesehead was the most sought-after hat in town. Well, in the state, actually. And the nationally televised Packers games helped increase demand for the hats throughout the Dairy State—and the image spread throughout the country.

Today, making Cheeseheads is a full-time job for Bruno, who manufactures a multitude of cheese products from his own company, Foamation. The original hat was on display for a time at the Wisconsin Historical Society, and new ones are still rolling off the assembly line for a new generation of fans. Foamation has sold products in all 50 states and in more than 30 countries. Cheeseheads have been worn by high-profile politicians (what better way to win a vote in Wisconsin?) and celebrities, as well.

Cheese Spread

You can still get the original Cheesehead wedge-shape hat, but now it comes in a youth version and an even smaller size for babies or pets. There are even mini Cheeseheads (measuring two inches from point to point) that are just perfect for your Barbie or GI Joe. There's also a patriotic Cheesehead in fashionable red, white, and blue—complete with stars and stripes.

Wisconsin's Three UFO Capitals

❈ ❈ ❈ ❈

The three cities that claim to be Wisconsin's official UFO capital will guarantee orbiting visitors a happy landing.

Extraterrestrial Elmwood

The Pierce County hamlet of Elmwood earned worldwide fame in the 1970s for its UFO sightings. The most spectacular occurred in 1975, when a police officer witnessed a huge, suspended "ball of fire." In total, at least 50 sightings have been recorded here. To celebrate this notoriety, Elmwood's annual UFO festival is held in July, with a nighttime parade and a UFO Watch.

Blastoff in Belleville

Another police officer, this time in the southern Dane County town of Belleville, kicked off a UFO frenzy in January 1987. The officer reported seeing an object flashing the colors of the American flag. At least three other sightings were reported that year, and five more occurred in 2001. The city of 1,500 holds its UFO Day Festival in October, with a UFO parade, "glow bowling," and costume contest.

Space Brothers of Dundee

Wisconsin's third UFO capital is not actually a town but a tavern, Benson's Holiday Hideaway in Fond du Lac County. Its extraterrestrial heritage begins in 1959 when an area resident witnessed a UFO flying over nearby Long Lake. The faithful began to gather, and a yearly festival in July features local celebrities like "UFO Bob" Kuehne, who claims he can communicate with the aliens that appear over the tavern. Attendees wear headbands with sparkly antennae or the more traditional aluminum foil hats to block alien mind probes.

Talkin' Wisconsin

When You Say WIS-CON-SIN, You've Said It All!"
—*"You've Said it All" or "Bud"*

"Madison! It never leaves the hearts of those who have sampled its many delights. White sails on sparkling waters. Autumn arboretum rambles. Saturday mornings at the Farmers' Market. Theater, music, art. All in Madison, a city of endless possibilities."
—*Jerry Minnich, Madison author and publisher*

"Wisconsin is a beautiful state, and though I am obligated as an Illinois resident to rib its residents, it is hard to escape the fact it produces some of the nicest people in the Midwest."
—*From* Oddball Wisconsin *by Jerome Pohlen*

"It is possible, even probable to be told a truth about a place, to accept it, to know it and at the same time not to know anything about it. I had never been to Wisconsin, but all my life I had heard about it, had eaten its cheeses, some of them as good as any in the world. And I must have seen pictures. Everyone must have. Why then was I unprepared for the beauty of this region, for its variety of field and hill, forest, lake? I think now I must have considered it one big level cow pasture because of the state's enormous yield of milk products . . . . I remembered that I had been told Wisconsin is a lovely state, but the telling had not prepared me."
—*John Steinbeck in* Travels with Charley in Search of America

"What did that feel like when you went into a barn on a windy day . . . when the wind was blowing around the corners and rustling under the eaves,

when the pigeons were cooing up on the hayfork track? I often talk about it as being in the middle of an orchestra with the music all around you."
—*Jerry Apps, author of* Barns of Wisconsin, *in an interview for Wisconsin Public Television*

TV Shows Feel at Home in Wisconsin

❋ ❋ ❋ ❋

Quick, name a U.S. city that's been the setting for a television show. New York, Los Angeles, Chicago, and Miami will certainly come to mind. Then there's San Francisco, Las Vegas, Seattle, and even Dallas. But don't forget Milwaukee and a handful of other Wisconsin cities. It may lack the glitz and glamour of some of our nation's big TV hubs, but Wisconsin is the site of several prominent TV shows.

Happy Days Are Here Again

Between 1974 and 1983, millions of Americans tuned in to ABC to watch the nostalgic sit-com *Happy Days*. For a half-hour each week, they could step into simpler times and the lives of Richie Cunningham, his family, and his friends in 1950s Milwaukee.

Happy Days could have been set almost anywhere, but Milwaukee was perfect for the wholesome Midwest tone the show projected. It was not too big (danger and glamour just wouldn't be right for this gang). Yet Milwaukee was not so small that it was boring; the cast had more to do than watch the grass grow. While the downtown skyline was not often shown, the characters proudly displayed their local sports loyalties with Marquette University and UW Madison pennants, sweaters, and letter jackets. Home run hitter Hank Aaron of the Milwaukee Braves even appeared in one episode as himself.

From Small Beginnings

Happy Days actually got its start as a single episode of *Love, American Style* called "Love and the Happy Days." The show's popularity, however, eventually resulted in four spin-offs: *Laverne & Shirley, Blansky's Beauties, Mork and Mindy,* and *Joanie Loves Chachi.* The most notable of these was *Laverne & Shirley,* which also took place in Milwaukee.

Penny Marshall and Cindy Williams starred as the title characters Laverne DeFazio and Shirley Feeney in this ABC comedy that ran from 1976 to 1983. The girls were first introduced on *Happy Days* as friends of Fonzie, and the show took place during the same time period—the late 1950s through 1967.

The pair were friends and roommates who worked as bottle-cappers at the fictional Schotz Brewery. And what better setting than Milwaukee for a job like that? In fact, the TV brewery was modeled after Milwaukee's Schlitz Brewery, and Laverne and Shirley lived on Knapp Street, an actual street near the Schlitz plant.

As times change, so do locations, and after five years in the beer city, Laverne and Shirley lost their bottlecapping jobs to automation. The duo moved to Los Angeles, where they continued "Making Our Dreams Come True," as the show's theme song suggests.

Other Cities, Other Shows

A handful of other shows took place in real Wisconsin cities. *Step by Step,* a comedy, set in Port Washington (near Milwaukee), starred Suzanne Somers and Patrick Duffy as a newly married couple trying to blend their families together. The show lasted seven seasons in the 1990s.

Another 1990s show that took place in Milwaukee was *A Whole New Ballgame*, about a professional ballplayer who worked as a sportscaster during a players strike. The show starred Corbin Bernsen with Julia Campbell as his station manager. Unfortunately, the show lasted only about as long as the baseball strike.

Set in beautiful Madison in 1995, *The George Wendt Show* starred—if you didn't already guess—George Wendt, who had just finished a long run as Norm on *Cheers*. But even that wasn't enough to keep this show on the air. It was canceled after seven episodes.

American Dreamer did a little better, lasting one whole season in 1990. Robert Ulrich played Tom Nash, a newspaper columnist who lived in Kenosha and wrote for a Chicago newspaper.

Wisconsin jumped into the limelight one more time in 2008 with *Aliens in America*, set in Chippewa Falls. The plot featured a teenage boy whose mom agreed to host a foreign exchange student hoping that the newcomer would help her son infiltrate the in-crowd. What she didn't expect was a Muslim teenager from Pakistan—with a few problems of his own. *Aliens* got the axe after a single season.

Maybe If It's Not Really in Wisconsin

So do fictional Wisconsin cities fare any better? Well, yes and no. *A Minute with Stan Hooper*, set in the made-up Waterford Falls was pretty much a bomb. It was cancelled after only six episodes.

Life with Louie, an animated show, managed to last three seasons in fictional Cedar Knoll. Based on the childhood of actor Louie Anderson, the comedy focused on eight-year-old Louie and his adventures growing up in Wisconsin with his parents and ten siblings.

And remember *Picket Fences*? Created by David E. Kelley, this one was a drama that lasted four seasons. Bizarre crimes were the norm for the residents of Rome, a fictional small town, not too far from Green Bay. The show's all-star cast included Tom Skerritt, Kathy Baker, Lauren Holly, Holly Marie Combs, Ray Walston, Don Cheadle, Marlee Matlin, and other familiar faces.

Hitting the airwaves in 1998, *That '70s Show* was another hit sitcom that derived its success from a burst of nostalgia. Viewers eager to relive the peace, love, and hippie decade made *That '70s Show* a hit. The series revolved around a group of teenagers growing up with their families in the fictional Point Place in 1976. The show lasted a solid eight seasons.

Good Clean Fun

Speaking of longevity, the popular soap opera *The Young and the Restless* has been on since 1973. Genoa City is home to the Newman and Abbott clans, both wealthy from the cosmetics industry and competing for power and money. And don't forget love—there's forbidden romance, on-again, off-again relationships, fairy tale endings, and star-crossed lovers all right in the Dairy State.

Wisconsin Cow Chip Throwing Fun

✳ ✳ ✳ ✳

Wisconsin has its chocolate chips and potato chips—and then there are the cow chips.

Cow chips are, simply put, the waste product of a cow's herbivorous diet. You know, cow droppings. Wisconsin is known as the Dairy State, so it stands to reason that there are a lot of cows around. And a lot of cows means a lot of... well, you get the picture. At the Wisconsin Cow Chip Throw in Prairie du Sac, the chips are front and center. There are a lot of activities to please the family at this festival, though it's the chip-throwing contest that is the highlight.

Whatever Gave Them that Idea?

Winters were cold and lonely in Wisconsin for the early settlers. When trees were scarce—or too big to cut down—the pioneers looked for alternate heating fuel sources. They discovered that cow chips (chock full of grasses and minerals) could be used for fuel. After they dried, they were odorless and they burned with intense heat and no sooty residue. They were so valuable to the settlers that they were even used to trade for food and other necessities.

Wisconsinites don't use cow chips much these days to heat their homes, but each year thousands of people gather to celebrate and have fun with them. There's plenty to do if you're not into chucking chips—just look for the Trojan Cow. It's 20 feet tall, and kids can climb inside. There is live music, good food, races, and a parade, too.

But let's get to the main event. Contestants select their chips from the Meadow Muffin Wagon. The best ones are about six inches around and fairly dense. Chips are usually tossed like a flying disk, and each competitor gets two throws. The winner is simply the competitor with the longest throw. There are two things to remember when competing. First, contestants can't wear gloves. Second, if they're brave enough, they can lick their fingers for a better grip.

Wisconsin's Federal Fearmonger

❋ ❋ ❋ ❋

Wisconsin has produced many notable U.S. senators, but the state also claims one very infamous senator, Joseph Raymond McCarthy, best known for his sensational communist witch hunt.

A Promising Youth

Born to a farming family in rural Grand Chute on November 15, 1908, McCarthy was a bright but restless youngster. He dropped out of school after graduating from eighth grade and started his own chicken farm. Unfortunately, his birds fell victim to disease, and at the age of 20, McCarthy went back to school.

Somehow, he crammed an entire high school education into nine months, while also managing a grocery store in Manawa. He earned such stellar grades that Marquette University accepted him as a law student. At Marquette, he was known as "Smiling Joe" for his good humor and became a champion middleweight boxer, often felling larger opponents with his high-energy fighting style. McCarthy was so good that he even considered making a career in the ring, but a local boxing instructor talked him into getting his degree instead.

Throwing his energy into school, McCarthy dove into campus debate clubs where he proved he could be as much of a pit bull with his words as he was with boxing. After graduating in 1935, he became a lawyer in the small towns of Waupaca and Shawano and, by age 30, was elected judge in Wisconsin's Tenth Judicial Circuit.

Serving His Country

McCarthy put his legal practice on hold to join the Marines in 1942 and serve in World War II. He was an intelligence officer in the South Pacific and saw action as part of a bombing raid crew, which earned him a second nickname, "Tailgunner Joe."

McCarthy would later falsely say he carried ten pounds of shrapnel in his leg, but in truth, he returned to Wisconsin unscathed and determined to regain his circuit judgeship. In 1946, he dared to run for the Republican candidacy for the U.S. Senate against the popular 21-year incumbent, Robert M. LaFollette Jr. McCarthy barely squeaked through to win the nomination and became the youngest U.S. Senator at that time at age 38.

The Beginning of the End

The 1950 Senate election may have spurred McCarthy's monumental decline. Perhaps grasping for a campaign issue, McCarthy made the shocking claim that he had a list of 205 government officials who were communists. The government's House Un-American Activities Committee had already paved the way for such suspicion with its investigations of the Hollywood entertainment industry starting in 1947. The Senate opened hearings on McCarthy's allegations in March 1950, but McCarthy never proved his case. In 1952, the Senate turned the tables and began investigating McCarthy.

Although the committee found him guilty of unethical actions, his loyal base still reelected him in 1952. Ironically, McCarthy was made Chairman of the Committee on Government Operations and Investigations. "Tailgunner Joe" kept looking for communists, even going so far as to accuse the U.S. Army and the Eisenhower presidential administration. However, hearings broadcast via the new medium of television in 1954 helped discredit McCarthy. By December of that year, he was officially condemned by the Senate for abuse of power. He finished the two and a half years of his term, largely powerless and unpopular. At the same time, McCarthy began to drink heavily and suffered various physical ailments.

McCarthy succumbed to hepatitis on May 2, 1957. His grave in Appleton's St. Mary's Cemetery is marked by a gray granite headstone that simply reads "United States Senator." He left behind a wife, Jean, an adopted daughter, Tierney, and a new word that's still in use: "McCarthyism." Thanks to this term, Joseph McCarthy's name will forever be associated with the act of aggressively hunting for certain people based on unsubstantiated charges.

Fast Facts

- Archibald McArthur (1844–1925) of Dodgeville mystified everyone. The fashionable young lawyer had everything and was going places. In his middle age, he abjured it all to become a miserly, vegetarian recluse living on 50 cents a day. He left most of his $250,000 estate to a near stranger.

- Only one parent and child have served in the U.S. Senate simultaneously: Henry Dodge (D-Wisconsin, 1848–57) and his son Augustus Dodge (D-Iowa, 1848–55).

- When the glaciers retreated, they left numerous depressions with a shape that gives a long strip of eastern Wisconsin its modern name: Kettle Moraine. The Potawatomi, who called Kettle Moraine "The Great Spirit Washbowl," said it would fill with water after protracted northerly winds. It's located just south of Palmyra.

- Oh, to be in Waukesha in 1978–79 during the Kangaroo Panic, when locals reported a rash of kangaroo sightings. The state Agriculture Department even warned citizens against kangaroo-borne diseases. No 'roos were ever caught, though, and the explanation seems to involve practical jokers and poor deer identification.

- Burlington has a Liars' Trail, a path of bronze plaques through town all containing falsehoods. The local Liars' Club collects whoppers and has an annual competition to see who can tell the biggest fib. The competition is for amateurs only—no politicians.

- What would you do if a 55-ton boulder bounced into your bedroom? Fortunately, Fountain City residents Dwight and Maxine Anderson weren't sleeping at the time, and the rest of the house wasn't harmed. The Andersons sold the property to friends, who now operate it as a curiosity.

- Green Bay Packer fans experience badgerlike snarling fits at the words "Dan Devine." In 1974, the beleaguered head coach told Time that locals had shot his dog. In 2000, he finally admitted his exaggeration. The Devine dog had attacked a neighbor's ducks, and the neighbor felt terrible about the accidental shooting.

Waters of Wisconsin

❋ ❋ ❋ ❋

Wisconsin life and recreation often revolve around the water. This water-lovin' spirit has long been a prominent part of Wisconsin.

Water World

The Great Lakes, which cover 4.5 million acres, border Wisconsin. Inland lakes, numbering 15,081, account for almost an additional million acres, or about 3 percent of Wisconsin's total area. Wisconsin also hosts about 200 miles of the Mississippi River and has more than 12,600 other rivers and streams. Here are two Wisconsin water distinctions:

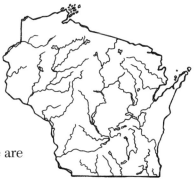

- With 28 lakes in its network, Eagle River is considered to have the largest chain of lakes in the world.

- Spanning more than 32,000 acres, Horicon Marsh is the largest freshwater Cattail Marsh in the U.S. In 1991, it was deemed one of only 15 wetlands of international importance.

Breaking the Ice

The vast majority (about two-thirds) of what we know as Wisconsin was buried beneath a sprawling 5,000-foot-thick blanket of ice 15,000 years ago. This period of glacial dominance gradually diminished as unstable temperatures caused widespread melting in alternation with partial refreezing. This created water-filled pockets in lowlands and eventually created Lake Superior, Lake Michigan, the Fox River, and the Wisconsin River, among other bodies of water.

A River Runs Through It

The Anishinaabe Native Americans had a different explanation for how the Wisconsin River was formed. Their early tribal lore tells of a giant serpent that dwelled in the dark forests surrounding Big Lake. One day, the snake decided to embark on a massive migration. He slithered his colossal body across the land, cracking earth and creating tributaries with his tail. His path became the Wisconsin River.

Lake Michigan and Lake Superior

Let's get fresh! Not only is Lake Michigan the largest freshwater lake contained entirely within the U.S., it also hosts the largest freshwater dune ecosystem in the world! Lake Michigan's water surface area extends 22,300 miles and reaches as deep as 925 feet.

On the other hand, Lake Superior, as its name implies, exceeds all the other Great Lakes in size and scope by far! According to the Wisconsin Department of Natural Resources, Lake Superior is so massive, you could theoretically pour the other four Great Lakes into its gigantic basin and still have room for three more Lake Eries. It's also the coldest and deepest, descending more than 1,300 feet.

The Size of a Winnebago

Like the big family campers of the same name, Wisconsin's Lake Winnebago is the largest of its kind and can cover miles and miles. Specifically, it is the largest of Wisconsin's non-great lakes. The surface area of Lake Winnebago is about 137,700 acres, and it boasts 85 miles of shoreline. Lake Pepin, Lake Petenwell, Lake Chippewa, and Poygan Lake round out the state's top five largest lakes.

What's in a Name?

The names of many Wisconsin lakes and rivers were derived from Native American names or European encounters with natives in the 17th and 18th centuries. For example, the Menomonee River comes from the Chippewa word *Manomini-sibi* from *omanominig*, which means "wild rice people." Little Buttes des Morts Lake was named for a Meskwaki (Fox) burial ground. Meaning "Hill of the Dead," it was the site where the French massacred hundreds of people. Wazee Lake gets its name from the Ho-Chunk word for "tall pine," many of which can be found at nearby Black River State Forest.

While it's Lake Michigan today, this body of water had something of an identity crisis in the past. It was previously called "Lake of the Stinking Water," "Lake of the Puants" (French for *Indian*), and even "Lac des Illinois," which roughly means "Lake Illinois."

Imitation being the highest form of flattery, several Wisconsin lakes share names. When someone says "Meet you at Mud Lake," you may want to ask for clarification. There are 116 Mud Lakes in Wisconsin! In the state, there are also 82 Bass Lakes, 59 Long Lakes, and 49 Spring Lakes. One can also *find* 42 Lost Lakes!

Approximately 60 percent of the lakes in Wisconsin do not have an official name. These anonymous lakes typically consist of less than ten acres. Some assume a body of water that modest in size would be described as a pond as opposed to lake. What's the difference? Well, there are a range of factors to be considered when differentiating a lake from a pond. One must evaluate inhabiting plant and animal life, temperature, water movement, and oxygen levels. The simplest way to identify is depth. Lakes are too deep for sunlight to penetrate to the bottom. Ponds, however, are shallow enough for light to reach the bottom, allowing aquatic plants to carry out photosynthesis.

Go Fish

Wisconsin is the second most popular fishing destination in the country. Skilled anglers hook everything from bass to Muskellunge ("musky" or "muskie" for short). Back in 1949, Louis Spray reeled in the largest musky ever recorded—a whopping 69 pounds. It was caught in Hayward, otherwise known as the Musky Capital of the World! Boulder Junction also prides itself as the Musky Capital of the World; the slogan is even a registered trademark on the website of the town's chamber of commerce (whose phone number happens to be 1–800–GO–MUSKY). To celebrate their claim to fame, Boulder Junction has held its Musky Jamboree annually since 1957.

Clinton's "Mad Man"

❊ ❊ ❊ ❊

Driving along Interstate 43 in southern Wisconsin near Clinton, it rises on the horizon like a magnificent vision. You look once, twice, even three times, not believing what you're seeing. It's a sight unlike any other: a truck in a tree.

The Truck in the Tree began as a simple request to a father from his son for a tree house. A creation of the "Mad Man of Wisconsin," a play on Clinton resident Mark Madson's last name, the turquoise and white 1959 half-ton Chevy Fleetside pickup truck has been wedged between two basswood trees along the Interstate since 1994. It stands as a sentry to Madson's maniacal, motley collection of reworked vehicles, statues, and sculptures made of old parts and more.

Surprising Sculptures, Creative Cars

Madson has long been a creative tinker, recreating new from old and looking at things from a fresh perspective; in fact, he calls himself an "upside-down and backwards guru." His foray into the reconstructive arts began in the seventh grade (Madson is now in his 50s), when he took the motor off the family lawn mower, rigged it to his bike, and embarked on a weeklong adventure.

A welder by trade, Madson's skill set serves him well. One of his earliest public creations was a mailbox made from a Chevy 427 big block engine that took top honors in the Super Chevy best mailbox contest. Stolen just three months after making its public debut in 1989, Madson eventually tracked down the thieves and recovered his creation. It now stands next to his Harley in his living room, which is part living space and part museum. The lawnmower bike, reworked from Madson's seventh grade adventure, is also there.

Through the years Madson, often using his son's questions and requests as inspiration, has created a number of thought-provoking anomalies. One example is a 600-pound, 427-cubic-inch big-block engine, dubbed the "Answer Is Blow'n In The Wind." It sits on a skinny pole that doubles as a wind vane and anemometer, a device that measures wind speed. Indicative of Madson's line of thinking, he said of the Answer: "Many people have asked me how I got that long skinny pole to hold that engine up there for so long. I simply say, the pole isn't holding the engine up, the engine is holding the pole down!" There's also the 1969 Dodge Charger, painted by local technical college students to look exactly like the General Lee from *The Dukes of Hazzard.* It sits atop a tavern in nearby Allens Grove named the Boar's Nest, just like the bar the Dukes frequented on the show.

One of Madson's more recent creations is the Packer Mobile, a 1978 Cadillac Eldorado Biarritz that he debuted in 2008 when the Pack was headed toward a 13–3 season. He drove almost 400 miles roundtrip to Green Bay to watch his football team cream the Lions.

Four hundred miles isn't a bad drive…unless it's late December and you are driving across the Upper Midwest in a convertible with its top down. During the drive, it was 13 degrees out, with a driving wind chill factor of about 40 below! The Packer Mobile featured a six-foot flagpole bearing a Packers flag, as well as an 11-foot flame-painted surfboard, a blue shark fin, and bullhorns. The Packer Mobile is actually Madson's sixth conversion of this Cadillac-turned-convertible, the last of which was dedicated to Jimmy Buffett.

Madson's experience and creativity has garnered him appearances on television shows such as *Ripley's Believe It or Not, Junkyard Wars,* and the Discovery Channel's *Monster Nation,* where he turned a car into a cube with some creative crushing.

❋ ❋ ❋ ❋

- *Wisconsin Shriners are not excused from upholding the state tradition of displaying something big and colorful. The Milwaukee Tripoli Shrine Temple on Wisconsin Avenue looks very much like a mosque, complete with minarets. There's even a camel sculpture outside to help those who don't quite grasp the Middle Eastern motif.*

From the Badger State to Tinsel Town

❋ ❋ ❋ ❋

Is it something in the water? Or perhaps in the cheese? Whatever Wisconsin's secret might be, this state has played a part in the start of some of America's favorite television and silver screen stars. Here are a few Wisconsin-born celebrities.

Heather Graham

This big-eyed, strawberry blonde rollerskated her way through 1997's *Boogie Nights*. She also swing danced her way into the broken heart of Mike Peters (played by Jon Favreau) in the 1996 hit *Swingers* and appeared in 1999's *Austin Powers: The Spy Who Shagged Me*. Graham is from Milwaukee.

Kathy Kinney

Cleveland, Ohio, has long wanted to claim the *The Drew Carey Show's* mumu-wearing Mimi as its own. The Buckeye State can have the character, but Kinney, the actress who brought wisecracking Mimi to life, is a Stevens Point native, born there in 1954. (Ironically, this Wisconsinite is allergic to cheese.)

Willem Dafoe

Maybe it was a good thing tyrannical director Michael Cimino fired Dafoe from his first movie role, a bit part in the 1981 film *Heaven's Gate*. The expensive flop ultimately folded United Artists, yet Dafoe went on to roles in more than 75 films, eventually nabbing Academy Award nominations for Best Actor in a Supporting Role for 1986's *Platoon* and 2000's *Shadow of the Vampire*. He also played the role of Jesus in 1988's *The Last Temptation of Christ* and the Green Goblin in the *Spiderman* films.

Pettit Center Keeps Fast Pace

✳ ✳ ✳ ✳

Did you ever wonder where those American speed skating stars at the Winter Olympics learn to skate like that? For many of them, it's right here in Wisconsin at the Pettit National Ice Center in Milwaukee.

A Top-notch Track

The state-of-the-art facility opened on December 31, 1992, right next to State Fair Park. Named for Jane and Lloyd Pettit, philanthropists from Milwaukee, it sits on the site of the former outdoor Wisconsin Olympic Oval. The outdoor facility was in operation from 1967 to 1991 and was the training facility for many competitive speed skaters and Olympic medal winners. As you can imagine, the new climate-controlled rink is a vast improvement. Although the U.S. national team is based in Salt Lake City, Utah, the Pettit Center is also a prime training location for U.S. athletes. In fact, it has special significance to athletes preparing for the 2010 Winter Olympics in Vancouver since it is the only indoor oval at sea level—just like the facility in Vancouver.

Since its opening, the nonprofit Pettit Center has hosted numerous national and international speed skating competitions. In 2005, the U.S. National Short Track Championship drew a crowd from 33 states. Events that year, including the World Cup speed skating competition, are estimated to have generated $2.5 million for the community. Of the U.S. speed skaters that participated in the last  four Olympic games, all of them have either trained or competed at the Pettit Center. This includes familiar names such as Dan Jansen, Bonnie Blair, Apolo Anton Ohno, Shani Davis, and Chad Hedrick.

Something for Everyone

If you think the Pettit Center is just home to past and future Olympians, you've got it wrong. In fact, the center's mission statement makes it clear that they support both the health benefits and physical development of skating for interested people of *all* ages and *all* abilities. They strive to promote the sport of skating to the public, including people who skate for exercise and enjoyment, not just competition. Only after stating that do they mention the added goal of preparing amateur athletes for local, state, national, and international speed skating competitions.

❋ ❋ ❋ ❋

- *The Pettit National Ice Center cost $13 million to build.*

- *The building is 200,000 square feet; the arena is 155,000 square feet. Most importantly, there are 97,000 square feet of ice.*

- *The 400-meter Olympic oval was designed for long-track speed skating.*

- *There is seating for 3,000 around the oval.*

- *The Pettit also houses two international-size rinks for hockey, figure skating, and short track speed skating. Both measure 100 feet by 200 feet.*

- *The Pettit Center has one of the largest skating schools in the nation and one of the largest adult hockey leagues in Wisconsin.*

- *Wheelchair hockey is also played in the Pettit Center.*

- *Would you be surprised to learn that the facility houses a 450-meter, two-lane jogging track? This track surrounds the ice oval and is home to the Badgerland Striders Running Club and the Mustangs AAU Track and Field Club.*

- *More than 500,000 people visit the Pettit Center annually.*

- *Speed skating is the fastest means of human travel that doesn't utilize gravity or mechanical aids.*

Wisconsin Olympic Athletes Are Golden

❋ ❋ ❋ ❋

Wisconsin hasn't hosted the Olympic Games, but that doesn't mean it hasn't produced its share of Olympic athletes. Do you remember these Olympians from Wisconsin?

- **Dan Jansen (West Allis) Speed Skating 1984, 1988, 1992, 1994:** Dan is known for his dramatic gold medal win in the 1,000-meter race in the 1994 Olympics in Lillehammer, Norway. His best Olympic showing before 1994 was fourth place in the 500 in both 1984 and 1988.

- **Bonnie Blair (Pewaukee) Speed Skating 1984, 1988, 1992, 1994:** Actually a transplant from Champaign, Illinois, Bonnie came to Wisconsin to train at the Pettit Center right after graduating high school. She won gold and bronze medals in 1988 and two gold medals in both 1992 and 1994. After retiring from competition, she moved to Wisconsin. Currently, her medals reside in a coffee table in her Pewaukee home.

- **Chris Witty (West Allis) Speed Skating 1994, 1998, 2002:** Chris took part in her first Olympic games when she was 18 and placed 23rd in the 1,000-meter race. By 1998, she had won a silver medal in the same event. She also won a bronze in the 1,500 meter. In 2002, she achieved gold in the 1,000-meter race in Salt Lake City. With competition in her blood, Chris went to the 2000 summer Olympics as well and placed fifth in cycling.

- **Casey Fitzrandolph (Verona) Speed Skating 1998, 2002:** Casey started skating one month after watching Eric Heiden in Lake Placid. His success led him to the 1998 Olympics where he placed sixth, seventh, and thirty-first. In 2002, he came in seventh in the 1,000-meter but achieved his dream in the 500-meter race where he won gold.

Taste of Wisconsin

The Incredible, Edible Pasty

Think portable food is the best thing since sliced bread? Long before stores were flooded with handheld convenience foods, the wives of Wisconsin's 19th-century miners were cooking up their own pocket-size delicacies.

So, What Is It, Exactly?

Called a pasty—that's pronounced "pah-stee," not "pay-stee," by the way—these pastry pockets were ideal sustenance for miners. They were hearty, traditionally filled with meat (when it was available, of course), potatoes, onions, or any root vegetable capable of handling Wisconsin's short growing season and long winter storage. (Carrots and turnips have also been known to show up in pasties.)

Generally, to make pasties, wives would roll out some dough, use an overturned plate or pie tin to cut the dough in a circle, fill it, fold it into a half-moon shape, then seal and crimp the edges. Because of the way a pasty was made, its size was perfect: big enough to fill a hungry miner's belly but small enough to fit in his pocket, where the freshly baked pasty would warm him, and his body heat could, in turn, help keep the pasty warm.

The pocket-size pasty also eliminated the need for a miner to haul a lunch pail into the cramped mine shaft or clamber out to fetch it up top. Come lunchtime, he could simply sit down where he was and munch—no pail, plate, or utensils necessary. Perhaps the pasty's most miner-friendly feature was that its hard, crimped edge acted as a handle. Miners, who were covered head to toe in grime, could simply hold the pasty by that edge and take easy, filth-free bites.

Overseas Origins

Who invented this ingenious treat? Credit goes to Cousin Jack—a.k.a. Cornish miners. Prompted by the collapse of the copper mining industry in Cornwall, England, many miners in the early 1830s began making their way to Wisconsin after hearing that lead mines were opening up and were hungry for workers. Some say the nickname "Cousin Jack" originated because so many immigrant miners, upon getting jobs for themselves, asked if there was also a job available for their cousin Jack back in Cornwall. Others say it originated from the way Cornish folks called each other cousin when greeting each other, Jack being simply a common Cornish name. For the next 20 years, Cornish miners and their families streamed into towns like Shullsburg and Mineral Point, bringing along their hard rock-mining expertise and the ways, language, and, of course, food of their culture.

Notoriously superstitious people, the Cornish explained much as the work of giants, pixies, and fairies, and like much in their lives, pasties and mines weren't exempt from the reaches of their superstitions. Cornish miners believed in what they called "knockers," spirits living in the mines that were roused by the crash and bang of the miners' picks and shovels against the rock. Here, a pasty's handle edge came in handiest. Much like the Native Americans who would bury a fish in the garden as an offering to the gods, Cornish miners would toss their uneaten crimped edge into the mine as an offering to appease the knockers and ensure their own safety. Did it work? Hard to say; mining is an inherently dangerous job, and deaths weren't unheard of. But considering pasties have survived more than a century and are still served up as a favorite Wisconsin dish even today, it's probably safe to say that tossing the knockers a piece of crust didn't hurt, but a whole pasty now and again might have been a better bet.

❋ ❋ ❋ ❋

- *In 1985, a group in Cornwall, England, made a pasty that was more than 32 feet long.*

- *Brenda Wootton, a Cornish folk singer, released an album in 1971, called* Pasties & Cream, *featuring the song, "There's Something About a Pasty."*

- *Pasties are also popular regional treats in areas of North America outside of Wisconsin, including Michigan's Upper Peninsula and parts of eastern Pennsylvania.*

Baseball's Rodney Dangerfield

✻ ✻ ✻ ✻

The late Rodney Dangerfield, who claimed that he never got any respect, has a kindred spirit—Bob Uecker, the legendary voice of the Milwaukee Brewers, who also didn't get any respect during six Major League seasons.

A Less-than-Stellar Career

For his career as a player, Bob Uecker hit just above the Mendoza Line—a baseball term that describes a batting average of .200. "The highlight of my career?" Uecker asks rhetorically. "In '67 with St. Louis, I walked with the bases loaded to drive in the winning run in an intersquad game in spring training."

Uecker says his deficiencies at the plate were so obvious that "when I came up to bat with three men on and two outs in the ninth, I looked in the other team's dugout and they were already in street clothes."

A catcher with four Major League clubs—including the Milwaukee Braves from 1962 to 1963—Uecker's play behind the plate would have won him a Tarnished Glove, rather than a Gold Glove, at the end of a season. "The way to catch a knuckleball," he joked, "is to wait until it stops rolling, and then pick it up."

Success at a New Position

But after Uecker took off the tools of ignorance for good, unlike Dangerfield, he got plenty of respect—and notoriety. Uecker made several appearances on *The Tonight Show* with Johnny Carson and starred in Miller Lite beer commercials as a member of the Miller Lite All-Stars, which included Dangerfield, Billy Martin, Mickey Spillane, and John Madden, among others. He eventually returned to his native Milwaukee and started doing play-by-play broadcasts for the city's new American League team, the Brewers.

Known as "Mr. Baseball," Uecker also ventured into the world of acting. For five seasons in the 1980s, Uecker played the role of George Owens in the sitcom *Mr. Belvedere*. But Uecker's portrayal of wisecracking play-by-play announcer Harry Doyle in the 1989 hit movie *Major League* brought him stardom on the big screen. *Major League* went on to gross $50 million and produce two sequels: *Major League II* and *Major League: Back to the Minors* (Uecker reprised the role of Harry Doyle in both sequels).

Few can match Uecker's abilities as a play-by-play announcer in real life. He received the annual Ford C. Frick Award in 2003 from the Baseball Hall of Fame—an award given to a broadcaster for making major contributions to baseball.

Naturally, Uecker's acceptance speech was chock-full of self-deprecating humor. Describing the day he was born, Uecker said, "I remember it being very cold. It was January. I didn't weigh very much. I think the birth certificate said something like 10 ounces. I was very small. And I remember the coldness on my back from the asphalt. And I was immediately wrapped in swaddling clothes and put in the back of a '37 Chevy without a heater. And that was the start of this Cinderella story that you are hearing today."

❋ ❋ ❋ ❋

- *After the Braves relocated to Atlanta, Bob Uecker lost one game for them all by himself. He committed catcher's interference, allowed two crucial passed balls (in one inning), and threw a ball into centerfield. The two runs scored off of his errors were the Braves' margin of defeat that day.*

- *In addition to playing for the Braves in both Milwaukee and Atlanta, Bob Uecker also played for the Philadelphia Phillies and the St. Louis Cardinals.*

Bragging Rights

Taped Crusaders on the Ball

Sitting quietly in the corner of an otherwise loud space is, perhaps, the world's largest tape ball, at home in a Madison body shop. It now weighs at least 150 pounds and keeps growing all the time. Several years in the making, it now takes two people to shimmy it out of its corner.

Just steps away from an auto painting booth, the ball is made completely of used tape from the painting process; tape and plastic is used to block off parts of the car that shouldn't be painted, such as the windshield or door handles. The project began as a way to keep the tape out of the garbage.

But Is It the World's Largest?

In 2005, someone put a 60-pound ball of tape on eBay and dubbed it the "world's largest ball of tape"; it was scooped up for $900. In 2006, a young Canadian got minor league hockey teams to contribute used tape to his ball. He purportedly created a seven-foot-tall, 1,862-pound ball of hockey tape, but he never made the call to Guinness.

The current record holders for the world's largest ball of tape are two New Zealanders who spent two months building their version. Dubbed the "largest of its kind" when completed in 2007, it weighed in at 53 kilograms and has a circumference of 2.5 meters; in the American system, it weighs a measly 116.845 pounds and is 8.2 feet around.

The Madison body shop's ball puts the Aussies to shame weight-wise. As for circumference, the body shop's employees haven't bothered with spherical perfection, so that's more difficult to measure. For now, the employees are elated to know their ball is bigger than Guinness's record holder, but in light of the young Canadian's poorly documented feat, they are still content with the second-best distinction and with owning the world's "probably-largest" ball of tape.

The Beasts Are Back

✻ ✻ ✻ ✻

"If you go into the woods today, you're sure of a big surprise," says the line from the old song "Teddy Bears' Picnic." Today, it applies to Wisconsin's great outdoors as rebounding populations of bears, cougars, and wolves surface in the least likely spots.

Bizarre Bears

The citizens of Wauwatosa, an urban area adjacent to Milwaukee, were shocked in April 2005, when a worker at Schwaab Stamp and Seal discovered a 154-pound black bear peeping through a window at him as it stood on its hind legs. The bruin then ran up a tree near 114th and Burleigh streets, where a tranquilizer-toting team from the Milwaukee County Zoo nabbed him. A series of sightings leading up to the incident suggested the bear had come from Kaukauna.

Until the last decade or so, most people assumed black bears were found only in northern Wisconsin. But the state's estimated bear population in 2000 was 12,700, more than double the number from the 1985 bear census. On top of that, male bears require almost 30 square miles of personal territory, and they are roaming farther and farther south to find it.

It doesn't seem that Wisconsin's bears are suffering for lack of food, however. One huge, deceased bruin sparked a battle between a Boyceville farmer and state wildlife officials over ownership of its 700-pound carcass in February 2009. To compare, an average black bear weighs about 350 pounds.

The farmer said he ran over the bear with his combine in his Dunn County cornfield the previous November. But an autopsy showed the bear had been shot twice before the farm machine hit it. The shooter turned out to be a former neighbor who had been allowed to hunt deer on the property, and the Department of Natural Resources (DNR) decided to keep the pelt and skull as evidence.

Catcalls

Like bears, cougars also need their space and are starting to show up in areas once thought too civilized for them. Residents near Milton, in Rock County, began reporting cougar sightings and tracks in January 2008. Over the next several months, other witnesses spied a cougar farther east, in Walworth County.

In April, to the surprise of zoologists everywhere, police sharp-shooters shot a cougar in the Roscoe Village neighborhood of Chicago. DNA tests comparing the carcass with blood found in southern Wisconsin confirmed it was the same animal.

Other brushes with cougars include sightings in the Springdale Estates area of Pewaukee in 2004 and numerous other reports that have been made to the state's wildlife officials since 1985.

But not all reports are genuine. So many people have created fake cougar sighting reports that Wisconsin's Department of Natural Resources devoted a web page to the hoaxes, some of which made the rounds on the Internet before they were detected. A popular chain e-mail in 2008 showed a man holding a large, dead cougar, claiming the man shot the big cat north of Antigo, in Pelican Lake. In truth, the photo was from a wildlife magazine and the dead cougar was actually downed in the state of Washington.

A Wood County taxidermist who was hired to mount a cougar that died in a game farm inspired another round of tall tales. When he stopped at a tavern with the cat carcass in his vehicle in March 2008, a number of bar patrons saw the dead cougar, and soon, people were saying they had seen it doing everything from eating a dead horse to attacking pets.

Crying Wolf

Timber wolves were thought to be extinct in Wisconsin after 1960 due to over-hunting. But today, they are back in strong enough numbers to create a problem for farmers by mauling livestock. Their population in the state is now estimated at around 600. Like the bear and cougar, the wolf has journeyed farther south than expected. One is suspected of having killed a horse in Jefferson County in 2009.

"Wildlife Officials Say Evidence Points to a Wolf" read headlines in a Wisn.com news article posted on January 31, 2009. Earlier that week, a rural Watertown woman found her horse mauled to death. Its attacker left tracks that DNR experts identified as wolf prints.

Wolf sightings and predations have become common in the state's northern counties. State reimbursements for livestock destroyed by wolves amounted to almost $120,000 in 2007. The timber wolf no longer enjoys protection as an endangered species, and some groups want the government to grant a wolf-hunting season.

Citified Coyotes

Other big predators are enjoying boom times, too. Coyotes, native to Wisconsin but once scarce in the southern counties due to over-hunting, are now commonly seen around Milwaukee and its suburbs.

As early as 1999, a Franklin man found mowing his lawn a scary proposition as a coyote watched him from the yard's edge on three separate days. And a mother in Mequon contacted wildlife officials because she feared for her children's safety after a coyote began visiting her backyard deck. The state's coyote population is estimated at around 20,000, and full-grown males can weigh up to 40 pounds. Adding to the trepidation is that these animals chase their prey at a speedy rate of 25 miles per hour!

Hogs Wild

While bears, cougars, wolves, and coyotes are merely returning to their former habitats, one new, non-native species is gaining a foothold in the western part of the state. Wild hogs now rampage through southwestern Wisconsin, gobbling corn crops and destroying plants and trees. Authorities believe an elk farm owner may have imported them from Texas in 2002. The dangerous porkers sport nine-inch tusks and may weigh more than 400 pounds.

Peshtigo Fire Sparks Devastation

✣ ✣ ✣ ✣

In the early evening of October 8, 1871, one of the worst fires on record began in Peshtigo. Before it was over, it claimed more lives than any other natural fire in the history of the United States. That year was one of the driest on record, with only two measurable rainfalls between July and September, and the extreme heat and drought caused many to pray for rain. But the prayers weren't answered soon enough, so when fire struck, it was devastating. Oh, and there happened to be a big fire in Chicago on that very same night.

A Forgotten Tragedy

Most people have heard of the Chicago Fire, with its story about how Mrs. O'Leary's cow kicked over a lantern and started a fire that is now a part of history. Cow or no cow, that fire was the most destructive blaze ever to hit a metropolitan area, causing 250 deaths and property damage estimated as high as $200 million. Also consider Chicago's urban advantages at the time, and it's no wonder that this is the fire we hear about. Telegraphs, trains, and other "modern" means got word of the disaster out to the rest of the country. In contrast, Peshtigo, located in northeastern Wisconsin, had much more modest property values and very limited means to spread the word about its fire. Sadly, it also had no way to stop the terrible fire that consumed the town, forests, and surrounding farmland and left anywhere between 1,200 and 2,400 souls dead.

Boomtown Burns Out

Peshtigo, Wisconsin, was on the verge of becoming a boomtown. Situated on a railroad line and near Lake Michigan, the town was thriving thanks to the many nearby forests and the booming lumber industry. In fact, the world's largest woodenware factory was located in Peshtigo. Even with all of its economic success, the town was still no match for Mother Nature.

Weather can certainly be unpredictable, and back then, forecasting was more about feeling the heat and listening to the wind than long-range prediction. That's not to say there was no advance notice. Creeks had dried up, and small fires were commonplace. In fact, fires occurred so often that ships on Lake Michigan had to use their foghorns miles from shore because the smoke hung so thick. Perhaps people grew so accustomed to these conditions that nothing seemed out of the ordinary.

In fact, the dry conditions were a benefit to the lumber business. Rainless days were a good time to harvest more timber, and settlers and lumberjacks alike cut trees and left in their wake piles of sawdust and tree waste, known as slash. No problem, really—until the slash caught fire. As if to add to the impending trouble, the drought had also caused trees to lose their leaves early, and dry leaves carpeted the forest floor—one more accelerant when the fire hit.

The Beginning of the End

At about 8:30 on that fateful night, survivors recalled hearing a loud roar. The wind had kicked up and formed firewhirls (small fire tornadoes) that spread with unprecedented speed. In fact, witnesses later called the disaster a "tornado of fire." Hurricane-force winds uprooted trees, tore the roofs off houses and barns, and sent families fleeing in panic. Flames burst high into the air, and smaller individual fires came together as one, gaining momentum. Temperatures reached as high as 2,000 degrees. The fire was so powerful that some debris that got caught up in the updraft was later found as far away as Canada.

Alarming News

The lumber mills used their steam whistles as alarms to call to the tugboats out in the harbor, but the fire raged too fast to be stopped. The town's lone horse-drawn steam pump was no match for nature's fury. With no quick way to escape to safety, the residents of Peshtigo were essentially trapped in a town made of wooden buildings and sidewalks. The sawdust that covered the roads and the beautiful forests surrounding the town were suddenly horrible agents of death.

People ran from their homes and some found refuge in wells and streams, while others lay facedown on the ground. Most residents headed to the Peshtigo River or Green Bay. Sparks and debris blew onto the river, so people could only raise their heads above water for short periods. In total, the Peshtigo Fire spread over 2,400 square miles or one and a half million acres. By 10:00 that night, most of Peshtigo was gone. By daybreak, only one building—a house under construction with wood too green to burn—remained standing.

Unlike Chicago, in Peshtigo there was no cow to blame. Lightning is not thought to have been responsible, and no one really knows the exact cause of this terrible fire. It may have just been the right conditions for such an event. After all, Chicago was also alight with flame that night, along with other towns in Michigan. Dry conditions in the Midwest may have been all it took. Weather historians who study the blaze have speculated that meteor showers may have played a part. These showers are common in fall, and any sparks hitting the dry forest floor could have started numerous small fires that joined and spread in the windy conditions that night.

And the next day? The blaze burned until the winds died down and the fire reached Green Bay. And the rain? It finally came. But before it did, the little town of Peshtigo, once bustling and lively, had been destroyed. A local newspaper called it a "scene of devastation and ruin that no language can paint and no tongue describe."

❋ ❋ ❋ ❋

- *On October 8, 1878, in addition to Peshtigo and Chicago, there were disastrous fires in three Michigan towns: Holland, Manistee, and Port Huron.*

- *"Fighting Bob" La Follette was a feisty Wisconsinite, but did you know he was also the type to run into burning buildings? When the Capitol caught fire in 1904, La Follette took charge of evacuating records from the doomed structure. Nearly everything was saved, thanks to his efforts.*

Fast Facts

- Only one Big Ten team has ever won consecutive Rose Bowls: Wisconsin's own Badgers, in 1999 (against UCLA) and 2000 (against Stanford). Madison's team has played in six Rose Bowls, winning their first in 1993 against UCLA.

- W. D. Kenzie of Beloit saw John Wilkes Booth flee Ford's Theatre after Lincoln's assassination on April 14, 1865. He later helped start conspiracy theories surrounding the event. Called on to identify Booth's body 12 days later, Kenzie said the authorities had the wrong guy. Even today, some people still support Kenzie's view.

- The early Wisconsin territorial legislature was a serious pigsty. And that isn't a figure of speech. In the 1830s and '40s, pigs used to run around underneath the legislative chambers, squealing loudly enough to disrupt proceedings. As if that wasn't ignoble enough, the legislators tended to settle arguments with gunfire.

- Who decides how much an inch really is? According to James Burnette of Black Creek, the government's version of the measure is incorrect. He has constructed numerous signs to attract people to his property, which contains lots of exhibits to prove his point.

- In the late 1830s, some folks decided it was time to dig a canal between the Rock River and Lake Michigan. Forty miles is a long way for a canal. In the end, the proponents only dug 1.25 miles of canal before railways made the idea obsolete.

- Ghost nuts should visit Kemper Hall in Kenosha. The legend goes that students of this former girls' school killed a mean nun named Sister Mary Terese, whose ghost now prowls the place. One problem: Records show that no Sister Mary Terese ever taught there.

- Writers: Suppose The Washington Post called and offered you a chance to blister your own self-published novel with a savage review. You know you'd do it. In 2003, this happened to UW-Whitewater English professor Robert Burrows, author of a ponderous satire on the Bush administration. Sales exploded as the book gained cult status.

The Wright Stuff

✳ ✳ ✳ ✳

"Every great architect is—necessarily—a great poet. He must be a great original interpreter of his time, his day, his age." That quote is attributed to Wisconsin native Frank Lloyd Wright, perhaps the greatest and most influential American architect of all time. In a life that spanned more than 92 years, Wright would experience paramount professional and creative success and satisfaction. He would also endure horrific personal heartache and strife.

The Student Becomes the Master

"Form follows function—that has been misunderstood. Form and function should be one, joined in a spiritual union."

In Richland Center, Wisconsin, Frank *Lincoln* Wright was born on June 8, 1867; he later changed his middle name after his parents divorced. Frank studied engineering at the University of Wisconsin-Madison for two semesters before moving to Chicago to try his hand at architecture.

After six years of absorbing the style and lessons of his mentor, architect Louis Sullivan, Frank embarked on his own path. Early in his career, he and his wife Catherine lived in Oak Park, a suburb of Chicago, where he built a studio adjacent to their home. During his Oak Park studio days, he worked on more than 125 commissions and developed into a supremely confident visionary. Frank championed an open concept style of "prairie" homes, characterized by their low, horizontal lines. Some of his designs from that period included the Avery Coonley house, the Darwin Martin house, the Ward Willits house, and the Robie house.

Some of his early non-residential masterpieces included the Larkin Building in Buffalo, New York, and the Unity Temple in Oak Park. He became a strong proponent for "organic architecture" in which a building's design flows cohesively with the nature around it.

Adultery! Exile!

"Early in life I had to choose between honest arrogance and hypocritical humility. I chose the former and have seen no reason to change."

Frank was master of his professional domain, but his domestic life was decidedly messy. Though married with enough children to fill...well, a house... Wright fell in love with the wife of a client for whom he was designing a home. The society that had praised and admired the architect now condemned him as an adulterer. Shunned by those around them, Frank and his mistress Mamah Cheney ditched their families in 1909 and fled to Europe.

When the lovers returned to America more than a year later, they settled down in Spring Green, Wisconsin, where Frank had spent childhood summers with relatives. There Frank designed a retreat so the couple could live away from the judgment and gossip of others. He built his famous Taliesin home on a hill overlooking the valley of the Wisconsin River.

Unfortunately, Taliesin would not prove to be the sanctuary that Frank had intended. Tragedy struck in 1914 while Frank was in Chicago overseeing a construction project. Julian Carlton, a disgruntled former servant, set fire to Taliesin. Mamah, her two visiting children, and four others tried to escape the flames, but an ax-wielding Julian blocked the only exit. He murdered seven people that day. This event devastated Frank's world.

Haunted! Cursed!

"I believe in God, only I spell it Nature."

Haunted by his loss, Frank threw himself into his work, completing the Midway Garden commission in Chicago and spending several years in Tokyo, building the impressive Imperial Hotel. When the Great Kanto Earthquake of 1923 ravaged Tokyo, Frank's Imperial Hotel was one of the few buildings left standing. He also took comfort in the arms of sculptor, and alleged morphine addict, Miriam Noel. She resided with him at the newly built Taliesin II.

Frank's legal wife Catherine finally granted him a divorce in 1922, and the next year he engaged in an ill-advised marriage to Miriam. She left him by 1924. While still married to Miriam, Frank became enamored with Olga (Olgivanna) Milanoff Hinzenberg, a ballet dancer 33 years his junior. In another juicy scandal, Olgivanna and her daughter Svetlana dashed overseas to be with Frank at Taliesin. Her Russian architect hubby tried to have Frank arrested in violation of the Mann Act (a law that banned trafficking women across state lines), but the charges didn't stick.

In 1925, Olgivanna gave birth out of wedlock to Frank's seventh child. That same year, the Taliesin home fell victim to a second fire, this time an accident. Rumors ignited that Frank and the home were cursed.

Rebuilding a Life

"The longer I live, the more beautiful life becomes."

The resilient architect finally married his live-in love Olgivanna on August 25, 1928. He rebuilt Taliesin a third time. Taliesin III, deemed a National Historic Landmark in 1976, still stands today. It is open for public tours and has been described as Wright's "auto-biography in wood and stone."

The next several decades would be highlighted by some of Wright's greatest professional triumphs. This included the machine-inspired and beautifully curved Administration Building of the S. C. Johnson & Son Company in Racine, Wisconsin. There were also his less flashy Usonian houses for the middle class. He designed his Fallingwater masterpiece, a breathtaking house built on a waterfall, and it graced the cover of *Time* magazine in 1938. And in 1943, he was commissioned to design the Guggenheim Museum. Throughout his life, Frank traveled tirelessly, and his designs live on all over the world, but Wisconsin was always central to his heart.

You Can Thank Wisconsin

Great Wisconsin Inventions

Some ways the Badger State made the average American's life even better.

The Answering Machine

In 1898, a Danish inventor received a patent for Europe's first automatic answering machine. Soon, American inventors worked to develop their own devices. The American Telephone & Telegraph Company (AT&T) fought to convince the Federal Communications Commission (FCC) that such gadgets could threaten the national phone system and peoples' privacy. So, in the 1930s the FCC outlawed the installation of any foreign attachment to its network. In 1948, Elm Grove's Joseph Zimmerman found a way around this rule. His Electronic Secretary Model R1 mechanically lifted the telephone receiver off its hook and sent sound through the air—not FCC wires—via a phonograph record, which played an outgoing greeting. Then, the caller's message was recorded on a spool of steel wire.

Garbage Disposal

Architect John W. Hammes of Racine tinkered in his basement workshop until 1927, when he built an out-of-sight in-sink implement for pulverizing leftover food scraps so they would wash down the drain. In 1935, he patented the device and, in 1937, founded the In-Sink-Erator Manufacturing Company. By 1993, the company—then called InSinkErator, a subsidiary of Emerson Electric—had sold more than 50 million garbage disposals.

Malted Milk

Brothers James and William Horlick's first infant formula wasn't perfect. The extract of wheat and malted barley they'd dried and combined was nutritional, but it required milk for mixing, and milk in the late 1800s wasn't always in safe supply. But then the Racine-based brothers figured out how to reduce milk to a dry powder. Their recipe was patented in 1883 as Diastoid and renamed Malted Milk in 1887. The formula's heavy caloric and nutritional content and "just add water" ease made it a hit among new mothers, invalids, and even explorers. In fact, Antarctic adventurer Admiral Richard E. Byrd named a mountain range after William Horlick.

Hammerin' Hank's Last Hurrah

❋ ❋ ❋ ❋

Over the years, Milwaukee baseball fans have certainly seen their share of stars trot out to the field from the home team's dugouts at County Stadium and Miller Park, but one stands above the rest.

A Proud Baseball Tradition

Hall of Famers Robin Yount, Paul Molitor, and relief pitcher Rollie Fingers were mainstays on the only Brewers' squad to win a pennant so far. The 1982 team, which then played in the American League (the Brewers moved over to the National League in 1998), featured a potent offense under manager Harvey Kuenn and were affectionately known as "Harvey's Wallbangers."

The 2008 "Brew Crew," led by big left-hander CC Sabathia, and young sluggers Prince Fielder and Ryan Braun, gave fans something to cheer about other than Bernie Brewer (the team mascot) and the Klement's Sausage Race. After enduring a stretch where they enjoyed only one winning season in 15 years, they finished second in the National League Central Division, notching 90 wins and earning their first postseason berth since 1982. Only time will tell if future Brewer teams will match (or surpass) the accomplishments of the 1950s Braves' teams—the Golden Era of baseball in Milwaukee.

Home of the Braves

The Boston Braves moved to Milwaukee in 1953, and the city welcomed its new team with open arms. More than 1.8 million fans poured into County Stadium that first season (establishing a single-season N.L. attendance record) to see the Braves finish with a 92–62 record. Future Hall of Famer Eddie Mathews belted a league-leading 47 home runs and pitcher Warren Spahn led the N.L. with 23 victories.

The Braves would play only 12 more seasons in Milwaukee before moving to Atlanta in 1966. They won an average of 88 games each year—posting 90 or more victories four times—while winning back-to-back National League pennants in 1957 and 1958, as well as the 1957 World Series.

A Superstar in the Making

Milwaukee's young left fielder, Hank Aaron, earned the National League Most Valuable Player award in 1957, after leading the league in home runs and RBI. Three years earlier, the Braves put the unproven Aaron in left field after Bobby Thomson, whom Milwaukee acquired during the off-season, broke his ankle.

Thomson never re-gained his starting job. And Aaron? Well, he became one of the game's immortals—breaking the legendary Babe Ruth's all-time home run record in 1974 and remaining baseball's home run king until 2007 with 755 career homers.

Interestingly, Aaron returned to Milwaukee in the mid-1970s to finish his storied career. A trade late in 1974 made Aaron a Brewer, and he became the team's designated hitter. By that time, however, Aaron was in his early 40s. Hammerin' Hank's numbers dropped off considerably during his final two big league seasons in 1975 and 1976.

But Aaron treated the city to one more nugget of history before calling it quits after the 1976 campaign. On July 20, 1976, Aaron ripped a slider from California Angels pitcher Dick Drago and put the ball over the left-field fence at County Stadium for what would be his final Major League home run.

Richard Arndt, who worked as a part-time grounds-keeper with the Brewers, grabbed the ball. He wanted to give the ball back to Aaron but ended up keeping it because he wasn't able to hand the ball to Aaron in person. That decision cost Arndt his job, but he ended up cashing in years later. Arndt sold the ball for $650,000 in 1999.

White Buffalo Miracle

❋ ❋ ❋ ❋

When Dave and Valerie Heider decided to raise buffalo on their hobby farm in the late 1990s, they had no idea what fate had in store for them.

Follow the Star

Hoping to earn a little extra money for their retirement years, the Heiders raised buffalo in their spare time and kept their day jobs in Janesville. Then in August 1994, one of the buffalo cows prepared to give birth and her white calf was not just a surprise—she was a miracle. And that's how she got her name.

The Heider family considered Miracle's appearance to be a bit unusual, but they were totally unprepared for the attention that soon descended on their little farm. It turns out that white buffalo are very significant in Native American mythology. The Associated Press picked up the story, and soon people from all over the country wanted to see the baby calf that was causing such a stir.

In fact, the day after the story hit the presses, the first Native Americans had arrived in Janesville. To the Native American tribes of the Midwest, a white buffalo is akin to the second coming of Christ, according to a Lakota medicine man who saw the calf. They wanted merely to see her, pray, and leave an offering.

What's It All About?

Buffalo, of course, were very important to certain Native American peoples. They relied on the beasts for food, clothing, and shelter, as well as tools and utensils. But even more important for this story, in light of everything buffalo added to their lives, Native Americans forged a spiritual relationship with the buffalo that did not exist with other animals.

The Legend of the White Buffalo varies a little depending on who tells it, but the most important points remain the same. Long ago, when the Sioux inhabited the Great Plains, a group of hunters went out in search of game. Some say the hunters saw a beautiful woman, while others say they saw a white buffalo that then turned into a woman.

The woman instructed the hunters to return to their village and tell people that she would be coming. They did and she came, bringing a sacred pipe. Before leaving, the White Buffalo Calf Woman promised she would return as a white female buffalo calf. This event would symbolize a new harmony among people of all colors.

Along Came a Miracle

So imagine the excitement among Native Americans when a white calf was born. While some said she should have been born to one of the Native American nations, others thought the fact that she was born on a farm owned by a "white man" was significant—possibly a necessity for restoring peace among nations.

Whatever the reason that Miracle was born on the Heider farm, it seemed to be a stroke of luck. The Heiders had never heard the white buffalo tale before her birth, and Dave Heider himself admits he saw dollar signs when she first appeared. But once the family saw the religious and cultural significance that Miracle held, they changed their minds. They considered Miracle a special gift and went so far as to open their farm to visitors. Onlookers were not allowed within the gates—and in fact, the Heiders eventually needed to install a sturdy fence to protect the buffalo and to hold the numerous gifts and offerings that visitors brought with them and draped over the fence to honor her.

And people did come—thousands of them. They came from all over to pay their respects, satisfy their curiosity, and to meditate. One man even came all the way from Ireland.

The family had opportunities to sell the calf but turned down each offer. Ted Turner, who owns a large private buffalo herd, made an offer. So did Ted Nugent, who wrote a song about a white buffalo. Circuses and carnivals came calling, as well, but in each case, the answer was no.

Miracle was never about money to the Heiders. They didn't sell posters or mugs. They didn't even charge admission. They finally sold photos of the calf for a dollar, if only to discourage visitors from taking their own pictures and selling them for profit.

One in a Million ... or So

The reason for all the uproar is that a white buffalo, as you may have guessed, doesn't come along every day. In fact, the last documented white buffalo died in 1959. And just for the record, Miracle was not an albino, a genetic oddity; she had brown eyes. One source says the odds of the birth of a true white female buffalo are as low as one in a million. Other sources maintain that the chance is considerably less than that. In any case, your odds of winning the lottery are quite possibly higher.

Miracle lived a relatively short life (she died of natural causes at age ten), considering many buffalo live as long as 40 years. During her short life, she didn't remain white but changed color four times. This too was part of the ancient prophecy, to unify the four peoples of red, white, black, and yellow.

Native Americans believe Miracle lived up to her name as the return of the White Buffalo Calf Woman. No matter what, she was surely a symbol of hope. Today, you'll find a statue of the White Buffalo Calf Woman erected in her honor on the Heider's farm in Janesville.

Monster Moo-vies:
Wisconsin-related Fright Flicks

✳ ✳ ✳ ✳

Wisconsin may be half a continent away from Hollywood, but local actors, filmmakers, and scenic locations have done the Dairy State proud—especially when it comes to films involving the monstrous and the macabre. Keep in mind that this is only a partial list of freaky Wisconsin flicks, and the cameras are still rolling.

- *The Amityville Horror* (2005): A house on Silver Lake Road in Salem served as the exterior environment for this MGM remake about a very haunted house in Amityville, New York.

- *Aswang: The Unearthing* (1994): Most of the scenes of this gory movie about a vampirelike Filipino monster were filmed in Milwaukee. Cowriter and director Barry Poltermann is a Lake Geneva-area native.

- *The Beast of Bray Road* (2005): A bloody take on the sightings of a werewolflike creature described in Linda S. Godfrey's 2003 book of the same title. It was written and directed by Milwaukee native Leigh Scott.

- *Blood Harvest* (1987): This murder fest was directed by Wisconsin filmmaker Bill Rebane and shot in the state. It's also notable for starring the already horrific Tiny Tim as "Marvelous Mervo."

- *Blood Hook* (1986): A fishing contest runs amok when a humongous hook starts snagging the fishermen. The film was directed by Jim Mallon, a UW-Madison alum. It was shot in Hayward, which is home to a fishing museum—housed in a giant fiberglass musky.

- *The Boogeyman: The Devonsville Terror* (1983): A story about the curse of an ancient witch in the fictional small New England town of Devonsville. Part of it was filmed in Wisconsin, and Bill Rebane was a co-producer.

- ***The Capture of Bigfoot*** (1979): Bill Rebane directed Troma Entertainment's nod to Sasquatch. It was shot on location in Gleason and finds the hairy one at a ski resort.

- ***Damien: Omen II*** (1978), ***Omen III: The Final Conflict*** (1981): These sequels to the original film, *The Omen,* were shot at Northwestern Military and Naval Academy in Lake Geneva and Catfish Lake in Eagle River.

- ***Fever Lake*** (1996): In this horror film, teens learn to never spend time in a cursed house. It was filmed in Twin Lakes and at Carthage College in Kenosha.

- ***Frankenstein: The True Story*** (1973): This adaptation of Mary Shelley's story starred Agnes Moorehead, who had lived in Reedsburg and Soldier's Grove for several years in the mid-1920s.

- ***The Giant Spider Invasion*** (1975): Bill Rebane created this arachnid romp, his best-known film, in Merrill and Gleason. In the movie, massive, interdimensional spiders overrun Merrill and disrupt the Gleason Days fest.

- ***Meet the Applegates*** (1991): Neenah and Oshkosh were the shooting locations for this film about a family of human-size bugs living in suburbia.

- ***Mindwarp*** (1992): After the Apocalypse, horror abounds. Some of this science-fiction thriller was shot in East River.

- ***The Monster of Phantom Lake*** (2006): A comedy about a creature spawned by (fictional) atomic waste in a Mukwonago lake, written, directed, and edited by Christopher R. Mihm.

- ***The Pit*** (1981): This horror mystery was filmed in Beaver Dam. It's about a nasty preteen who begins feeding townsfolk to some monsters he finds in the woods.

- ***Psycho*** (1960): Alfred Hitchcock's classic thriller was based on Robert Bloch's novel of the same name. Bloch's inspiration for the character of Norman Bates was Ed Gein, the mild-mannered murderer of Plainfield. Bloch lived in Milwaukee and Weyauwega.

- **Rana, Legend of Shadow Lake (1975):** A part human, part frog lake monster terrifies a small Wisconsin community in this Bill Rebane shocker.

- **Shadow of the Vampire (2000):** Willem Dafoe, a native of Appleton, was born in 1955. He starred as Max Schreck in this inventive tale of the filming of *Nosferatu,* the classic 1922 vampire movie. Dafoe has also appeared in the *Spider-Man* movies and numerous other major films.

- **Young Frankenstein (1974):** This horror spoof, directed by Mel Brooks, starred Gene Wilder, who was born Jerome Silberman in Milwaukee on June 11, 1933.

❋ ❋ ❋ ❋

- *New Berlin had a teenage witch in the mid-1850s. Her name was Jennet, not Sabrina, and she was more of a diviner than a witch (an important distinction; just ask a real witch). She did Ouija-type readings before the actual board's invention and communed with spirits—just the usual stuff.*

- *Madisonian Sam Sanfillippo, for reasons best known to himself, has a unique leisure pursuit: stuffing and mounting rodents for his Squirrel and Chipmunk Museum. There's a topless chipmunk dancing troupe, a poker game, a squirrel pianist…you get the idea. Interestingly enough, the museum is located in a funeral home.*

- *As he sat down to eat in his Milwaukee home on March 2, 1876, Dr. John Garner had a terrible premonition of doom. Sometimes we should heed those. Sarah Wilner, a disgruntled and grief-mad patient from Ohio, called at his door and shot him to death right after dinner.*

- *In the 1860s, a mysterious, deranged young woman walked into an Oconto County logging camp. Was she an escaped mental patient? A runaway? Naming her Crazy Jane, the county jail hired her as a janitor for room and board. To this day, we don't know who Crazy Jane really was.*

Quiz

So you think you know all about the Badger State? Then try this Wisconsin Cultural Literacy Quiz!

1. Wisconsin has been one of the United States for more than 150 years. How long was it part of French territory?

a) More than 100 years
b) Between 50 and 100 years
c) Less than 50 years

2. There are 15,057 lakes in Wisconsin. How many are named?

a) Almost all of them
b) Around half
c) Fewer than half

3. Which Wisconsinite was Louis Armstrong's favorite musician?

a) Steve Miller (Milwaukee)
b) Rowland "Bunny" Berrigan (Fox Lake)
c) Les Paul (Waukesha)
d) Liberace (West Allis)

4. In the late 1800s there was quite a ruckus in front of the Music Hall on Bascom Hill. Who was making all the noise?

a) Prostitutes plying their trade
b) The school marching band
c) Barking stray dogs
d) A group of ROTC buglers

5. Which is true?

Fact A: Kenosha native Orson Welles attended grade school in Madison.

Fact B: Welles considered returning to his home state to run for the U.S. Senate.

a) Fact A
b) Fact B
c) Both A and B
d) Neither

6. It's not the humidity. It's the heat. Or lack of it. What is Wisconsin's annual average temperature?

a) 98.6 degrees Fahrenheit
b) 42.4 degrees Fahrenheit
c) 24.2 degrees Fahrenheit
d) 55.1 degrees Fahrenheit

7. Which was the first state to adopt an income tax?

a) Illinois
b) Nebraska
c) Wisconsin
d) New York

ANSWERS: 1. a, 2. c, 3. b, 4. a, 5. c, 6. b, 7. c

104

Grand Old Party Begins in Ripon

❋ ❋ ❋ ❋

Today, in the little town of Ripon, about 50 miles northwest of Milwaukee, there is a large sign on the front of a one-room schoolhouse that proclaims "Birthplace of the Republican Party." And in a 1954 speech, President Dwight D. Eisenhower credited the party's founding to a meeting that took place 100 years earlier at that very spot. So it must be true, right? Well, yes and no.

Trying Times

It was a time of turmoil in our nation, and there is no doubt that other areas were having anti-Democrat powwows of their own. Jackson, Michigan, and Pittsburgh, Pennsylvania, are two of the other cities that have laid claim to the title of Republican birthplace. Yet after careful analysis over the years, it appears as though Ripon's party started just a bit earlier than the other events. Even the Republican Party itself credits Ripon as the home of the first informal meeting of the party. The first 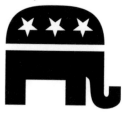 official meeting of Republicans occurred in Jackson a few months later, and Pittsburgh hosted the first national GOP convention two years after that.

Out with the Old, In with the New

Decades before the Civil War actually broke out, the institution of slavery had become a controversial topic—especially in the northern states. The Missouri Compromise of 1820 had closed the Kansas and Nebraska territories to slavery, but in 1854 Democrat Stephen Douglas introduced a bill that would amend the law and allow settlers to make their own decision regarding slavery in the territory.

So on March 20, 1854, attorney Alvan E. Bovay of Ripon organized a group of people interested in the politics of the day. It is said he went door to door to recruit citizens for his meeting, and he managed to round up 54 of the 100 eligible voters in Ripon. They met at the Little White Schoolhouse, where, at Bovay's urging, these former members of the Whig, Democrat, and Free Soil Parties pledged their allegiance to the antislavery movement and the new Republican Party.

Bovay's friendship with New York publisher Horace Greeley gave the newcomers a boost. In June 1854, Greeley publicly used the term "Republican" for the first time in an editorial against slavery. With Greeley's help, the name—and the values it represented— quickly spread throughout the country.

History Preserved

The Little White Schoolhouse has been moved three times since that famous meeting. In 1908, the Ripon Historical Society, the Ripon Commercial Club, and the Ripon City Council came together to save the schoolhouse. In 1973, the schoolhouse was placed on the National Register of Historic Places. A year later, the U.S. Department of the Interior declared the site a historic landmark for its role in the formation of the Republican Party.

Today, the Little White Schoolhouse still stands in Ripon and is open to the public as a museum. No matter what your political affiliation may be, a visit to the schoolhouse is an important glimpse into our nation's history.

❀ ❀ ❀ ❀

- *When Wisconsin was drafting its first constitution, an early version promised unheard-of property rights for women. What a woman had before marriage, or gained herself during marriage, would be hers. Fearing the downfall of social order, the all-male electorate voted down this draft in April 1847.*

Braves, Bears, and Minor League Brewers Meant Baseball in Milwaukee

❋ ❋ ❋ ❋

You know the old joke: A teenager looks at his parents and says, "You mean Paul McCartney was in another band before Wings?" Well, the same could be said for Milwaukee baseball. Although the city was home to a Negro League team, a minor league team, and a Major League team, to today's youth Milwaukee baseball will always be associated with the Brewers.

There's More to a Name

The Brewers of today aren't even the first ones in Milwaukee. Various ballclubs in Milwaukee began using the name in the 1880s. However, for most fans, the designation belongs to the minor league team that played there from 1902 until 1952 when the American League Braves relocated from Boston. Those Brewers played at Athletic Park near Eighth and Chambers. The ballclub belonged to the American Association and had a modest following, but fans couldn't help hoping that a Major League team would come their way. The city built Milwaukee County Stadium in 1953, and the Brewers were all set to move in, until Lou Perini decided to move his Boston Braves to Wisconsin.

How 'Bout Them Bears?

But wait—something's missing. Thirty years before the Braves, the city—in the middle of its 50-year love affair with the minors—played host to another team for one year. They were the Milwaukee Bears, a franchise of the Negro National League. It was 1923, and like the Brewers, they played their home games at Athletic Park.

Newspaper coverage for the Bears was unpredictable. One day there would be a full story with box scores and the next day, no report at all. The minor league Brewers got more space and so did amateur teams. Even high school and sandlot games got more notice than the Bears. With so little publicity, the team was never able to build enough fan support. Attendance, in turn, was so poor that the Bears played most games on the road and never even finished the season. Their record was 12–41, good enough for last place.

Winners Take the Field

So Milwaukee baseball lovers pledged their allegiance to Brewer baseball until 1953, when their wildest dream came true. The Major Leagues came to Milwaukee in the form of the Boston Braves. It was a match made in heaven. The Braves were sick of playing second fiddle to their American League brethren, the Boston Red Sox, and Milwaukee was thrilled to have its own big league team at last. This was the first time since 1903 that a major league franchise had changed cities—but it wasn't to be the last.

The Braves didn't disappoint. In their first year at County Stadium, they drew a record-setting 1.8 million fans and finished with a 92–62 record. Over the next few seasons they got even better. With hitters like Eddie Mathews and Hank Aaron alongside pitchers Warren Spahn and Lew Burdette, the Braves were on their way to glory.

In 1957, the team won the National League pennant and then took on the New York Yankees in the World Series. It took a full seven games, but the Braves were victorious, winning their first World Series in 40 years. In 1958, they won the pennant for the second year in a row but lost out to the Yankees in the World Series.

That early success was never duplicated, but Milwaukee still loved the Braves. Unfortunately, a change of ownership ruined the relationship between the team and the city. Perini sold the team to William Bartholomay in 1962, and the new owner began to shop around for a location with a bigger television market. Atlanta fit the bill, and by 1966 the team had left Milwaukee for greener pastures. But they left behind a legacy of pride—the Milwaukee Braves never had a losing season. Milwaukee did not go without baseball for long. In 1970, the city got its second Major League team, the Brewers.

Houdini Escapes Obscurity in Appleton

❋ ❋ ❋ ❋

A magician and escape artist of world renown,
Harry Houdini spent his early years in Appleton.
In fact, he frequently told people that he was born there.

A Wisconsinite at Heart

Harry Houdini was actually born in 1874 in Budapest, Hungary, the son of a Jewish rabbi named Mayer Samuel Weisz. The future magician was really named Ehrich Weisz. A job opening in Appleton brought the family to the United States in 1878.

It was the hope of a better future that brought the Weisz family to the U.S., but the good times didn't last long in Appleton. Unfortunately, Houdini's father was fired four years after they arrived and the family then moved to Milwaukee. Although he was young, the time in Appleton may have been the best—and most normal—of Houdini's life. Maybe it was his fond memories of early childhood that prompted Houdini to later call Appleton home.

Traveling circuses were a popular entertainment of the day, and Houdini quickly became enthralled. The way he told it, Houdini started his performing career in a neighborhood show—as a tightrope walker who called himself "Prince of the Air."

From Pauper to Prince

After his father's dismissal and subsequent move from Appleton, Houdini's childhood became less idyllic. At a very young age he set out working odd jobs to help provide for the family. In his pre-teen years he worked shining shoes, selling newspapers, and doing jobs that drove him to succeed in his own adult life. According to one story, he ran away to join the circus at the age of 12, but there is nothing to validate the tale.

You could say Houdini had more talent than schooling. His first foray into the world of magic occurred when he was 17. He partnered with Jack Hayman, and they called themselves the Houdini Brothers (after magician Jean Eugene Robert-Houdin). Hayman soon lost interest, and Houdini's brother Theodore took his place. He too was later replaced, this time by Houdini's future wife, Bess.

Success was slow in coming to Houdini, but after acts full of card tricks, illusions, and unspectacular box escapes, Houdini found his niche—and his ultimate claim to fame. He became known as the Handcuff King and offered to escape from any pair of handcuffs that the audience could produce. He succeeded and became widely known as a master of escape. Today, Houdini remains famous for performing the Water Torture Cell, the Milk Can Escape, and an act called Buried Alive before his untimely death in 1926.

Back to His Roots

When Houdini was getting started, he performed his magic in dime museums—places that featured mostly up-and-coming acts and has-beens. After he made a name for himself, Houdini vowed he'd never play in a dime museum again. Museums have changed since then, and Houdini would probably be pleased with a prominent place in an institution of culture and history. And it seems fitting that Harry Houdini has received such an honor in Appleton.

Thanks to Houdini's loyalty and love of Appleton, it is only natural that it would be the first American city to honor Harry Houdini in some way. The Outagamie Museum in Appleton has long had an exhibit devoted to the magician's life. The museum features devices from his famous acts, such as leg irons, a straitjacket, and handcuffs. But best of all, they have recreated Houdini's most famous tricks and allowed guests to experiment with them, revealing a lot of his secrets—much to the dismay of many magicians!

Fast Facts

- Serving with the famous Iron Brigade at Gettysburg, the 7th Wisconsin Volunteers sustained 77 percent casualties at McPherson's Woods in the Battle of Gettysburg—without giving ground until ordered! One can argue that, but for the Iron Brigade's tough and early stand, the Union might have lost the battle.

- In 1967, nine Juda High School kids died on their senior trip in New Orleans when a plane smashed into their hotel. One, Nelva Jean Smith, was best remembered for her love of music. Locals therefore memorialized the young music lover with a life-size granite piano tombstone near Brodhead.

- The typical north Wisconsin lumber village generally looked like the set of a Hollywood western. However, when a 1923 fire took out Elcho's main drag, mill baron Charles Fish showed his Wisconsin style: He rebuilt the downtown in Tudor English style. Some of the old buildings still stand.

- Jim Otto of Wausau was the last NFL offensive lineman allowed to wear a jersey not numbered between 50 and 79. The iron man center wore number 00 for the Oakland Raiders from 1960 until his 1974 retirement. He also won entry to the Pro Football Hall of Fame in his first eligible year.

- Lorena Hickok, a journalist from East Troy, may or may not have been Eleanor Roosevelt's lover. Let's put it this way: A lot of Mrs. Roosevelt's surviving letters to "Hick" sound anything but platonic. But since her husband was fooling around, can we really fault Eleanor?

- Dungeons & Dragons, the seminal fantasy role-playing game, came from Lake Geneva. Gary Gygax and Dave Arneson created the game together in 1974. It was the forerunner of every multi-player fantasy game played today—and it's still going strong!

- In Wisconsin Dells there's a surreal tourist attraction called Adventures in Time. The basic theme is that you ride a time capsule chasing Time Bandits.

Eden in Wisconsin

❋ ❋ ❋ ❋

North of La Crosse, in Galesville, near the Mississippi River, is an imposing statue of the Reverend David O. Van Slyke, an itinerant 19th century preacher and Methodist missionary. His flowing cape is caught, frozen in the wind, and in one hand he holds a book; in the other an apple. Here is a man who must have had something to say to the ages. And so he did. In 1886, Van Slyke published news of a remarkable discovery that, he noted, he had arrived at by entirely scientific methods: Galesville, he claimed, was at the center of the Biblical Garden of Eden. Really.

In Love with Nature

David O. Van Slyke was born in 1818. At age 44, he enlisted in the 30th Wisconsin Infantry to serve as a chaplain in the Civil War. At the end of the war, he returned home to Galesville to do missionary work. He built a house and started a farm. And he became increasingly bewitched by the area's natural beauty, especially its rivers and high bluffs.

"I, as a matter of pleasantry, used occasionally to say to my friends, this is the Garden of Eden," Van Slyke recalled. "At this suggestion I smiled."

After a time, however, he came to look at the bluffs framing his pleasant garden valley as a wall. He noticed that the whole region between La Crosse and Winona, Minnesota, was bracketed and contained. Biblical scholars had long been disappointed in trying to find a real location for Eden in the arid Middle East. Perhaps there might be clues, which if carefully sifted, could provide actual, scientific proof that Galesville was in fact the biblical birthplace of humanity!

Finding Proof Everywhere

Van Slyke was not disappointed in his search. Nearly everywhere he looked, he was able to find proof of his theory. His starting point was Genesis 2:8–14, which noted that although four rivers ran into Eden, only one ran out. That described Trempealeau County, making the Mississippi into the Bible's Euphrates River. In fact, where else on the planet, he wondered, was there such a compact yet complex water system?

Well-traveled visitors passing through by steamboat often told Van Slyke that the area was the most beautiful they had ever seen. Moreover, the soil was excellent, yet poor in "money mineral wealth, as these, if easily obtained, are corrupting in their tendencies." Among the bluffs one must also "look out for snakes, for how could you have such a garden without a 'serpent'?" Van Slyke noted that the region "has been notorious for rattlesnakes from time immemorial." He said, in fact, that the bluffs were known to Native Americans as "Rattlesnake Hills."

The preacher began to share his developing theory in a series of columns in the *Galesville Independent*, "to invite general inspection and criticism." More discoveries followed.

The climate was neither too warm nor too cold. Yes, it could be a struggle during the winter, but surely a wise creator put gentle impediments in the way of humanity's growth. Also, the area was seemingly protected from tornadoes and "yet so free from malaria." Also, it was obviously a land of milk and honey. For example, butter from the nearby towns of Arcadia and Alma had just won first and second place in an international competition at St. Louis.

Yes, it was a large area for just Adam and Eve to roam, but "did you ever think how long they lived, how many children they probably had, what a numerous family before the first pair died, numbering into the thousands?" By contrast, across the Mississippi Van Slyke observed that the farms of Minnesota were "rough and rugged" and home to "Fallen Humanity." Van Slyke concluded that the great flood must have come, and Noah and his family rode the ark from Galesville around the world, finally landing on top of Mount Ararat in Turkey.

Spreading the News

In 1886, Van Slyke collected his research in a lengthy pamphlet entitled "Found At Last: the veritable Garden of Eden, or a place that answers the Bible description of that notable spot better than anything yet discovered." Somewhat unfortunately, his book carries one additional, idiosyncratic proof: The creator would surely have placed Eden at the center of the earth—and Galesville is in the central time zone!

Van Slyke was mocked, of course, but he retained a good sense of humor about it. Why, of course the clues were perhaps a bit obscure! Did his detractors expect Eden to be marked by a sign? If so, they would be disappointed. "Evidently not a Lo here, or a Lo there," he sniffed.

In the end, however, Van Slyke's main argument was simply that "the scenery is simply GRAND." So, Eden must be located roughly between La Crosse and Bluff Siding, Wisconsin. "We CAN and HAVE proven it, on scientific principles."

Van Slyke died in 1890, but his booklet is often reprinted by Galesville merchants to promote the idyllic qualities of their town. Whether or not Galesville was Eden, Van Slyke was not the last resident to compare it to paradise. Visitors can judge for themselves—but remember to look out for rattlesnakes.

❋ ❋ ❋ ❋

- *The Gideons, of hotel Bible fame, got started in Boscobel. Traveling salesmen John Nicholson and Sam Hill first shared a room there of necessity in 1898 and realized their religious commonality. They met again the next year and founded the Gideons in Janesville—to provide lodgers with wholesome reading.*

- *The Cistercian monks of Sparta support their abbey by refilling ink and toner cartridges. If you think about it, it's an ingenious way to keep the place fiscally sound. The business is called LaserMonks, and its slogan is "Commerce with Compassion." You go, brothers!*

Lawrencia Bembenek: Run, Bambi, Run!

❋ ❋ ❋ ❋

"Bambi." Laurie Bembenek would be the first to tell you she hates that nickname. It's all part of the image portrayed by the prosecution when she was on trial for murder. They suggested that she was a materialistic second wife—and a cold-blooded, calculating murderer.

A Murder in Beer City

Milwaukee isn't typically known as a hotbed of crime. It's a pretty "safe" place compared with other cities. Maybe that's why Lawrencia Bembenek's case garnered such a following—from the murder to her conviction, to her escape and ultimate release. It all began on May 28, 1981, when Christine Schultz was found murdered in bed in her Milwaukee home. The victim was the ex-wife of Fred Schultz, a detective for the Milwaukee Police Department. Laurie was his second wife—and the only one with motive, means, and opportunity to commit the crime, according to the district attorney.

Although all of the evidence was circumstantial, it still mounted against Bembenek. Fred Schultz had an alibi for the time of the murder, while Laurie did not. There was no sign of a break-in at the Schultz home, but Laurie had access to Fred's key. Even more incriminating, she had access to Fred's off-duty revolver. As a former police officer, she knew how to use the gun. And finally, a wig with fibers similar to those found at the crime scene was found in the plumbing system of Laurie's apartment building.

The case drew national attention. It had all the hallmarks of a steamy crime drama—a love triangle gone wrong, a second wife fighting for what should have been hers, and a former Playboy bunny and model turned vindictive.

Presumed Guilty

With no alibi, Bembenek's best defense was the eyewitness testimony of her 11-year-old stepson, who said the murderer was a heavyset, wig-wearing man with broad shoulders. There was also the matter of possible police retribution. Laurie had been fired from her position on the police force. The police said it was for possession of marijuana while she said she had stood up to sexual harassment.

None of that seemed to matter. The jury had heard enough. Laurie Bembenek was found guilty in March 1982 and sentenced to life in prison at the Taycheedah Correctional Institution.

For years she maintained her innocence but was unable to get her conviction overturned. She eventually met and became engaged to Nick Gugliatto, the brother of a fellow inmate. In July 1990, she escaped with Gugliatto's help and they ran to Thunder Bay, Ontario, Canada, where they lived secret lives for three months. At that point, the couple was featured on an episode of *America's Most Wanted,* and people recognized them, leading to a quick arrest. Back in Wisconsin, Laurie pleaded no contest to second-degree murder and was sentenced to time served. She was free.

Life After Prison

Since that time, more evidence has been found that exonerates Laurie. For starters, there was semen at the scene, making it likely that Christine was raped and the murderer was male. Also, the bullets recovered didn't match the service revolver Laurie was thought to have used. Finally, her husband had prior contact with a criminal who later told friends that he committed the crime.

Since her release, Laurie has found it hard to adjust to the outside world. She's had problems with drugs and alcohol and has had difficulty finding work. Scheduled to appear on the *Dr. Phil Show* in 2002, she felt claustrophobic in her hotel room and jumped from a window. Her leg was injured so badly that it had to be amputated.

Laurie has written a book and been the subject of a made-for-TV movie. But despite the infamy, Laurie's most fervent desire is still elusive—that her conviction be overturned.

Gangster's Paradise

✻ ✻ ✻ ✻

Throughout the 1920s and '30s, Wisconsin's Northwoods were the place for bad guys looking to escape the heat—literally and figuratively—of Chicago. After the Chicago & North Western Railroad expanded due north into Wisconsin's wooden hinterlands, Chicagoland's elite came to vacation on the crystal-clear lakes. But they didn't come alone. For gangsters and their henchmen, the Northwoods were both a summer playground and a year-round hideout. Today, numerous communities have their own stories of gangster legend and lore. Here's a lineup of the most memorable.

Public Enemy No. 1

After serving eight-and-a-half years for robbery and assault, John Dillinger took off on a ten-month crime spree that earned him the title "Public Enemy No. 1." He and his gang rampaged across the Upper Midwest, busting cronies out of the slammer, robbing banks, murdering lawmen, and escaping from the FBI each time. Possibly needing a quiet vacation, Dillinger and accomplices headed to northern Wisconsin. On Friday, April 20, 1934, they showed up at Little Bohemia in Manitowish Waters.

The owner of a nearby resort tipped off the feds, and G-men headed north. But what happened just two days later would disgrace the Bureau. Driving into the resort, headlights off, the lawmen met some Civilian Conservation Corps workers who were leaving the resort after dinner. Figuring Dillinger and his partner-in-crime, Baby Face Nelson, were inside the car, the lawmen called for the driver to stop. Unable to hear the order, the car didn't stop and the lawmen opened fire, killing one of the innocents. When Dillinger and his band heard the gunfire, they made a hasty escape. Nelson, in a nearby cabin, escaped along the shoreline of Star Lake. Both parties forced nearby neighbors to provide getaway cars.

Both Dillinger and Nelson were killed within the year. But Little Bohemia Lodge remains on Highway 51, the main thoroughfare to and through the Northwoods. It still serves breakfast, lunch, and dinner, with a heaping helping of history.

The Capones

"Big Al" Capone turned 21 the day after the Volstead Act, the legislation that made alcohol illegal, went into effect. This seems like an ironic twist for someone who would go down in history known as a bootlegger, gangster, and criminal mastermind.

The Northwoods wasn't a temporary escape for Big Al, as it served as his permanent getaway. He didn't even try to cover up this fact, dubbing his Couderay retreat "The Hideout." His home on the shores of Cranberry Lake came complete with a gun turret alongside the driveway, openings in the stone walls for machine guns, and a personal jail. Booze runners from Canada would land their planes on the lake, and Capone's gang then took care of the distribution.

Al's older brother, Ralph "Bottles" Capone, was the director of liquor sales for the mob and covered his tracks by operating Waukesha Waters, a distribution company for Waukesha Springs mineral water. But Ralph had another passion: bookmaking. Ralph was less vicious than his brother, but bookmaking got him into trouble. He landed in prison in the early 1930s for tax evasion, coincidentally the same charge that sent Al to Alcatraz, where he was imprisoned

for seven-and-a-half years. When Big Al was released in November 1939, he was so stricken with syphilis that he was unseated as leader of the criminal underworld. He died seven years later.

Later, Ralph lived in Mercer, from 1943 until his death on November 22, 1974. He managed the Rex Hotel and Billy's Bar and owned a house that had previously belonged to his brother. Ralph sponsored community Christmas parties, donated food and gifts to the needy, contributed to churches, and financed high school class trips. Despite his criminal history, locals remember him mostly for his kindness and charity. He also earned at least $20,000 a year from an Illinois cigarette vending machine business and was repeatedly investigated by the Internal Revenue Service. After 1951, Ralph Capone didn't even bother to file tax returns. At the time of his death he owed $210,715 in back taxes.

The Most Vicious

Few gangster aficionados know the story of John Henry Seadlund, dubbed "The World's Most Vicious Criminal" by FBI director J. Edgar Hoover. A loafer from Minnesota, Seadlund turned to crime after a chance meeting with Tommy Carroll, a veteran of Dillinger's gang. To make fast cash as a new criminal, Seadlund considered kidnapping wealthy Chicagoans vacationing in the Northwoods and demanding ransom. But after joining with a new lowlife, James Atwood Gray, Seadlund's kidnapping plot expanded to include a professional baseball player. The plan was to kidnap the St. Louis Cardinals' star pitcher Dizzy Dean, but Seadlund gave up when he realized how hard it might be to get ransom from Dean's ballclub.

Kidnapping ballplayers didn't pan out, so Seadlund abducted a retired greeting card company executive while heading out of Illinois in September 1937. After getting ransom, he exacted a kidnapping and murder scheme on the retiree, leaving him and accomplice Gray dead in a dugout near Spooner. He was caught when marked bills from the ransom were used at a racetrack the following January.

Beyond Bigwigs

Northwoods legend and lore extends beyond the mob's biggest names. During Prohibition, federal agents found and confiscated major gang-run stills in towns across Wisconsin's northern third. Elcho was the purported home to a mob doctor who traded bullet removal for booze, and Hurley was a gangster hot spot, as it was a "wide-open" town that flouted Prohibition and laws against prostitution. Wisconsin's Northwoods mob stories are as big as its fish tales.

Talkin' Wisconsin

"There is a hoary joke they tell in the far reaches of Wisconsin whenever an Alberta Hook weather system swings down from Canada across Lake Superior to slam a wintry punch at the state. Amid the hail, frozen rain, and snow, the lament goes up, 'I'm gonna put a snow shovel on my shoulder and walk south, stopping when the first person says, "What's that you're carrying?"'"
—*From* Off the Beaten Path: Wisconsin *by Martin Hintz*

"When viewed from the air, Wisconsin's lakes are diamonds sprinkled on a velvet green mosaic of rich pine green. Shell, Rice, Red Cedar, Long, Spooner, Grindstone, Chippewa, Big Round, Clam, and all the other bodies of water dapple the land in their glittering finery. Ribbons of braided silver—the rivers and streams—spiderweb their convoluted journeys through the textured scenery."
—*From* Fun with the Family in Wisconsin *by Martin Hintz and Stephen V. Hintz*

"Oh Wisconsin, land of my dreams. Oh Wisconsin, you're all I'll ever need. A little heaven here on earth could you be? Oh Wisconsin, land of my dreams."
—*"Oh Wisconsin, Land of My Dreams," Wisconsin Official State Ballad, Erma Barrett, Lyrics*

"Wisconsin is an extraordinary place. Its gently rolling hills and pastoral settings offer a countryside as beautiful as any in the world. Its cool deep woods and clear blue lakes are a paradise for outdoor enthusiasts."
—*From* On-the-Road Histories: Wisconsin *by Mark D. Van Ells*

"They say in Minnesota that when offered something, you refuse three times before accepting; in Wisconsin I've seen it run up to six or seven offers, depending on what it is."
—*From* Wisconsin Curiosities *by Michael Feldman*

"Madison has the most magnificent site of any inland town I ever saw."
—*Horace Greeley, 19th-century newspaper publisher, 1855*

Timeline

(Continued from p. 36)

1854
The Republican Party is formed when a group of antislavery activists meet at the Little White Schoolhouse in Ripon.

1856
Fur trader and Milwaukee founding father Solomon Juneau is poisoned by a rival fur trader while visiting the Menominee peoples for their annual U.S. government treaty payment.

1857
The railroad arrives in the Wisconsin Dells. The terminus point is named Kilbourn City, but the name refuses to stick, and the town is officially named Wisconsin Dells in 1931. Today it is a popular recreation area and one of the Midwest's most popular tourist attractions.

February 1858
A fistfight on the floor of the U.S. House of Representatives is defused by laughter when Wisconsin Congressman John F. Potter snatches the wig off another congressman's head and declares, "I've scalped him, boys!"

September 1862
George Merrick, a Wisconsin steamboat pilot, ferries U.S. troops up the Mississippi to help suppress the Sioux Uprising in neighboring Minnesota.

October 1871
A massive forest fire burns through six Wisconsin counties and into Michigan, claiming more than 1,200 lives. This fire will come to be known as the Peshtigo Fire, the worst in North American history.

1871
P. T. Barnum, creator of the three-ring circus, founds "The Greatest Show on Earth" in Delavan.

1878
The family of master escape artist Harry Houdini moves to Appleton. Despite being born Ehrich Weisz in Budapest, Hungary, Houdini claimed Appleton as his birthplace throughout his life.

March 1880
Neenah resident John Stevens receives a patent for his grain-crushing mill.

July 8, 1881
The ice cream sundae is born in Two Rivers when druggist Edward Berner pours chocolate sauce over ice cream. There is some doubt to this story, however, as at least a half-dozen other U.S. towns claim to be the sundae's birthplace.

January 10, 1883
General Tom Thumb, famed small person and P. T. Barnum exhibit, emerges unscathed from the devastating Newhall Hotel fire in Milwaukee. More than 70 people were not as lucky and lost their lives in the blaze.

September 1894
A massive fire sweeps through Minnesota and into Wisconsin, burning approximately 300,000 acres and claiming hundreds of lives.

(Continued on p. 146)

Lady Liberty Emerges from Lake Mendota

❋ ❋ ❋ ❋

What is the Statue of Liberty? If you said the people of France gave it to the United States, you'd be correct. On the other hand, if you said a bunch of University of Wisconsin students worked three days to erect it on Lake Mendota in Madison, you'd also be correct.

Start with a Pail and Shovel

It all began when students Leon Varjian and Jim Mallon decided to rebel against the establishment and bring fun to student government. The pair ran for office as part of the Pail and Shovel Party (the name refers to their campaign promise to convert the $70,000 student budget into pennies and allow students to dig through it with pails and shovels).

Varjian and Mallon also promised that they would buy the Statue of Liberty and bring it to Lake Mendota. The platform of absurdity was just crazy enough to spark the interest of the student body, who elected these party leaders by a definitive margin. And then the fun began.

It Came to a Head

In keeping with their outrageous campaign promises, Varjian and Mallon spent student money freely—on toys and toga parties— drawing the ire of former student government leaders who used the student newspaper, the *Daily Cardinal*, to voice their complaints.

The battle came to a head one morning in February 1979 when Lady Liberty appeared on the frozen Lake Mendota. Well, let's back up—the head, arm, and torch of the statue appeared on Lake Mendota. Varjian and Mellon had made good on their promise. Appearing to rise from the water, the statue was created out of chicken wire, papier-mâché, and plywood and moved onto the ice. Postcards of the scene were an immediate hit and can still be found in Madison.

A Dime a Dozen

While students and locals were caught up in the delight of it, Pail and Shovel critics denounced student government for spending $4,500 on such a folly. Varjian claimed the expense amounted to a mere dime per student and offered to pay back anyone who asked for their portion. (Sixty students responded, and Varjian wrote each a check for ten cents.) The debate raged for three weeks. Then, in the dead of night on March 2, Lady Liberty was torched and burned down. No one was ever caught, but oddly enough, the *Daily Cardinal* had a photographer on hand who captured the event on film.

A Return to Life

The Statue of Liberty came to life again the following February, much to the delight of many Madisonians. This time it was bigger and cost $6,000. It was finally retired after the Department of Natural Resources declared it a fancy fishing shanty and demanded its removal. Lady Liberty remained in storage until 1995 when the Hoofers outdoor recreation club decided to bring it back for UW-Madison's 1996 Winter Carnival. Volunteers worked for more than a month to recreate the statue's 40-foot-high torch and 38-foot-wide crown with 25 sheets of plywood and 300 pounds of plaster.

And the Pail and Shovel Party?

Lady Liberty may have been retired, but the group was not entirely out of ideas. In September 1979, students were greeted on the first day of classes by 1008 plastic pink flamingos covering Bascom Hill.

Fast Facts

- Bill Veeck became so famous in Cleveland and Chicago that it's easy to forget he bought his first ball team in Milwaukee. From 1941 to 1945, the Brewers (then a minor league team) became Veeck's gag and promotion laboratory. He gave Milwaukee a good show—and three AA pennants.

- The 28 submarines built in Manitowoc for World War II tallied 32 confirmed kills of enemy ships during the conflict.

- You may have had a premonition that famed psychic Jeane Dixon was from Wisconsin. If you're really attuned, you have already divined that she was born in 1904 in Medford under the name Lydia Emma Pinckert.

- Milwaukee had 38 years with Socialist Party mayors in charge between 1910 and 1960. The rest of the country, if it knows, can't understand why. The answer may lie in the progressive streak that came to Wisconsin with waves of northern European immigrants.

- A Wisconsin firm used to make asbestos-lined warmers for baby bottles. The Hankscraft Company, located first in Madison then in Reedsburg, made these as late as the 1950s. Hankscraft is still around, but it's long since exited the baby-bottle-heater business.

- Emmy-winning actress Tyne Daly, born in Madison in 1946, comes from a very successful Wisconsin acting family. Her father James, of Wisconsin Rapids, is also an Emmy winner. Her brother Tim was an Emmy nominee.

- Among the Union soldiers sent into the infamous 1864 Battle of the Crater during the Siege of Petersburg was a Wisconsin regiment: the 29th USCT (United States Colored Troops), composed predominantly of black Wisconsinites.

- Standout Packer guard "Fuzzy" Thurston of Altoona was a fixture of Vince Lombardi's Packers teams. He was also a witty man. A reporter asked Thurston how he prepared for the 1967 NFL Championship (the infamous Ice Bowl) and its subzero weather. Fuzzy's reply: "About ten vodkas."

Exploring Cave of the Mounds

❋ ❋ ❋ ❋

Let's face it; sometimes "educational" trips are boring for kids and the same can be true for adults. Old buildings often smell, well, old. History and science can be interesting, but sometimes it's overwhelming to hear so many facts and figures all at once. And sometimes everything exciting is behind glass, which certainly takes away from the fun.

But if you're traveling through southern Wisconsin, it's well worth a stop at Cave of the Mounds just off Highway 18/151 in Blue Mounds. You don't have to be a spelunker to enjoy this cave. Science and nature come to life in an underground cave just waiting to be explored. The only caveat here is that it's okay to look, to ooh and ahh, and even to take photos, but absolutely, positively DO NOT TOUCH the cave walls and rock formations!

A cave is just a cave, right?

Wrong! The Cave of the Mounds is actually a National Natural Landmark.

How did it get that designation?

The United States Department of the Interior and the National Park Service gave that honor to Cave of the Mounds in 1988 to recognize it as a site that possesses exceptional value in terms of illustrating our nation's natural heritage. Such landmarks must also help visitors to better understand their environment.

What do those people look for?

They do an extensive study of a potential site, which needs to be one of the best examples of a certain geologic or biotic feature within a given region. Cave of the Mounds fit that perfectly!

What is Cave of the Mounds sometimes called?

The "jewel box" of American caves. The variety, colors, and delicacy of the cave's formations make it unique.

What makes it so colorful?

A mixture of minerals found in the water created the cave's colors. Gray and blue formations are caused by magnesium oxide. Iron oxide produces red and brown.

Does anyone sleep in the Dream River Room?

No, it's just the fanciful name given to one of the areas of the cave. The wide array of beautiful colors found throughout the cave inspired other imaginative names such as Gem Room, Cathedral Room, and Painted Waterfall.

Does the cave go any further than where the tour goes?

No one really knows. Some rooms wind for hundreds of feet, and some people believe that they may lead to other passages and even other caves.

Is the cave old?

You could say that. The cave itself began to take shape one to two million years ago. Yet, that's nothing compared to the rock it was formed in, which dates back 400 million years.

How did Cave of the Mounds get its name?

The name comes from two large hills, called Blue Mounds, in southern Wisconsin. The cave lies under the East Mound.

How was it discovered?

It was actually an accident! On August 4, 1939, some workers were removing limestone from a quarry in the Blue Mounds area. They set off a blast that suddenly revealed the underground cave.

What did they see?

Something totally unexpected: a limestone cave full of mineral formations, which opened into even more rooms.

What happened next?

So many people came to check out the new cave that it was finally closed to the public in order to protect it.

So did they protect it?

Yes. While it was closed, the cave was made accessible without hurting the cave itself. Wooden walkways and lights were installed. In May 1940, Cave of the Mounds was opened to the public.

So what's so cool about it?

Well, everything. You'll get a tour guide who'll tell you all about the rock formations and the underground stream. And there are amazing stalactites and stalagmites to see up close.

Which is which again?

Stalactites are columns that grow from the ceiling down. (Remember, they hold on "tight" to the ceiling.) Stalagmites grow up from the ground (trying with all their "might" to reach the ceiling).

Speaking of cool, what should visitors wear on the tour?

The cave is the same temperature all day, all year round. It's 50 degrees, so you might need a sweater in the summer, but it feels pretty cozy in the Wisconsin winter months.

Is the cave open year round?

Yes. It's open daily in the spring, summer, and fall, but it's only open weekends in the winter.

Where is it?

Cave of the Mounds is in Blue Mounds, just off Highway 18/151. It's about 20 miles west of Madison.

How many people visit Cave of the Mounds?

More than 59,000 visited the Cave in the first eight weeks it was open! Today, thousands visit every year and millions have come through since it opened in 1940.

What else can you do at the cave?

Visitors can take advantage of a beautiful outdoor setting that offers picnic areas, rock gardens, and walking trails.

A Game of Bridge

❋ ❋ ❋ ❋

In the mid-19th century, what we now know as Milwaukee was actually comprised of two communities divided by the Milwaukee River. The west side of the river was called Kilbourntown, and the east side was known as Juneautown. Unfortunately, an intense rivalry existed between the leaders of the two towns. Their feud culminated in a bitter disagreement over bridge rights and provoked acts of sabotage and violence in 1845. This conflict became known as the Bridge Wars.

The Players

Byron Kilbourn was a key player in Milwaukee's Bridge Wars saga, and he played dirty. He shrewdly recognized Milwaukee's immense potential as a port town. So the aggressive businessman plotted with a corrupt land surveyor to have the land west of the Milwaukee River included on his federal land survey. As a result, he stole the land from the Potawatomi, who rightfully owned it. Kilbourn's quest for world (or at least port of Milwaukee) domination was stunted by the one man who could trump his hand, Solomon Juneau.

Juneau originally came to Milwaukee from Montreal to work for the American Fur Trading Company. His career flourished, and soon he was operating his own successful trading post. At a land auction in Green Bay, Juneau purchased the rights to the land east of the Milwaukee River, where his trading post was located. Under the tutelage of savvy and wealthy businessman Morgan Martin, the charismatic Canadian Juneau realized his aptitude for real estate development. He also proved to be a diplomatic peacekeeper and interpreter, mediating between Native Americans and white settlers.

East vs. West Side Story

In 1840, the Wisconsin legislature mandated that a bridge be built to replace the inefficient ferry system that brought people across the Milwaukee River. Kilbourn feared that this new bridge would help boost Juneautown's independence and put a damper on his little monopoly. Furthermore, both towns argued over payments for the bridge as it was constructed. The bickering escalated for five years.

Kilbourn decided that the pesky Chestnut Street Bridge, sitting where the Juneau Avenue Bridge resides today, would have to go. The bridge blocked Kilbourntown's access to Lake Michigan, which it needed in order to expand trade routes. Juneautown, on the other hand, relied on the Chestnut Street Bridge to gain access to food and commerce from the west bank. Kilbourn petitioned the town board to have the bridge destroyed, but his request was denied on May 7, 1845. When the legal recourse failed him, Kilbourn, with a strong dose of can-do attitude, took matters into his own hands.

With a twirl of his mustache, Kilbourn arranged for his posse to demolish parts of the Chestnut Street Bridge and, for good measure, the Oneida Bridge. Folks in Juneautown retaliated by destroying two smaller bridges, effectively cutting off Kilbourntown from the east and south. Scuffles ensued over the next several weeks, resulting in many injuries but, fortunately, no deaths.

Bridging the Gap

In a heartwarming, after-school-special kind of resolution, all parties agreed that the fighting was futile and they would have to join forces to move forward. Juneautown and Kilbourntown, along with Walker's Point on the south side, unified. Together, with a population of approximately 10,000 people, they became the incorporated City of Milwaukee on January 31, 1846. Solomon Juneau was elected the first mayor of the new city. Not to be one-upped by his rival, Byron Kilbourn ran for mayor two years later and won.

Local Legends

If you're ever in Wisconsin's northern forests, especially if you happen to be near Rhinelander, be sure to beware the fearsome Hodag. But what exactly is a Hodag?

The Hodag is an unusual creature that was discovered in 1893. It is savage and ferocious. It walks on four legs, is anywhere from seven to eight feet long, weighs roughly 265 pounds, and has two horns on its head and a row of spines down its back and tail. It appears to be somewhat like a dinosaur, yet it's covered with short, dark fur. Fortunately, the Hodag is exceedingly rare. It was thought to be a lumberjack's tall tale, something like Paul Bunyan, until one was captured by a man named Gene Shepard.

Or at least, that's what Shepard said. The story of the Hodag is also very much his story, too.

Gene Shepard was born in 1854, in Hortonia. He grew up in south central Wisconsin and eventually settled near Rhinelander, where he worked as a timber cruiser—a surveyor and estimator for the logging industry. He was so successful that he eventually was able to live a rather independent lifestyle, but his real genius took an unusual form: He loved to play practical jokes.

This was the age of the humbug. Audiences enjoyed the miraculous, even when they knew they were being fooled. For example, in 1869, a famous and popular New York attraction was the Cardiff Giant, which was a huge "petrified man" supposedly discovered underground by well diggers. When P. T. Barnum, of circus fame, was unable to purchase the stone giant for his own exhibit, he had another one carved and put it on display as the original.

Shepard's bizarre temperament led him to occasionally pretend to be a hobo. He entertained business associates by serving them roast beef and afterward "revealing" that it had actually been dog meat. He doused ordinary moss with cheap perfume and sold samples of it as a naturally scented rarity. In short, he was the ultimate hoaxer.

The Lore of the Lumberjacks

Lumberjacks already spoke of the Hodag and also told stories of other strange beasts, such as the Gumberoo, the Whirling Whimpus, and the Side Hill Gouger. But in 1893, Shepard claimed to have actual proof of the Hodag's existence. According to Shepard, he and a party of hunters had cornered a specimen of the beast and, after a fierce battle, finally destroyed it with dynamite. The charred remains were exhibited in town for all to see—if they paid first.

Three years later, a Hodag was finally captured alive, after being drugged in its den with chloroform. Shepard and his crew dragged it back to Rhinelander and exhibited it in a pit. The moment of capture was documented in a photograph, which became a popular postcard—the first of countless Rhinelander Hodag souvenirs.

The Hodag was subsequently shown inside dim tents at fairs in Antigo, Wausau, and even at the Wisconsin State Fair, amazing all (for the cost of a dime) with its slow, mechanical movements and guttural growls. Supposedly, the Smithsonian Institution even inquired about the creature. Shepard finally removed the specimen to a hut on his Rhinelander property, where it was accidentally destroyed in a fire.

Legacy of the Beast

Shepard passed away in 1923, but the Hodag lives on, as the City of Rhinelander's official mascot. The beast serves as the city's goodwill ambassador, and the high school's teams call themselves the Hodags. An annual Hodag Country Festival is held. The beast's image is featured on local advertising and even police cars, and several Hodag statues are on display in the area.

Was it all a hoax? Shepard is said to have admitted as much, but it is a fact that the legendary Hodag of the lumberjacks looks quite a bit like another supposedly mythical creature, the "water panther" of the Ojibwa (Chippewa). It's shown in Native American pictographs throughout the Great Lakes area. Images portray a long and low creature just like the Hodag, with two horns and a row of spines down its back.

Fast Facts

- Wisconsin had three teams in the All-American Girls' Professional Baseball League, which is famous for being featured in the film A League of Their Own. There were the Kenosha Comets, the Racine Belles, and the Milwaukee Chicks. However, only the Comets spent their entire baseball existence (1943–1951) in Wisconsin.

- The only female Wisconsin soldier killed in action in World War II was Ellen Ainsworth of Glenwood City. A nurse at Anzio (1944), she calmly moved wounded soldiers away from heavy shellfire despite her own grievous injuries. She died six days later and received the Silver Star posthumously.

- A Wisconsinite became one of the first elected female heads of state to lead her nation in wartime. Golda Meir (then Golda Mabowitz), a Ukrainian immigrant, lived in Milwaukee from the age of 8 until she was 14. She would later serve as Prime Minister of Israel during the Yom Kippur War of 1973.

- Carrie Chapman Catt, born 1859 in Ripon, headed the National American Woman Suffrage Association when it achieved its goal in 1920. During its final meeting, she founded the League of Women Voters to educate and focus the newly enfranchised electorate.

- If you watched TV in the 1980s, you came to know Gena Rowlands from the commercials for Gloria (in which she played a former gangster moll) as a feminine fist wrapped around a blasting revolver. Born in Madison in 1930, Rowlands achieved a filmography that now stretches over 50 years.

- One of America's most prominent neo-pagan/Wiccan priestesses, Selena Fox, is based in southern Wisconsin. She got her Master's in Counseling from UW-Madison and has run Pagan Spirit Gathering (a Wiccan religious festival) on her 200-acre sanctuary since 1981.

- Wisconsin's first paid physician was an African American woman named Marianne LaBuche. A St. Louis transplant, she practiced at Prairie du Chien from about 1790 to at least 1827. The soldiers of Fort Crawford considered her far superior to local Army doctors!

Butter Battles in the Dairy State

✳ ✳ ✳ ✳

The "Oleo Wars" between butter and the butterlike substitute oleomargarine are a little-known footnote to Wisconsin history. This is puzzling because the war is still being fought to this very day, some 40 years after the combatants officially laid down their "sticks."

A Likely Battleground

In the early 1870s, wives on dairy farms made butter, and variations in equipment, churning skills, and cleanliness resulted in a finished product of widely varying quality. During this time, oleomargarine arrived on the scene with little fanfare. The French product was cheaper than butter, far more consistent in quality, and kept for longer periods. Slowly but surely, oleomargarine tempted the taste buds of quality-conscious consumers, even if many hid their fondness from fellow citizens. An oleo vs. butter battle loomed large.

The Battle's Beginnings

In 1872, Wisconsin dairy producers banded together to form the Wisconsin Dairymen's Association (WDA). This protectionist organization eventually zeroed in on oleomargarine and the alarming headway it had made into the butter market. In 1880, former WDA president Hiram Smith warned farmers that "oleomargarine is giving better satisfaction than most dairy butter as now made." To protect their industry, Wisconsin dairy leaders decided to improve their own product and to launch a preemptive strike against oleomargarine for added insurance. The battle lines had been drawn.

In 1881, Wisconsin passed its first anti-margarine law, which required that butter and oleomargarine be marked as such to avoid confusion between the two. In 1886, the state passed even more stringent legislation, which added a stiff tax and imposed labeling and packaging restrictions upon oleomargarine. In 1895, Wisconsin brought forth yet another law. It required restaurants and hotels to display signs announcing that margarine was sold on the premises. It also prohibited the manufacture and sale of oleomargarine—whitish in its normal state—that had been colored yellow to mimic butter.

Fighting Words

To turn consumers against oleomargarine, butter proponents drew wretched pictures of farmers being driven off their farms because of the evil spread. In turn, margarine backers noted that their product was as "wholesome as butter" and reminded the state assembly of documented cases where spoiled butter had been reprocessed and sold as fresh. They also informed consumers that creameries routinely colored their butter to make it more yellow. In answer to unsavory drawings depicting oleomargarine as a three-headed monster, "oleophiles" reportedly fired back with artwork showing diseased, dirty dairy cows being milked in mucky barnyards.

In 1915, a new wave of anti-margarine propaganda featured illustrations of sickened rats that had ingested vegetable oils—a prime ingredient in oleomargarine. This opportunity to demean oleomargarine presented itself after a University of Wisconsin study of vitamins went public. It suggested that laboratory rats fed milk fat were healthier than those that had ingested vegetable oils.

Oleo Makes Headway

World War II saw a changing tide in the Oleo Wars. Due to stronger food rationing penalties against fats than against vegetable oil, oleomargarine made substantial inroads into the butter market. By war's end, oleomargarine was commonly found on tables throughout Wisconsin, and the stigma of being a poor man's spread had vanished.

A growing resentment against unfair taxation on oleomargarine was also gathering steam. More than a few consumers were irked that an economical food was effectively being denied them due to petty, protectionist policies. Plainly, the war had battles left to fight.

In the mid-1950s, oleomargarine was still being heavily taxed in Wisconsin. The uncolored oleomargarine tax rate of 15 cents per pound was significant in a time when minimum wage was 75 cents an hour. This led oleomargarine-loving Wisconsinites to smuggle the product from out of state. Newspaper photos from the period show people cramming their cars with Illinois-bought oleomargarine to take bring into Wisconsin. A state official estimated that a ton of margarine came across the Illinois-Wisconsin border each week.

Concessions

By 1967, opinions among Wisconsin state legislators began to change. Aware of oleomargarine's popularity, they brought forth a bill that would eliminate the ban on the sale of colored margarine but still retain a tax of $5\frac{3}{4}$ cents per pound through 1972 (the tax was ultimately extended to December 31, 1973). After that, oleomargarine would be tax-free. The bill passed in the state assembly on April 6, 1967, and went into law on July 1, 1967. For the first time in 72 years, colored oleomargarine was legal in Wisconsin. But was it?

Despite the repealed ban, dairy protectionism continued well beyond the 1960s. In fact, butter's parting shot has survived right up to this day. As proof, an obscure law, officially designated Wisconsin Statute 97.18(4), states: "The serving of colored oleomargarine or margarine at a public eating place as a substitute for table butter is prohibited unless it is ordered by the customer." The law is used as a trump card by dairy-backers and is applied sporadically, usually only after a butter-loving patron turns in an offending restaurant.

Such an event occurred in 2004. Wisconsin citizen Nels Harvey ordered a baked potato at a Ponderosa Steakhouse in Menomonee Falls and was horrified to see that it was covered with margarine. When he asked for butter, the server replied that there wasn't any.

Harvey sprang into action. The 71-year-old filed a complaint with the Waukesha County Department of Health and Human Services. Within hours, an inspector dispatched to the offending restaurant demanded that butter be made available. Despite the steeper price of butter and the fact that no one other than Harvey seemed to care, the owner complied with the request.

Legendary Wisconsinite: John Muir

❋ ❋ ❋ ❋

The man who kept America's wildernesses wild began as just a boy in the woods of Wisconsin.

Son of the Midwest

Mention the name John Muir, and people instinctively think of the West: The vast, snow-capped mountain ranges of the Sierra Nevada, Mount Rainier, Arizona's petrified forest, the Grand Canyon, and, of course, the wild glacier-carved wilderness of Yosemite, where Muir took President Theodore Roosevelt camping in 1903. Muir's thousand-mile walks and multiyear explorations of these wild places are legendary, as is the role he played in protecting and preserving them for the future. But as much as Muir influenced the shaping of the American West, it was Wisconsin that shaped him first.

Muir wasn't supposed to have grown up in Wisconsin. He was born in Dunbar, Scotland, in 1838. His father yanked Muir and his brother out of school and uprooted the family for a move to the New World, aiming to settle in the backwoods of Canada when Muir was just 11 years old. But on the rough six-week sail across the Atlantic, the elder Muir heard other emigrants talk of Wisconsin and Michigan. The prospects were better, they said, and the soil richer. There were woods, they had heard—but not as dense as Canada's, where a man could spend his whole life clearing a patch of ground to farm.

By the time the ship arrived on American shores, Muir's father was losing his lust for Canada. What was the ultimate nail in the family's Canada trip? While docked in Buffalo, New York, the elder Muir met a grain dealer. He asked the man where his grain originated. Most, the man replied, came from Wisconsin. Muir's father made his decision on the spot. The family sailed up the Hudson, through the Erie Canal, and across the Great Lakes, finally arriving at the gateway to Wisconsin's storied oak savannahs, Milwaukee.

Love at First Sight

The Muir clan headed inland, settling beside the Fox River, just northeast of Portage. The day John Muir set eyes on the landscape that would be his new home, he and his brother discovered in a tree a blue jay's nest, full of green eggs and just-hatched fledglings.

"This sudden splash into pure wilderness—baptism in Nature's warm heart—how utterly happy it made us," he recalled in his 1913 book, *The Story of My Boyhood and Youth.* "Nature streaming into us, wooingly teaching her wonderful, glowing lessons, so unlike the dismal grammar ashes and cinders so long thrashed into us. Here without knowing it, we were still at school; every wild lesson a love lesson, not whipped but charmed into us. Oh, that glorious Wisconsin wilderness!"

Under his father's stern command, Muir did not attend school in Wisconsin, but rather, toiled on the family's farm. He managed to escape now and again to savor Wisconsin's woods and waters. One of his favorite haunts was along the Fox River and Pucaway Lake, where he marveled at the "millions of ducks" who congregated in the surrounding wild rice marshes. It was there he began his long love affair with bird-watching.

By 1856, the farm's soil had been depleted, and Muir and his family moved six miles southwest, to a place that would come to be known as Hickory Hill Farm. Muir's first task? Digging the family a well. Dynamite proved ineffective in blasting through the thick layers of sandstone below the soil, so his father put the young Muir to work. Day after day, from sunup to sundown, the teenager crouched in the ever-deepening hole, cutting away at the sandstone with a hammer and chisel. The task almost killed him. One day, roughly 80 feet down, the earthen hole filled with carbonic acid gas, knocking Muir nearly unconscious. Luckily, Muir's father, suspicious of the sudden quiet, peered down the cavernous hole, realized his son was in danger, and hauled young Muir out in a bucket. Instead of sympathy, however, his father tossed piles of straw into the hole to stir up the poison and carry down some pure air. Within the next day or two, Muir was sent back in, toiling on until, 90 feet down, he finally hit water.

To secure more time to himself—and away from the endless demands of his father—Muir struck a deal with his dad: he could have all the hours to himself that he wished, so long as they were gotten before his workday began. Thrilled, Muir took to waking up at 1:00 A.M. each day, relishing the quiet hours before the rest of the family awoke and satiating his curious mind by reading books and building wild contraptions he dreamt up. Among them was a rotary saw powered by the water of a dammed brook, unique door locks and latches, an automatic horse feeder, a clock-set firelighter, and, perhaps most famous of all, an alarm clock that not only told the time but connected to his bedstead to launch him onto his feet at a designated hour.

Encouraged by neighbors who thought his mechanical inventions were the work of a genius, Muir decided to take his clocks to the State Fair in Madison in hopes of securing a job in a machine shop. They were a hit, and Muir was hired to work in a machine shop in Prairie du Chien. Within a few months of starting his new job, however, he had set his sights on another goal—college.

Higher Education

At age 22, Muir enrolled at the University of Wisconsin in Madison, where he quickly gained notoriety for his inventions, including a desk he had whittled from wood, which accelerated his studies by pushing a new book in front of him after several minutes had elapsed. Though Muir scrimped and saved to pay for his tuition, room and board, and other school supplies—often surviving for weeks at a time on bread, potatoes, and molasses—he didn't work toward a degree. He simply took whatever classes interested him: Greek, Latin, chemistry, math, and physics were among his favorites. However scattered his curriculum at the University of Wisconsin, it was there that a seminal moment occurred that would forever alter the course of his life.

One June day a fellow student who loved "imparting instruction" (read: know-it-all) called Muir over to see a flower he had plucked from a nearby locust tree. He showed Muir the subtle characteristics that revealed, to the trained eye, the giant, thorny hardwood's relation to a weak, spindly pea vine. The revelation that nature's designs were not singular or similar by coincidence, but rather, unified with boundless variety, astounded Muir. He rushed into the woods and meadows, wild with enthusiasm for botany, a line of study he believed revealed traces of God's thoughts.

Without regard for a diploma or future employment, Muir decided to leave school to explore the world's wildest corners. It was not without some sadness that he left the place that had ignited his life's passion. As he recalls in *The Story of My Boyhood and Youth,* "From the top of a hill on the north side of Lake Mendota, I gained a last wistful, lingering view of the beautiful University grounds and buildings where I had spent so many hungry and happy and hopeful days. There with streaming eyes I bade my blessed Alma Mater farewell. But I was only leaving one University for another, the Wisconsin University for the University of the Wilderness."

❋ ❋ ❋ ❋

"No University, it seemed to me, could be more admirably situated, and as I sauntered about it, charmed with its fine lawns and trees and beautiful lakes, and saw the students going and coming with their books, and occasionally practicing with a theodolite in measuring distances, I thought that if I could only join them it would be the greatest joy of my life. I was desperately hungry and thirsty for knowledge and willing to endure anything to get it.
>   —John Muir speaking of the University of Wisconsin
>   in The Story of My Boyhood and Youth

"In every walk with nature one receives far more than he seeks."
>   —John Muir

"Take a course in good water and air; and in the eternal youth of Nature you may renew your own. Go quietly, alone; no harm will befall you."
>   —John Muir

Between a Rock and a Weird Place: The House on the Rock

❉ ❉ ❉ ❉

If you've ever said to yourself, "Gee, I wish there was a big house full of fake antiques, a giant plaster squid, the world's largest carousel, and a fully automated pipe organ 'played' by mannequins," then do we have the place for you! You can thank Alex Jordan Jr., a man who decided to build a house and fill it with everything listed above and a whole lot more. But is the House on the Rock an obsessive collection? A weird museum? A potentially haunted house? The answer? Yes.

I'll Show That Frank Lloyd Wright!

The House on the Rock is a tourist attraction near Spring Green. It's not a house per se, and although part of it is located on an outcropping of rock, the grounds of this attraction comprise buildings and structures that rest on 240 acres of farmland. So begins an attempt to describe a place that defies description.

The tale begins with Alex Jordan Sr., an aspiring architect and fan of the legendary Frank Lloyd Wright. The story goes that sometime around 1920, the elder Jordan had designed a women's dormitory for the University of Wisconsin. He took the plans to Wright's well-known property, Taliesin, to show them to his hero and perhaps land a job. Wright, who was not known for his warmth or diplomacy, snapped, "I wouldn't hire you to design a cheese case for me, or a chicken coop." Jordan was none too pleased with this assessment and vowed to get back at the big shot who had spurned him, though the "revenge" would actually be taken by his son, Alex Jordan Jr., years later.

In 1953, the younger Jordan spotted an odd piece of land outside of Spring Green called Deer Shelter Rock. A virtual chimney of rock, it stood 450 feet tall and offered a 70 by 200-foot expanse at the top. Jordan saw it as the perfect place to build a house that would ultimately gain as much attention as any Frank Lloyd Wright house. He began building immediately with funding from his dad.

The original section of the House on the Rock was completed in 1959, and it garnered plenty of attention. The house featured nine rooms with low-slung ceilings, fireplaces, and indoor waterfalls. The rooms spill into each other, and the whole place is incredibly dark. The decor has an Asian feel, but because Jordan favored accumulation over typical Asian minimalism, the effect is unique. Carpeting runs throughout the house, even on the walls in some places.

Let's Go Crazy!

Why the expansion? By 1962, curious people were paying 50 cents a head for a tour of the strange house built on the rock. Jordan Jr. figured that to bring in more people, they'd have to offer more, so five rooms were added.

Jordan supposedly hated to travel, but that didn't stop him from amassing a huge collection of antiques and artifacts over the years. Let the tourist beware: Some of the pieces on display at the House on the Rock are the real deal, such as certain toys and furniture, but others are fake, like the "Tiffany" lamps. With the help of friend and craftsman Don Martin, Jordan built whatever his heart desired and let the public think what they would.

Dim room by dim room, the collection reveals itself. The Oriental Art Room contains pieces similar to those found in the house's original section. The Blue Room and the Red Room contain fully mechanized organs, some with mannequins that "play" instruments in time to the music. There are doll rooms packed with dolls, dolls, and more dolls. The Model Circus Room, the Organ Room, and the Wildlife Room are all aptly named to describe their contents. A visitor can expect to find everything from taxidermic animals to carriages to grotesque masks hanging near old machine parts.

Jordan started plans for the Infinity Room in the 1960s, and it was completed 20 years later. This area is basically a superlong hallway that projects out from the main rock 218 feet into the air above the valley. Around Christmas, Santa Claus figurines greet guests at the doorway.

If it sounds weird, you're following along. The House on the Rock tour is said to take four hours and could take even longer if you actually attempted to look at everything. No visit would be complete without a peek at the largest indoor carousel in the world, which, at 80 feet in diameter, features 20,000 lights and 269 creatures (none of which are horses). The carousel revolves in a cavernous room to demonic merry-go-round music. No touching allowed.

There are no placards on items at the House on the Rock, no tour guides to explain origins or histories. The whole rambling structure seems to sort of live and breathe on its own. In defense of the curators (which included Jordan Jr. until his death in 1989), what could you really say about a three-level blimp hangar, dominated by a 200-foot-long sea monster battling a giant squid? Or all those topless angel mannequins that hang from the ceiling in the Carousel Room? Or the Cannon Room, featuring the world's largest cannon—an object so large the room had to be built around it?

See for Yourself

When Jordan Jr. passed away at age 75, it's believed that he left most of his fortune to his girlfriend of 45 years. Details of his life are murky, and the house he built (which he never lived in) was as mysterious as he was. As ostentatious as some might consider his life's work, he was a man who did not seek a lot of personal publicity.

The House on the Rock reportedly gets around a half million visitors every year, making it the most popular tourist attraction in Wisconsin and much of the Midwest. If you happen to be in the neighborhood, check out the nearby Alex Jordan Creative Center, where you can apparently commune with the spirit of the House on the Rock's creator, who claims he is still "present but not voting" regarding house matters.

From the Badger State to Tinsel Town

✳ ✳ ✳ ✳

Is it something in the water? Or perhaps in the cheese? Whatever Wisconsin's secret might be, this state has played a part in the start of some of America's favorite television and silver screen stars.

Chris Farley

Madison born and raised, Farley found his calling as a theatre student at Marquette University. Soon after he graduated, his natural aptitude for comedy sprung him from the Ark Improv Theatre in Madison to the acclaimed Second City Theatre in Chicago. He landed at the venerable *Saturday Night Live* in New York City in 1990, then quickly catapulted to the silver screen, where he went on to lead unforgettably funny films like 1995's *Tommy Boy* and 1996's *Black Sheep* along with best friend and fellow *SNL* cast member David Spade. Sadly, the hefty funnyman's career careened to a halt following a fatal 1997 drug overdose in his adopted city of Chicago. Farley is buried in Madison, where his family still lives today.

Kristen Johnston

Six foot tall, blonde and . . . a testosterone-fueled alien? Few actresses could pull off such a character, but Whitefish Bay-raised Kristen Johnston could and did—to great acclaim on television's wacky hit show *3rd Rock from the Sun,* which aired from 1996 to 2001. This funny lady continued to hone her humorous chops in the Austin Powers films, 1999's *The Spy Who Shagged Me* and 2002's *Goldmember,* as well as in 2000's *The Flintstones in Viva Rock Vegas.* She also appeared in the 2009 romantic comedy *Bride Wars,* starring Kate Hudson and Anne Hathaway.

Packers Make Ice Bowl History

✽ ✽ ✽ ✽

The Frozen Tundra and the Ice Bowl are both terms closely associated with Green Bay football and Lambeau Field, but how did those phrases really come about?

The Frozen Stage Is Set

It was New Year's Eve 1967, and the NFL Championship was on the line. The Green Bay Packers and the Dallas Cowboys wanted nothing more than to win the game, but Mother Nature had other plans. The mercury plunged to 13 degrees below zero—a record. But that was nothing compared to the 48-degree-below-zero wind chill. Thanks to the bone-chilling cold, the game would go down in history as the Ice Bowl.

Packers coach Vince Lombardi told his team that tough guys didn't care about the weather. But to keep play as normal as possible in the cold Wisconsin winters, he had taken the precaution of installing an $80,000 heating system beneath the field. Unfortunately, warm air sandwiched between the field and the tarp before the game, creating condensation. When the tarp came off, the arctic air hit the field and it turned into an ice rink—thus the Frozen Tundra.

The weather was unbelievably frigid. In fact, the commissioner actually checked with team physicians before deciding whether the game should be played. Once the game was underway, officials were forced to halt play after one referee's whistle froze to his lips.

A Hot Start

The Packers had home turf advantage—and were more accustomed to the freezing air—but the Cowboys were riding high after beating the Cleveland Browns a week earlier. Green Bay started quickly, taking a 14–0 lead early on. But by the second quarter, the Cowboys had adjusted to the bitter cold and forced two Packer fumbles, changing the momentum of the game. By halftime, the score was close at 14–10, and the air was colder than ever.

In the locker room, the focus was on warming up, and the coaches doled out heated words to their teams. But the third quarter scoreboard remained frozen, and there was no change until eight seconds into the fourth quarter, when the Cowboys scored a touchdown to take a 17–14 lead.

It seemed like the Packers' level of play had dropped as quickly as the temperature. They went more than 37 minutes without scoring, but with 5:04 remaining on the clock the Packers got the ball on their own 32-yard line. There, quarterback Bart Starr began the drive that would become the most famous of his career.

With less than a minute left on the clock, the Packers still had 11 yards to go. Starr and company managed to pick up another first down before getting stalled at the one-yard line. With the wind chill dipping to an incredible 50 below zero, running back Donny Anderson slipped on the icy turf, just one foot short of the goal line.

To Tie or Not to Tie

Trailing by three points with sixteen seconds on the clock, the Packers faced a tough decision. Would they try for a game-tying field goal and send the game into overtime? Bart Starr had other ideas.

Handing off the ball would be a risk on the icy field, so Starr called for the unthinkable—a quarterback sneak. Coach Lombardi had had enough of the arctic conditions, and if there was a way to avoid overtime, he was all for it. He gave the okay, adding, "Then let's run it and get the hell out of here."

Starr returned to the huddle and called the now-famous play. The quarterback lunged into the end zone—and into the record books—giving the Packers a come-from-behind 21–17 victory and their third consecutive championship.

Timeline

(Continued from p. 121)

1895
The OshKosh B'Gosh clothing brand is established by Wisconsinites James Clark, Frank Grove, J. Howard Jenkins, and George Jones.

January 1899
Representative Henry Daggett introduces a resolution in the Wisconsin state legislature to prohibit the tight lacing of women's corsets. His concern with women's undergarments is ridiculed, and the resolution dies in committee. Daggett does not attempt to run for reelection.

June 12, 1899
A massive tornado strikes New Richmond, killing 117 people. The death toll may have been elevated because the circus had just let out, and much of the town's population, along with visitors from other towns, was out on the streets.

January 28, 1901
Major League Baseball's American League is formed. It is initially comprised of teams from Milwaukee, Boston, Detroit, Baltimore, Philadelphia, Chicago, Washington, and Cleveland.

1903
Arthur, Walter, and William Davidson and William Harley build their first motorized bike in a Milwaukee basement.

1905
Sun Prairie native Georgia O'Keeffe enrolls in the School of the Art Institute of Chicago.

January 2, 1906
Robert M. La Follette takes his seat as a U.S. Senator representing Wisconsin. He will run as a Progressive candidate for President in 1924 and ultimately come to be regarded as one of the most influential members in the history of the U.S. Congress.

October 11, 1907
Cyprus, a freighter carrying iron ore from Superior, Wisconsin, to Buffalo, New York, sinks in a storm on Lake Superior. All but one of her crew drowns in the disaster.

1912
The Wisconsin schooner *Rouse Simmons* founders on Lake Michigan during a winter storm. The ship is loaded with 10,000 Wisconsin Christmas trees destined for Chicago. Helmsman Herman "Captain Santa" Schuenemann goes down with his ship.

October 14, 1912
Former President Theodore Roosevelt survives an assassination attempt while campaigning for reelection in Milwaukee. The would-be assassin is quoted as saying, "Any man looking for a third term ought to be shot."

August 15, 1914
Seven people are murdered at Taliesin, architect Frank Lloyd Wright's home, by a recently hired estate employee. The dead include Martha (Mamah) Borthwick Cheney, Wright's mistress, as well as her two children, three of Wright's associates, and the son of a fourth.

(Continued on p. 176)

Dairy Farming:
An Industry on the Mooove

❀ ❀ ❀ ❀

California cows may be happy, but Wisconsin cheese is still tops.

Humble Beginnings

When the earliest settlers traveled west to make Wisconsin their home, they found the rolling hills and rich soil perfect for farming. And wheat was the easiest crop to grow. It was relatively inexpensive and could be harvested twice a year, netting a decent profit. Unfortunately, it was tough on the soil, depleting it of nitrogen, which made the next round of growing harder—and then the bugs and pests moved in. Farmers had to try something else.

In the 1860s, most Wisconsin farmers had a single cow, which provided milk and butter for their own family. Many of the settlers came to the state from New York, which was the leading dairy producer at the time. They brought their knowledge of dairy farming with them, creating a new dairy tradition in Wisconsin.

In the beginning, milk, butter, and cheese were just items for barter; farm families would trade dairy products for other groceries and necessities. Over the years, the Wisconsin dairy industry expanded through scientific research done close to home. In fact, it was UW's Professor Stephen Babcock who first created a test for butterfat content in milk.

The dairy industry boomed. In 1867, there were 245,000 dairy cows in Wisconsin. That number jumped to 1.4 million by 1912. And cheese production, which was at about three million pounds in 1869, quadrupled over the next ten years. By 1915, Wisconsin was indeed America's Dairyland, producing more cheese and butter than any other state.

But that was then, and this is now. Wisconsin dairy farming went through some rough times in the 1970s and '80s when California—and their happy cows—exploded onto the scene. Out west, dairy farming was treated as big business rather than a family enterprise, and this method produced enormous success. In fact, by 1991 Wisconsin had dropped to second place in milk production.

To make matters worse, urban areas were growing and taking over farmlands. Farming was seen as unglamorous and a hard way to earn a living. In the 1990s, however, the Professional Dairy Producers of Wisconsin and the Wisconsin Dairy Business Association were both formed. These two groups were a huge boost to dairy farmers in Wisconsin. They fostered the growth and success of dairy farming by offering business, networking, political, and educational help to farmers.

Today, Wisconsin has found its own niche in a particular aspect of the dairy business—making cheese. Master cheese makers from the state have developed specialty cheeses that have been wildly successful across the country and the world. People today want convenience in their foods, and cheese makers in Wisconsin have had success marketing flavored cheeses (such as Italian, Mexican, or smoked cheese) that are ready to use without additional spices. They have also promoted ready-to-use shredded cheese and quality cheese slices.

Artisan cheeses are also becoming very popular. These specialty cheeses are handmade in small batches on farms, using milk from cows right there on the same farm. The result of such work is fine cheese for a more discriminating palate.

So while California cows are happy (or so the commercials say), Wisconsin farmers are happy. And so are the millions of people around the world who get to enjoy eating cheese made in America's Dairyland. Everyone should tip their caps—or cheeseheads—in respect to Wisconsin's fine dairy tradition.

Fast Facts

- There were no cows in North America until early settlers brought them over from Europe.

- Most pioneer families had only one cow, called a house cow, which produced just enough milk for the family's daily use.

- Today, there are about 94 cows per farm for a total of 1.26 million dairy cows in Wisconsin.

- The dairy industry in Wisconsin accounts for $20.6 billion of Wisconsin's economy.

- There are seven types of cows common in Wisconsin: Guernseys, Ayrshires, Holsteins, Brown Swiss, Herefords, Jerseys, and Milking Shorthorns.

- Who's who? You may think of all cowlike creatures as cows, but actually only females that have given birth earn that distinction. Babies are called calves (until they're about nine months old). Once they reach that age, males are referred to as bulls and females are called heifers—until they give birth. After that, they can rightfully be called cows.

- Cows use about half the food they eat to make milk.

- Cows eat about 75 to 80 pounds of food a day. And it must make them thirsty, because cows drink the equivalent of one bathtub full of water daily.

- One cow produces roughly 100 glasses of milk each day, or 200 gallons a month.

- Even though it's second to California, Wisconsin still produces 15 percent of the nation's milk.

- More than 68,000 people from around the world attend the World Dairy Expo held each year in Madison.

- Today 15,500 dairy farms in Wisconsin each produce about 18,850 pounds of milk per year. Ninety percent of that is used to make cheese—2.4 billion pounds of it. That's a big grilled cheese!

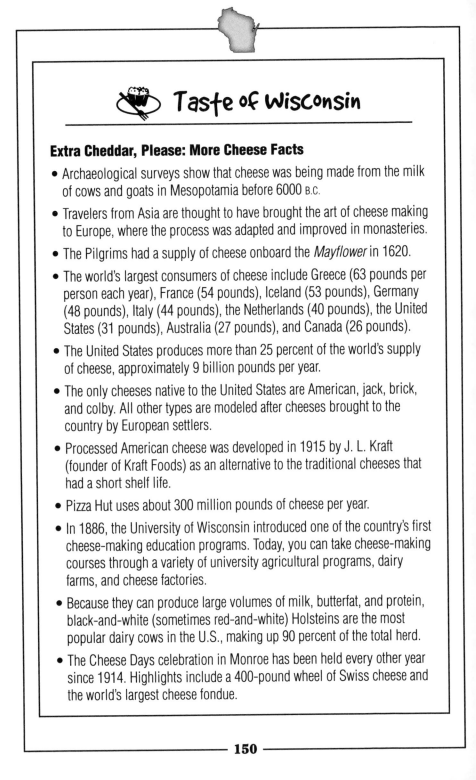

Taste of Wisconsin

Extra Cheddar, Please: More Cheese Facts

- Archaeological surveys show that cheese was being made from the milk of cows and goats in Mesopotamia before 6000 B.C.

- Travelers from Asia are thought to have brought the art of cheese making to Europe, where the process was adapted and improved in monasteries.

- The Pilgrims had a supply of cheese onboard the *Mayflower* in 1620.

- The world's largest consumers of cheese include Greece (63 pounds per person each year), France (54 pounds), Iceland (53 pounds), Germany (48 pounds), Italy (44 pounds), the Netherlands (40 pounds), the United States (31 pounds), Australia (27 pounds), and Canada (26 pounds).

- The United States produces more than 25 percent of the world's supply of cheese, approximately 9 billion pounds per year.

- The only cheeses native to the United States are American, jack, brick, and colby. All other types are modeled after cheeses brought to the country by European settlers.

- Processed American cheese was developed in 1915 by J. L. Kraft (founder of Kraft Foods) as an alternative to the traditional cheeses that had a short shelf life.

- Pizza Hut uses about 300 million pounds of cheese per year.

- In 1886, the University of Wisconsin introduced one of the country's first cheese-making education programs. Today, you can take cheese-making courses through a variety of university agricultural programs, dairy farms, and cheese factories.

- Because they can produce large volumes of milk, butterfat, and protein, black-and-white (sometimes red-and-white) Holsteins are the most popular dairy cows in the U.S., making up 90 percent of the total herd.

- The Cheese Days celebration in Monroe has been held every other year since 1914. Highlights include a 400-pound wheel of Swiss cheese and the world's largest cheese fondue.

Big A and Big O Invade Bucktown

✳ ✳ ✳ ✳

Door County and the Wisconsin Dells are two of Wisconsin's most popular tourist attractions. However, for a few years in the early 1970s, two of basketball's star attractions called Wisconsin—more specifically the Milwaukee Arena—home.

The Bucks Arrive

The National Basketball Association awarded Milwaukee an expansion franchise in January 1968, and the Milwaukee Bucks took the court later that year. Unfortunately, the Bucks were easy game for other NBA clubs, and they lost 55 games while only winning 27 during their inaugural campaign.

But as is usually the case in professional sports, if you're floundering near the bottom of the standings one year, you get a crack at the top pick in the college draft the next year. So after their first season, the Bucks won a coin flip with the Phoenix Suns—another expansion team with an equally dismal record. That coin flip changed the course of history for the Bucks.

Star Power

Milwaukee selected Lew Alcindor, a 7′2″ standout from UCLA, the most dominant big man to enter the league since Wilt Chamberlain. Alcindor, who would change his name to Kareem Abdul-Jabbar after converting to Islam a few years later, won Rookie of the Year honors, and the Bucks did a complete 180. They went 56–26 in the 1969–1970 season and advanced to the second round of the playoffs.

During the off-season, the Bucks unexpectedly acquired some additional star power. Oscar Robertson, one of the league's premier guards with the Cincinnati Royals during the 1960s, joined the Bucks in a deal that sent shock waves throughout the league. A rift apparently developed between Robertson and former NBA great Bob Cousy, who had taken over as the head coach of the Royals, thus opening the door to a trade. Rumors circulated that Cousy was envious of Robertson, who had broken several of Cousy's records.

Now, opposing teams could no longer concentrate solely on stopping Alcindor, the Big A, because they'd have to deal with Oscar Robertson, the Big O. Robertson proved to be a great complement to Alcindor. The 6'5" Robertson, who once *averaged* a triple-double with the Royals—30.8 points, 12.5 rebounds, and 11.4 assists per game in his second NBA year—provided about 20 points per game for the Bucks during the 1970–1971 season, while Alcindor averaged more than 31 points and 16 rebounds per game.

The Bucks Don't Stop

They, and the Bucks, were unstoppable. Milwaukee, coached by Larry Costello, put together a 20-game winning streak at one point during the season and breezed to the NBA's Midwest Division crown with a 66–16 record. The Bucks cruised through the postseason and swept the Baltimore Bullets to capture the NBA championship.

The Bucks dominated the Midwest Division in the 1971–1972 season, going 63–19. Abdul-Jabbar—who changed his name six months after the Bucks won the NBA crown—averaged nearly 35 points per game, while forward Bob Dandridge and Robertson checked in at 18.4 and 17.4 points, respectively. However, Milwaukee ran into the Wilt Chamberlain and Elgin Baylor-led Los Angeles Lakers in the playoffs. The Lakers dethroned the defending champs in the Western Conference Finals and went on to take the NBA title.

Abdul-Jabbar and Robertson teamed up for two more Midwest Division crowns. The Bucks did reach the NBA finals in 1974 but lost a tough series to Boston, four games to three. Robertson retired after the 1973–1974 season, and the Bucks slipped to 38–44 the following year despite Abdul-Jabbar averaging 30 points a game.

Abdul-Jabbar played one more season in Milwaukee but requested a trade to Los Angeles or New York early in the year, citing cultural reasons. So the Bucks shipped him to the Lakers after the season in exchange for four other players. His departure officially signaled the end of the most successful era in Bucks' history to date.

You Can Thank Wisconsin

Great Wisconsin Inventions

Two ways the Badger State made the average American's life even better.

Four-Wheel Drive

Overseas, guys like Ferdinand Porsche and automakers like Daimler Benz already had four-wheel-drive cars in development, but it wasn't until 1908, when Otto Zachow and William Besserdich developed and built the "Battleship" in their Clintonville machine shop, that the United States had the makings of its first successful four-wheel-drive automobile. Soon after, the pair began the Badger Four-Wheel Drive Auto Company (which would later become the FWD Corporation). It would eventually manufacture trucks with four-wheel-drive design that were considered a great asset to the U.S. military in the ensuing world wars.

Bucket Bagger

Unsettled by Hurricane Katrina's devastation in 2005, Edgerton welder Stacey Babiarz invented the Bucket Bagger, which can fill a 30-pound sandbag in less than 7 seconds—about 50 times faster than a person doing it with a shovel. The bucket, a front-load attachment that fits on any skid steer loader, is used to scoop up a large pile of sand, then a giant auger inside churns the sand across the bucket bottom, through a side port, and into the bag. Typically, Babiarz's invention sells for $5,400, but when heavy rainfall and floods threatened his own home and those of his south Wisconsin neighbors in June 2008, Babiarz donated his invention to help save his neighborhood.

Fast Facts

- *Angel Blows Nose on Wausau:* On October 17, 1983, young Todd Roll looked outside to see ropy strands of white snotlike stuff raining—or sneezing—from the heavens. It soon evaporated. As far as we know, the sample Todd collected and froze has never been analyzed. Someone should do that.

- The nation's northernmost Confederate cemetery is Confederate Rest, part of Forest Hill Cemetery in Madison. It is the resting place for Rebel soldiers who died in Camp Randall, a prison camp.

- America got a skewed view of Wisconsin from Jim Bouton's baseball memoir Ball Four (1969). Bouton's Seattle Pilots had Gene "Bender" Brabender, a hulking, grim-faced pitcher from Black Earth. He once said, "Where I come from we just talk for a little while. After that we start to hit."

- Wisconsinites might like to forget Aldrich "Rick" Ames who was born in 1941 in River Falls. He spied for the Soviet Union in very damaging ways during the Cold War. For his spying, he was sentenced to life in federal prison.

- Wisconsin's shortest gubernatorial term was four days. In 1856, in the wake of Governor William Barstow's resignation following a ridiculously tainted reelection campaign, Lieutenant Governor Arthur MacArthur governed for four days before the Supreme Court named Coles Bashford the new chief.

- A Madison doctor in the early 1900s suggested a smallpox remedy made from powdered, roasted toads. Never try this. Toad skin exudes enough poison that few animals can eat a toad, meaning this remedy probably made people sicker.

- Jefferson Davis, who would later get a job with high prestige and low retirement potential (President of the Confederate States of America, 1861–65), served near Madison as a young officer.

- The La Crosse Nursing Home reports a strange phenomenon. Now and then, a dementia patient will start asking, "Who's that little boy?" In most cases, shortly thereafter, a patient passes away.

Taste of Wisconsin

Wisconsin has long been associated with unusual foods and equally unique dining establishments. Consider this a foodie and novelty fan's Wisconsin must-visit list.

Safe House

This spy-themed restaurant is located...well, the exact location is top secret. Let's just say it's in a downtown Milwaukee building disguised as the home of International Experts Ltd. There is no Safe House sign, and when you enter, the doorman asks for the password. If you don't know the password, you can still gain access, but there's a price. And money is not the object. Performing a task such as push ups or hula hooping is more likely. Inside, expect oddities such as extra low toilets in the restroom. And if you try to use the phone booth, you may be transported through a secret passage to the back alley. Some notable celebrities have reportedly hidden out at the Safe House over its half-century of notoriety, including Mick Jagger, Keanu Reeves, Caroline Kennedy, and Penn & Teller.

The Sci-Fi Café

Greetings, Earthlings! Beam up to Burlington and visit the self-proclaimed "only sci-fi café in the Midwest." It's part old-fashioned ice cream parlor and part museum. It exhibits local evidence and lore pertaining to UFO activity and all things weird or unexplainable. Beyond offering breakfast and lunch, the Sci-Fi Café hosts seminars, tours, movies, and more. Explore the Haunted Cellar and learn about the physics-defying Burlington Vortex. Along with your sandwich and black cow, you can also enjoy a side of urban legend about the Bray Road Beast.

Al Johnson's Swedish Restaurant & Butik

Known to tourists as "the restaurant with the goats on the roof," Al Johnson's Swedish Restaurant is more like a visit to Little Scandinavia. Located in Door County's Sister Bay, the restaurant serves primarily Swedish and Norwegian flavorings on dishes imported from Porsgrund, Norway. An interior painting was done by renowned Norwegian artist Sigmund Arseth.

For more than 50 years, diners have endured the common two-hour wait to feast on Swedish pancakes, Swedish meatballs, and other house specialties. During the height of tourist season, Al's feeds about 2,400 people a day. And, yes, those are real live goats grazing on the grass roof.

It all started in 1973, when Al Johnson's practical joker friend Winkie Larson decided to put a goat on the restaurant roof as a prank. He climbed a ladder carrying a goat named Oscar. Ornery Oscar protested, wiggling and kicking, and both man and goat fell to the ground. Oscar was unhurt, though poor Winkie broke his collarbone. Undeterred, Winkie eventually succeeded in getting Al with the same prank. Ever since, Al keeps between five and seven goats on the roof during daytime hours, weather permitting.

Supper Clubs

In the 1920s, Milwaukee native Lawrence Frank opened the first supper club in Beverly Hills, California. Since then, the idea spread, and lots of supper clubs have popped up in Wisconsin. Any tour of the state's interesting eateries must include a supper club stop. The quintessential supper club is dark and dripping with outdated swank. There's always a long bar and plenty of white cloth-covered dining tables. Meals are far from à la carte; your steak and/or seafood entrée comes with a bread basket, relish tray, soup and/or salad, vegetable, and starch. No wonder Lawrence Frank is also credited with coining the term "doggie bag." Order a Brandy Old-Fashioned Sour at the bar, and enjoy an authentic Friday night fish fry.

Supper clubs tend to thrive in leisurely lake towns where people embrace the outdoorsy lifestyle, and that's often reflected in the decor. Dun Rovin Lodge in Hayward features a taxidermist convention's worth of stuffed and mounted animals and prize fish. As you gobble your chops, get an eyeful of Robert Malo's 70-pound, 4-ounce musky.

Turk's Inn Restaurant and Bar is located not far from Dun Rovin, but it feels like a world apart. While still considered a supper club, this restaurant forges a unique identity (or identity crisis) through its bizarre combination of classic Turkish food served in 1950s-inspired Asian kitsch decor. Lime green chairs and pink linen napkins pop when surrounded by heavily decorated red and gold walls and seemingly hundreds of knick-knacks, memorabilia, and family photos. Order lamb kebabs, and watch Marge, the petite owner, wheel a cart of three-foot skewers out of the kitchen.

The Biggest *M* of Them All

✻ ✻ ✻ ✻

How many towns can boast that they have the world's largest version of anything, much less a letter of the alphabet?

Ask anyone in Platteville to name their town's claim to fame, and they will answer—*M!* Platteville's landmark is a white limestone *M* reaching 241 feet in height and 214 feet in width. Set on the side of a hill, it is a remarkable site, visible for miles around. But who would go to the trouble of putting all of those stones on a hill? And why arrange them into the shape of an *M?*

It all started in 1936 when a couple of college students took a winter hike up the Platte Mound. They somehow got the idea of stamping out an enormous letter *M* in the snow. The *M* stands for the Wisconsin School of Mining, which was established in 1907 when the local mining industry was booming. A sudden freeze hardened their footprints, which preserved their work for weeks and caught the whole town's attention. Little did they know what their hillside stomping would inspire!

That spring, students began placing stones on the hill in the shape of an *M*. Eventually, an engineering professor arranged a field day, challenging his students to survey the hill and lay out a plan for the world's largest *M*. Over the course of six months, students carried more than 400 tons of limestone rocks up the Platte Mound.

In the fall of 1937, the *M* was completed just in time for homecoming. In celebration, the entire *M* was illuminated with oil candles, starting the tradition of M-Day. For decades, students prepared for M-Day by merrily hauling buckets of hydrated lime and water up the hill to give their big letter a good washing. While this practice had to be discontinued, due to the obvious dangers of splashing burning chemicals onto rocks, the lighting of the *M* has become the high point of the University of Wisconsin-Platteville's homecoming festivities—along with the after-lighting parties, which follow.

Wisconsin Olympic Athletes Are Golden

✤ ✤ ✤ ✤

Wisconsin hasn't hosted the Olympic Games, but that doesn't mean it hasn't produced its share of Olympic athletes. Do you remember these Olympians from Wisconsin?

- **Chelsie Memmel (West Allis) Gymnastics 2008:** Chelsie was part of the silver-medal-winning women's gymnastics team in Beijing. She was also part of the 2006 team that won a silver medal at the World Championships. At the 2005 World Championships, she was the first woman since 1994 to get first place in the all-around competition.

- **Paul Hamm (Waukesha) Men's Gymnastics 2000, 2004:** Paul was a nationally ranked diver before he trained on makeshift gymnastics equipment and went on to compete in the 2000 and 2004 Olympics. He won gold in the all-around competition in 2004 as well as the silver team medal. In 2000, he and his brother Morgan were the first set of twins to make the U.S. team. Paul withdrew from the 2008 Olympics due to a hand injury.

- **Morgan Hamm (Waukesha) Men's Gymnastics 2000, 2004:** Morgan competed along with his brother in the 2000 Olympics and was part of the 2004 team that won a silver medal in the team competition. Morgan was forced to sit out the 2008 games due to an ankle injury.

- **Garrett Weber-Gale (Fox Point) Swimming 2008:** Garrett won the gold medal in the Beijing Games in the 400-meter free relay and the 400-meter medley relay. In 2004, Garrett took the national title in the 100 free. He was also voted Big 12 Freshman of the Year in 2005.

- **Jim Montgomery (Madison) Swimming 1976:** Jim was the first man to break the 50-second mark in the 100-meter freestyle race. He earned that distinction in the 1976 Olympics, where he won three gold medals and one bronze.

Jeffrey Dahmer: "The Milwaukee Monster"

✳ ✳ ✳ ✳

The Oxford Apartments in Milwaukee are gone. The seedy complex at 924 North 25th Street was torn down in 1992 to prevent the site from becoming a ghoulish tourist attraction. But the empty lot still attracts visitors hoping to see a remnant of Apartment 213 and "The Milwaukee Monster." The small one-bedroom apartment was reputed to be tidy, clean, and home to charming serial killer Jeffrey Dahmer, his pet fish, and his collection of dismembered corpses.

Once Upon a Time

Jeffrey Dahmer was born in Milwaukee on May 21, 1960, and his family later moved to Ohio. He attended Ohio State University for one semester, then enlisted in the army in 1979. After being discharged for chronic drunkenness, he eventually moved back to Wisconsin, where he lived with his grandmother.

According to his parents, Dahmer started off as a sweet boy but became increasingly withdrawn during adolescence. They noticed his preoccupation with death, but they dismissed it. Friends knew he liked to dissect roadkill. Once he even impaled a dog's head on a stick. Another time, when his father noticed foul smells coming from the garage, Jeffrey told his dad he was using acid to strip the flesh from animal carcasses. Later, his stepmother realized that he might have been cleaning human bones.

There's a First Time for Everything

Dahmer committed his first murder in June 1978, at age 18. While still living with his parents in Ohio, he picked up a young male hitchhiker. The two had sex, then Dahmer beat the man to death, dismembered his body, and buried him in the woods. Later, Dahmer exhumed the body, crushed the bones with a mallet, and scattered them throughout the woods. His next three victims were all men Dahmer met at gay bars and brought back to a hotel or to his grandmother's house, where he seduced, drugged, and strangled them before sexually assaulting their corpses and cutting them up.

Bad Moves

In September 1988, Dahmer's grandmother kicked him out because he and his friends were too loud and drank too much. The day after he moved into his own apartment, Dahmer was arrested for fondling, drugging, and propositioning a 13-year-old Laotian boy. He was sentenced to a year in prison but was released after ten months. No one knew that he had already murdered four men.

After being released on probation for the assault, Dahmer moved back in with his grandmother. But as a stipulation of his early release, he had to find his own apartment. In May 1990, Dahmer moved to his now infamous home at the Oxford Apartments.

Modus Operandi

Living on his own, Dahmer stepped up his killing spree. Between May and July 1991, he killed an average of one person each week, until he had committed a total of 17 known murders. With few exceptions, the victims were poor, gay, nonwhite men. He would meet them in gay bars or bathhouses, drug them, strangle them, have sex with them, and then dismember them with an electric saw. He saved some parts to eat, and some skulls he cleaned and kept as trophies. He even experimented with creating "zombies" by drilling holes into his victims' heads and injecting acid into their brains while they were still alive. For the most part, he was unsuccessful, as only one man survived for more than a few hours.

On May 27, 1991, a 14-year-old Laotian boy escaped Dahmer's apartment and ran into the streets, half-naked, drugged, and groggy. Neighbors called the police, who escorted the boy back to Dahmer's apartment. Sweet-spoken Dahmer convinced the police that it was merely a lover's spat and that the boy was an adult. The police left without doing a background check on Dahmer. If they had, they would have discovered that he was a convicted child molester still on probation. After the police left, the boy, who was the brother of the boy Dahmer had been imprisoned for molesting, became his latest victim. The next week, when neighbors saw reports of a missing boy who looked like Dahmer's "boyfriend," they contacted the police and FBI but were told that he was an adult and with his lover.

The One that Got Away

Tracy Edwards was the lucky one. On July 22, police saw him running down the street with a handcuff on his wrist and stopped him for questioning. Edwards said a man was trying to kill him. He led the police back to Dahmer's apartment, where they found a human head in the refrigerator, an array of skulls in the closet, a barrel of miscellaneous body parts, a pot full of hands and penises, a box of stray bones, a freezer full of entrails, and snapshots of mutilated bodies in various stages of decay arranged in sexual poses. The police arrested Dahmer on the spot, ending his 13-year killing spree.

Crazy Like a Fox

At his trial, Dahmer's lawyer tried to convince the jury that his client was insane, emphasizing the heinousness of the crimes. Still, Dahmer was found sane and guilty of all 15 charges against him and was sentenced to 936 years in prison—15 consecutive life sentences.

And So We Come to the End

Dahmer was fairly infamous when he entered the Columbia Correctional Institute in Portage. He was kept out of the main prison population to protect him from other inmates. Even so, on November 28, 1994, he was assigned to a work detail with two convicted killers: Jesse Anderson and Christopher Scarver. When the guards checked in on them after a while, Anderson and Dahmer were dead; Dahmer's skull had been crushed.

Talkin' Wisconsin

" . . . . I ran out of gas west of Madison, and before I could lock my doors and hike off to a station, a guy named Terry pulled over, drove me to a pump, and brought me back to my car. For all Chicago has to offer, they don't have roadside assistance for spaced-out drivers, and for that reason alone, I love Wisconsin."
—*From* Oddball Wisconsin *by Jerome Pohlen*

"Oh, that glorious Wisconsin wilderness! Everything new and pure in the very prime of the spring when Nature's pulses were beating highest and mysteriously keeping time with our own! Young hearts, young leaves, flowers, animals, the winds and the streams and the sparkling lake, all wildly gladly rejoicing together!"
—*John Muir,* The Story of My Boyhood and Youth, *1912*

"Visiting the Wisconsin Historical Museum is like exploring my grand-mother's attic; I never know what I'll find."
—*From* Off the Beaten Path: Wisconsin *by Martin Hintz*

"I love to look at old barns in the winter. To me there's nothing more beautiful than a barn roof covered with snow contrasting with a deep blue winter sky with a few cows out in the barnyard in front of it all. To me that is a wonderful scene."
—*Jerry Apps, author of* Barns of Wisconsin *in an interview for* Wisconsin Public Television

"When French explorer Jean Nicolet landed near Green Bay in 1634, he walked ashore in Chinese silk robes brandishing pistols, in the mistaken belief that the Winnebago could show him a passage to Asia."
—*From* Wisconsin: The Spirit of America *by Joanne Trestrail*

"The great, dark trees of the Big Woods stood all around the house, and beyond them were other trees and beyond them were more trees. As far as a man could go to the north in a day, or a week, or a whole month, there was nothing but woods."
—*Laura Ingalls Wilder,* Little House in the Big Woods, *1932*

A Superior Tragedy:
The *Edmund Fitzgerald*

❈ ❈ ❈ ❈

Many ships have been lost to the Great Lakes, but few incidents have fascinated the world like the sinking of the Edmund Fitzgerald *off the shores of northern Michigan on November 10, 1975. The mysterious circumstances of the tragedy, which took 29 lives—all memorialized in a 1976 song by Gordon Lightfoot—have kept the story fresh to this day. The fateful journey began in Wisconsin.*

Least Likely to Sink

The 729-foot-long *Edmund Fitzgerald* was considered as unsinkable as any steamer. At its christening in June 1958, it was the Great Lakes' largest and most expensive freighter. Its name honored Edmund Fitzgerald, the president of Northwestern Mutual Insurance Company of Milwaukee, who commissioned the boat.

During the christening, a few incidents occurred that some saw as bad omens. As a crowd of more than 10,000 watched, it took Mrs. Fitzgerald three tries to shatter the bottle of champagne. Then, when the ship was released into the water, it hit the surface at the wrong angle, causing a wave that splattered the entire ceremonial area with lake water and knocking the ship into a nearby dock. One spectator died on the spot of a heart attack.

The Last Launch

The weather was unseasonably pleasant the morning of November 9, 1975, so much so that the crew of 29 men who set sail from Superior, Wisconsin, that day were unlikely to have been concerned about their routine trip to Zug Island on the Detroit River. But the captain, Ernest McSorley, knew a storm was in the forecast.

McSorley, a 44-year veteran of the lakes, had captained the *Fitzgerald* since 1972. He paid close attention to the gale warnings issued that afternoon, but no one suspected they would yield a "once-in-a-lifetime storm." However, when the weather report was upgraded to a full storm warning, McSorley changed course to follow a safer route closer to the Canadian shore.

Following the *Fitzgerald* was another freighter, the *Arthur Anderson*. The two captains stayed in touch as they traveled through winds measuring up to 50 knots (about 58 miles per hour) with waves 12 feet or higher. On November 10, around 1:00 P.M., McSorley told Captain Cooper of the *Anderson* that the *Fitzgerald* was "rolling." By about 2:45 P.M., as the *Anderson* moved to avoid a dangerous shoal near Caribou Island, a crewman sighted the *Fitzgerald* about 16 miles ahead, closer to the shoal than Cooper thought safe.

About 3:30 P.M., McSorley reported to Cooper that the *Fitzgerald* had sustained some minor damage and was beginning to roll to one side. The ships were still 16 to 17 miles apart. At 4:10 P.M., with waves now 18 feet high, McSorley radioed that his ship had lost radar. The two ships stayed in radio contact until about 7:00 P.M. when the *Fitzgerald* crew told the Anderson they were "holding [their] own." After that, radio contact was lost, and the *Fitzgerald* dropped off the radar. Around 8:30 P.M., Cooper told the Coast Guard at Sault Ste. Marie that the *Fitzgerald* seemed to be missing.

Evidently, the *Fitzgerald* sank sometime after 7:10 ı Ė Ę just 17 miles from the shore of Whitefish Point, Michigan. Despite a massive search effort, it wasn't until November 14 that a navy flyer detected a magnetic anomaly that turned out to be the wreck. The only other evidence of the disaster to surface was a handful of lifeboats, life jackets, and some oars, tools, and propane tanks. A robotic vehicle was used to thoroughly photograph the wreck in May 1976.

One Mysterious Body

One odd aspect of the tragedy was that no bodies were found. In most temperate waters, corpses rise to the surface as decomposition forms gas. But the Great Lakes are so cold that decomposition is inhibited, causing bodies to stay on the bottom.

In 1994, a Michigan businessman named Frederick Shannon took a submarine equipped with a full array of modern surveillance equipment to the site, hoping to film a documentary about the ship. His crew discovered a body on the lake bottom near the bow of the wreck, covered by cork sections of a decayed canvas life vest. However, this body may not be associated with the *Fitzgerald*. Two French vessels were lost nearby in 1918, and none of those bodies had been recovered either. A sailor from one of them could have been preserved by the lake's frigid water and heavy pressure.

What Sank the Mighty Fitz?

One theory is that the *Fitzgerald* got too close to the dangerous Six-Fathom Shoal near Caribou Island and scraped over it, damaging the hull. Another is that the ship's hatch covers were either faulty or improperly clamped, which allowed water in. Wave height may also have played a part, with the storm producing a series of huge swells known as the "Three Sisters"—a trio of lightning-fast waves that pound a vessel—the first washes over the deck, the second hits the deck again so fast that the first has not had time to clear itself, and the third quickly adds another heavy wash, piling thousands of gallons of water on the ship. Few ships can withstand this.

For Whom the Bell Tolls ...

On July 4, 1995, the bell of the *Edmund Fitzgerald* was retrieved and laid to rest in the Great Lakes Shipwreck Historical Museum in Whitefish Bay, Michigan. A replica bell, symbolizing the ship's "spirit," was left with the wreckage. Every year on November 10, during a memorial service, the original, 200-pound bronze bell is rung 29 times—once for each crewmember who perished.

The Sacred Altar of the Angler

❋ ❋ ❋ ❋

Wisconsin borders two Great Lakes and has thousands of smaller lakes. Wisconsinites fish in those lakes—and Hayward is where you'll find the National Fresh Water Fishing Hall of Fame.

Sounds Fishy

If you're thinking the Hall of Fame is just a bunch of fish heads on the wall and a collection of lures on display, think again. Hayward's hall is actually the international headquarters for the recognition, education, and promotion of fresh water fishing. The Hall of Fame and museum displays artifacts and recognizes lasting contributions to the sport. It also promotes programs and practices to improve the environment. And perhaps most importantly (for all the bragging fishers out there), it is the official record keeper for fresh water fishing records, with more than 3,000 world record entries to date.

Once you get to Hayward, you shouldn't have much trouble finding the Hall of Fame. Just look out for the famous Shrine for Anglers, which stands more than four stories tall—and is as long as a Boeing 757. Oh, and did we mention it's shaped like a fish? Yes indeed, the fiberglass-sculpted building is shaped like a giant musky with its toothsome mouth agape.

The Hall of Fame got its start in the 1970s thanks to an unlikely source—the Jim Beam Company. The whiskey distillers donated $250,000 in licensing fees from the sales of their fish-shape whiskey decanters to help keep the fish museum afloat.

Today, the attraction is host to more than 100,000 visitors each year, who come to view the 50,000 fishing lures, about 300 mounted fish, the huge collection of rods and reels, and 1,000 outboard motors on display. And for the more tenderhearted, there is a memorial to Herman the Worm, an ailing night crawler that was nursed back to health—by a fresh water fisherman, of course.

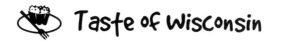

Taste of Wisconsin

It would be wise to stand down when your competition has a fight song... for its ice cream sundae birthright. Set to the collegiate anthem "On, Wisconsin!" the Sundae Fight Song represents Two Rivers' continued fight against "revisionist history" to herald its claim as the birthplace of the ice cream sundae.

A Sweet Tradition

Make no cones about it. Driving through Two Rivers, a city of nearly 13,000 on Lake Michigan, one can't miss the 28-square-foot state historical sign, a brown beacon recalling the magical event that gave birth to the ice cream sundae.

It was the summer of 1881, and George Hallauer, a Two Rivers native who had defected to Illinois, stopped by Edward Berners' soda fountain at 1404 15th Street while vacationing in town. Hallauer spotted a bottle of chocolate syrup normally used for ice cream sodas and asked Berners to put some atop his vanilla ice cream. Initially, Berners protested, saying it would ruin the flavor of the ice cream.

But Hallauer was adamant, and thus the ice cream sundae was born.

Selling for five cents each, sundaes were an instant hit. Berners went on to explore ice cream and topping pairings, giving his creations names like Flora Dora, Mudscow, and Jennie Flip. Word of his new concoction spread to the neighboring town, and Berners credited his ice cream counterpart in Manitowoc, George Giffy, with creating the term "sundae." Giffy only sold his ice cream treats on Sundays, until a sugar-sweet 10-year-old girl begged to have one . . . on a day other than Sunday. The story holds that in an effort to avoid blaspheming the Sabbath, the Sunday was renamed "sundae."

Even with a fight song and strong oral history of the invention, Two Rivers' claim comes with contention. Several other cities, including Evanston, Illinois; Buffalo, New York; even Baltimore, Maryland; have made weak claims to being home of the sundae. But Ithaca, New York, is the top threat to this coveted spot in American food history, unwilling to melt away from the heated competition.

Sundae Wars

City executives continue to banter, asking the other to back off from its claim. In 2006, the battle rose to a new level when Ithaca began promoting itself as the rightful birthplace. Two Rivers' representatives called on Ithaca to cease and desist. Then they started trading licks.

Ithaca placed an ad in Two Rivers' newspaper calling on the community to prove it. Two Rivers' city manager Greg Buckley countered, telling Ithaca to do the work.

And they did. The director of Ithaca's visitors' bureau combed through old newspapers and found an ad in *The Ithaca Journal* advertising a "Cherry Sunday," a new ten-cent "ice cream specialty" served at a little joint called Platt and Colt's. That ad ran in the April 5, 1892, issue, making Ithaca's claim to sundae dominance a full 11 years later than Hallauer's gustatory pursuit.

The road between Two Rivers and Ithaca was already a rocky one, but the barbs continued. Two Rivers introduced its Sundae Fight Song. Ithaca officials placed an ad in Two Rivers' local paper with a copy of Platt's 1892 ad, chiding: "Got proof? We do. Love, Ithaca."

Two Rivers bit back and placed a coupon in *The Ithaca Journal,* redeemable for a free sundae, but only in Two Rivers, and handed out pre-printed postcards addressed to Ithaca's mayor at the city's annual Sundae Thursday, encouraging residents to embark on a birthright-claiming blitz.

Despite continued efforts by Ithacans to slurp, er, rather, usurp, Wisconsin's claim, Two Rivers maintains that it is the rightful Birthplace of the Ice Cream Sundae. In any case, the reward remains just as sweet.

Fast Facts

- Ray Nitschke was certainly a savage Packer linebacker. It's perhaps less well known that off the field, Nitschke was one of the kindest, most gentlemanly guys you could hope to meet. He's fondly remembered for more than just his hard hits on the field.

- Baby boomers will remember May 15, 1972, when segregationist George Wallace's presidential run was cut short by four .38 bullets, one of which paralyzed him for life. The would-be assassin, Arthur Bremer, was from Milwaukee. His good behavior in the slammer earned him early release in 2007.

- When the new capitol in Madison was completed in 1869, a large recess in the ceiling directly over the chamber tended to collect dust. One legislator, seeing an effective way to punish the long-winded, rigged a rope that released the filth with one pull. If someone blathered on too long, they got a dust shower.

- From 1803 to 1810, a colorful business failure named Charles Reaume served as Justice of the Peace in Green Bay. The best way to influence his decisions was to bring whiskey to court. Despite this, Reaume's decisions (based in French and Native American custom) often resolved civil disputes peaceably.

- What good is an old granite quarry pit? A Montello realtor answered that question by diverting river water into one via four dramatic waterfalls, creating a beautiful lake from what was once an ugly hole.

- Born in Emerald, Hall of Fame baseball pitcher Burleigh "Ol' Stubblebeard" Grimes, who played for numerous teams between 1916 and 1934, was the last to chuck spitballs legally. On the mound he had the disposition of an irate badger; off the field he was as pleasant as one could hope for.

- An August 1976 lightning strike in Milwaukee uncovered an amazing find: a 1788 Massachusetts colonial penny, in excellent condition. No one knows how it got there, or if it really attracted the lightning bolt.

Wisconsin's Cartoon Heritage

✳ ✳ ✳ ✳

Wisconsin has many famous sons and daughters, but perhaps none are as well known as the creations of the state's cartoonists. Gasoline Alley's Skeezix, the bald and mute Henry, and Casper Milquetoast are all creations of cartoonists from Wisconsin who led the pack in the formative years of the American comic strip. A Wisconsin man is even considered to be the inventor of the daily comic strip.

It All Began in the Badger State

Clare Briggs was the earliest and most important of Wisconsin's famed cartoonists. Briggs was born in Reedsburg on August 5, 1875, well before the comic strip had been invented. Though his career eventually took him elsewhere, Briggs' intensely autobiographical work showed that his home would always be Reedsburg.

Briggs' historical importance lies in the work he did in 1904 and 1905. After working as a newspaper sketch artist, sign painter, and editorial cartoonist, he found himself in Chicago, working for William Randolph Hearst's *Chicago American*. With editor Moses Koenigsberg, Briggs devised a new way to use the Sunday comic supplement. Up to that time, comics existed only in colorful Sunday pages. They were huge, usually filling a whole sheet with just one title. Briggs thought of running a smaller black-and-white version every day. Readers would then have to buy the paper daily to keep up with the feature.

Briggs' comic was *A. Piker Clerk* (pun intended), the story of a racetrack enthusiast. It was the first daily comic strip. He later drew a Sunday strip called

Mr. and Mrs., about the troubles of a middle-class family. He is best remembered, however, for his whimsical single-panel cartoons. Briggs died of pneumonia in 1930, having already seen his work spin off into a small run of motion picture comedy shorts.

Little Pictures, Big Success

H. T. Webster, another famous Wisconsin cartoonist noted for his gentle humor, was creator of *The Timid Soul,* featuring Casper Milquetoast. Webster was born in West Virginia but moved to Tomahawk, Wisconsin, when he was young. There he did the things that all small boys do, including bragging about their future.

As the story goes, Webster was sitting around with his friends and they were deciding what jobs each would have. One boy, who already worked in a harness shop, declared that one day he would own the world's biggest harness shop, where he would sell horse collars inlaid with diamonds.

"Harold Webster," the boy sniffed, "all he's gonna do is draw little pictures."

"Little pictures!" yelled Webster. "I'm gonna draw big pictures, so big a million people can see 'em at once." Webster achieved and even surpassed his dream. His daily panels brought charm and wit to millions. Casper Milquetoast, the epitome of timidity, is his greatest creation. The character was embarrassment and paranoia personified. And his name even entered dictionaries to define just that.

King of Comics

Frank King, creator of *Gasoline Alley,* was born in Cashton in 1883. His family moved to Tomah when he was four. He drew pictures as a boy, practicing wash drawings and watercolors. King entered his work in the Monroe County Fair, using false names and entering in every possible class. He won in each case.

A sign King painted for a bootblack caught the eye of a traveling salesman, who arranged for the youth to be interviewed by a Minneapolis newspaper. His career as a cartoonist was launched. Later, in Chicago, he developed *Gasoline Alley,* with its familiar characters

Walt Wallet, Doc, Skeezix, and Aunt Phyliss. Some 14 million readers watched Skeezix grow up, marry, and have children of his own; King's innovation was to have his creations age. In 1941, *Newsweek* noted Skeezix's 20th birthday.

King often drew his characters taking walks in the Wisconsin countryside, especially in the fall. These strips were showcases for the cartoonist's style and gave the Sunday editions of *Gasoline Alley* a pastoral flavor. King died in 1969, but his comic lives on in newspapers today.

An International Star

Another classic that continues today is *Henry,* the silent, chubby boy with a talent for trouble. He first appeared in *The Saturday Evening Post* in 1932. Henry was "born" in downtown Madison. Carl Anderson, the son of a Norwegian carpenter, had knocked around the East Coast for years, narrowly missing fame several times. Finally he returned to his native Wisconsin, where he taught a cartoon class at the Madison Vocational School. In front of the class, Anderson developed the Henry character. William Randolph Hearst spotted the character in a German magazine and signed Anderson to adapt the feature for newspapers.

Anderson's fame came late; he was 70 years old when *Henry* achieved syndication. But once he made it, he made it big. The comic was an international favorite, because the boy's pantomime presentation transcended language barriers. Anderson's assistants took over drawing duties for the feature by 1942 because of the onset of his arthritis. He passed away in 1948.

❊ ❊ ❊ ❊

"Laugh and the world laughs with you."

—*Wisconsin poet*
Ella Wheeler Wilcox

A Staggering Spectacle

❉ ❉ ❉ ❉

What event mixes hardcore disciplined athletes with hardcore disciplined drinkers? The Riverwest Beer Run! It should be no surprise that Milwaukee, known as Beer City, is home to a race in which participants chug beer as they sprint, jog, walk... or stagger.

A Long-Running (and Drinking) Event

Since 1977, Milwaukee's Riverwest neighborhood has hosted the Locust Street Festival of Music and Art. About 20,000 people from Wisconsin and beyond flock to this big street party each year. Along with live music and arts and crafts booths, the block party is known for its Beer Run. This biathlon—the two events being running and drinking—is a 1.8-mile weaving course, and runners pitch and weave their way through Riverwest streets. Considering that many participants wear costumes, it's not viewed as a highly competitive race, unless the competition is to see who can slam their beer the fastest. In recent memory, enchanted fairies, spacemen, and a crew of plunger-gripping plumbers have stumbled across the finish line.

The run starts at 11:30 A.M. sharp, and preregistration is strongly encouraged, as it usually reaches its 900-runner limit early. The combination of beer and moderate exercise must be quite appealing to health-conscious drinkers. That Lakefront Brewery pint for breakfast? Why, that's just warming up.

Beer has actually become a welcome fixture at plenty of other races—usually at the finish line. But the official Riverwest Run entry form takes the beer component seriously and states, "Includes four mandatory beer stops for beer provided at tables along the route. Non-drinkers are welcome, but ineligible for prizes." Indeed, there are prizes (a fresh six pack, perhaps?) for the top three winners in each gender and age bracket. All contestants go home with a t-shirt and possibly a buzz. So it's the rare race where everybody wins!

Odd and Unusual Wisconsin Laws

❊ ❊ ❊ ❊

Wisconsin, if nothing else, is a state of laws. The state simply loves to legislate. The license plates may read "America's Dairyland," but Wisconsin is also America's Weird Law Land.

Don't Get Badgered by Legal Lingo

In Wisconsin, there are ordinances, statutes, and regulations restricting every possible contingency—even, for example, legally blind people who want to hunt deer with a rifle or crossbow. It is permitted by law.

Instead of deer hunting, why not go after goats? You'll find it more profitable. By law, anyone who catches a stray goat under four months of age in Wisconsin is required to be paid $5 by its owner—alive, not dead.

During your hunt, whether you're looking for deer tracks or goat tracks, stay away from train tracks! Besides rail employees, it's Wisconsin law that only newspaper reporters are allowed to walk by railroad tracks.

Among the things those intrepid reporters might see while walking the rails are trains, of course. Legally speaking, some of those trains may look pretty funny, too. For example, whenever two trains meet at an intersection, neither may proceed until the other has. That's the law, though it could take all day waiting for the first move.

And if you and a sweetheart happen to be riding one of those trains, keep the funny business to a minimum; in Wisconsin it's illegal to kiss on a train. Maybe that's why in old Hollywood films there's so much kissing at depots.

Does all this make the prospect of rail travel sound like too much trouble? If you're upset, we don't blame you. But whatever you do, as you depart the train, don't throw stones. Wisconsin outlaws throwing rocks at rail cars.

Perhaps you would rather travel by old-fashioned wagon instead. Hitch up your horse, but be careful: In Wisconsin, if you camp in a wagon on any public highway, you risk a fine of up to $10.

If you want live on the edge, and risk that whopping penalty by setting up house on the road, don't leave anything outside after dark. It is illegal to leave any material on a state highway after sundown—unless you mark it with a lantern that has enough oil to burn until daylight. It's the law.

Let's say that for whatever reason your local grocery store happens to be fresh out of lanterns and lantern oil. Please, please don't wave a burning torch in the air in its place! In Wisconsin, that's a Class A misdemeanor.

Yes, law in the Badger State foresees every possible eventuality. For example:

- Wisconsin previously defined rape as a man having forced sex with a woman he knows not to be his wife.

- You are required to have a license to make cheese. To make dangerously stinky Limburger cheese, the legislature wisely requires you to have a master cheese maker's license.

- Wisconsin may create no law prohibiting manually flushed urinals.

And finally, do remember that the State of Wisconsin takes its dairy industry seriously. Very seriously. Perhaps too seriously.

For example, take the state statute restricting the scourge of humanity, that evil, vile, great pretender, that seven-headed hydra, the beast whose name is 666, better known as ... margarine! Here is the actual law:

"The serving of oleomargarine or margarine to students, patients or inmates of any state institutions as a substitute for table butter is prohibited, except that such substitution may be ordered by the institution superintendent when necessary for the health of a specific patient or inmate, if directed by the physician in charge of the patient or inmate.

"Any person who violates any provision of this section may be fined not less than $100 nor more than $500 or imprisoned not more than 3 months or both; and for each subsequent offense may be fined not less than $500 nor more than $1,000 or imprisoned in the county jail not less than 6 months nor more than one year."

Timeline

(Continued from p. 146)

1917
The United States enters World War I. Wisconsin will send some 120,000 soldiers to Europe, becoming the first state to meet federal draft requirements.

1918
Frank O. King, the Cashton-born cartoonist for the *Chicago Tribune*, creates his *Gasoline Alley* comic strip.

October 1918
A deadly forest fire claims some 800 lives in Wisconsin and several hundred more in Minnesota.

1919
Wisconsin's Ringling Brothers merge their circus empire with that of P. T. Barnum, creating the Ringling Bros. and Barnum & Bailey Circus.

June 10, 1919
Wisconsin ratifies the 19th Amendment, giving women the right to vote. It is the first state to do so.

August 11, 1919
A group of athletes gather in the editorial room of the *Green Bay Press-Gazette* under the guidance of Curly Lambeau and George Calhoun to form the nucleus of the Green Bay Packers football team. They play their first game a month later, crushing the opposition in a 53–0 shutout.

October 23, 1921
Having obtained an NFL franchise earlier in the year, the Green Bay Packers play their first NFL game and defeat Minneapolis 7–6.

November 22, 1927
Carl Eliason of Sayner receives the first snowmobile patent.

1932
Celebrated architect Frank Lloyd Wright launches a school of architecture at his Spring Green home, Taliesin, with 30 students.

January 28, 1932
Wisconsin becomes the first state to provide unemployment compensation to its residents.

February 2, 1935
Leonarde Keeler, a detective who co-invented a polygraph machine, uses the new device on two suspects in Portage. Both are convicted. It is the first time in history that a conviction is handed down based, in part, on polygraph evidence.

1938
Wisconsin architect John Hammes launches the InSinkErator Company to produce and sell his invention, the under-sink garbage disposal.

January 19, 1939
Fort Atkinson resident Ernest Hausen plucks a chicken in 4.4 seconds, setting a record that remains unbroken to this day.

1941
Citizen Kane, the most famous film made by celebrated Wisconsin native and director Orson Welles, is released. It was considered a controversial flop until its 1950s rerelease.

(Continued on p. 194)

Wisconsin Dells Has Ducks in a Row

❀ ❀ ❀ ❀

Is it a boat? Is it a tank? Well, actually it's a little of both.

Fitting the (Duck) Bill

If you live or vacation in Wisconsin, you've probably heard of the Original Wisconsin Ducks. After all, they've been around for almost 60 years. One of the top attractions at the Wisconsin Dells, the amphibious Ducks transport more than 300,000 passengers a year through 8.5 miles of wooded terrain and scenic waterways. This one-hour excursion through the Lower Dells is calm and beautiful until you hit one of the two featured splashdowns—when your vehicle suddenly hits the water and becomes a boat. Now that's something to quack about!

❀ ❀ ❀ ❀

- *A Duck is a combination land and water vehicle with a steel hull and six wheels.*

- *General Motors developed the first Ducks during World War II to transport troops and cargo by land and sea to hard-to-reach areas.*

- *While they are affectionately known as Ducks, their real name is DUKW, which was a combination of military code letters for the* various aspects of the vehicle: D stands for 1942, the year they were designed; U is for utility or amphibious; K means it is front-wheel drive; and the W means it has two rear driving wheels.

- Ducks were used in Europe, North Africa, and the Pacific during World War II. They played a large role in the invasion of Normandy—2,000 Ducks transported troops and supplies to the shores of France.

- More than 21,200 Ducks were manufactured from 1942 through 1945, at a cost of $10,000 each. If that sounds cheap, compare it to the cost of a three-bedroom house, which cost less at that time.

- Each one of the Original Wisconsin Ducks is named after a military leader or WWII battle.

- The Duck's land motor is located in the front, and while in the water, the Duck operates by a rear propeller.

- Ducks are not small. They are 31 feet long and 8 feet wide, weighing in at 7.5 tons. They can reach speeds of 55 mph on land and 6 mph in the water.

- The Original Wisconsin Ducks attraction has more than 90 Ducks in its fleet, the largest in the nation. All told, there are about 300 Ducks still operating in the United States.

- More than 100 applicants each year apply for the position of Duck Driver. Only 60 get the call. Drivers must be at least 18 years old and have a commercial driver's license. Drivers must also have sufficient arm strength—there's no power steering.

- Duck Drivers go through an intensive six-week training—one week more than the soldiers who drove them in World War II.

- Drivers learn to work the double clutch in empty parking lots before venturing out on trails. All new drivers must also take the general manager on a tour before they get the nod to go it alone.

On, Wisconsin!

✻ ✻ ✻ ✻

"Minnesota, Minnesota, la, la, la, la, la." Oh wait—that's not right. But it might have been, if composer W. T. Purdy hadn't had a friend with ties to Wisconsin back in 1909.

A Gopher Anthem?

Purdy heard about a contest sponsored by a St. Paul, Minnesota, music store, seeking a new fight song for the University of Minnesota. The prize was $100. Purdy was a musician who belonged to the glee club and played the organ at Hamilton College in upstate New York. After he graduated, he moved to Chicago and took up residence at a boarding house. That's where he met a former University of Wisconsin student named Carl Beck, and the two became friends.

Purdy, who had never once been in Wisconsin, was trying out his jaunty new tune one day. Beck happened by just as Purdy was singing "Minnesota" and stopped in his tracks. Beck couldn't stand the thought that the song might go to his alma mater's rival, and he suggested substituting the words "On, Wisconsin" into the same tune—and the rest is history.

A Catchy Little Tune

The pair spent several evenings working on the new song, with Beck supplying the words. Unfortunately, the young men were a little short of cash and couldn't afford the $50 it would cost to publish the tune. They finally were able to come up with a $10 credit from a music plate engraving company, which they then used as a reference at the printer where they had 500 copies made.

The idea was to take their new song up to a Wisconsin football game and get the crowd excited about it. At the last minute, Beck was unable to make the trip and he sent Purdy off with a few letters of introduction and the bundle of sheet music. "On, Wisconsin!" was first sung by the glee club on November 10, 1909, and then again at a big pep rally the next day. The students loved it. The UW Band played the song at their homecoming game (against Minnesota, no less) on November 13, and there was no looking back. Students on street corners were heard singing, "Fight fellows, fight, fight, fight," long after the game was over.

New Words, New Purpose

The song instantly became a part of UW athletics, played at every game and sung around campus. But it wasn't until 1913 that the tune was used to create a state song. Judge Charles D. Rosa and J. S. Hubbard, editor of the *Beloit Free Press,* collaborated on the words. While it was widely accepted as the state song, it wasn't officially adopted until 1959. At that time, Representative Harold W. Clemens found out that there were only ten states without a designated state song and Wisconsin was one of them. He introduced a bill to make the song official. It passed and can now be found in Chapter 170, Laws of 1959; section 1.10 of the statutes.

Where Did it Go from There?

William Purdy sold his rights to the song in 1918 for less than $100, but it remained popular within Wisconsin and beyond. John Philip Sousa called "On, Wisconsin!" one of the best college marches around. Today, hundreds of high schools and colleges use the music, while substituting lyrics of their own.

At UW, the song was left untouched for many years until innovative band director Michael Leckrone made some changes to the arrangement in 1969. He holds the copyright to that version.

And what about the original? There have been numerous rumors over the years regarding who owns the rights to "On, Wisconsin!" Michael Jackson and Paul McCartney's names have both been mentioned as possible owners of the song's copyright.

Here's the scoop: U.S. Copyrights expire after a certain period of years, and currently all songs published in 1922 or earlier are considered to be in the public domain. This means that anyone in the

United States can use this song—at least the original version—free of charge. Half of the international rights, which govern its use outside the United States, are owned by Paxwin Music, which acquired them in 1960. Oddly enough, it seems that much of their royalty business comes from the fight song's use for ringtones, musical bottle openers, car horns, and other technology.

Edwin H. Morris, a division of MPL Music Publishing, owns 50 percent of the worldwide rights to the title. And to prove that there can sometimes be truth in rumor—MPL is owned by none other than Paul McCartney.

A Simple "No" Would Have Sufficed

A *New York Times* article dated February 1981 told of a letter written by then-Wisconsin governor Lee Dreyfus to Sir Paul. The governor asked if McCartney would consider giving up the song rights in honor of John Lennon, who had recently been killed. McCartney's attorney (and father-in-law) Lee V. Eastman responded by saying that "On, Wisconsin!" was part of a larger group of college fight songs. It would be impossible to separate that tune out because they had been purchased as an entity.

The lawyer definitely did not make any friends in Wisconsin with the rest of his answer. He went on to say that the song actually pulls in fewer royalties than the other fight songs because of the university's poor performance on the football field. As if that weren't enough, he then went one step further. Eastman said he should have told Governor Dreyfus to stop worrying about songs—and start worrying about getting a good football team.

Well, Dreyfus may not have been the one to do it, but less than a decade later, the football team regained national prominence. "On, Wisconsin!" has since been played in three Rose Bowl games and parades, as well as at numerous other televised games. The hockey team continues to be successful, and the basketball team has been in the NCAA tournament for many years running. Who's laughing—or singing—now?

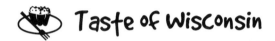

Taste of Wisconsin

A Diamond in the Rough

No prettier than a prune but tastier than a tenderloin steak, the wild morel mushroom is native to the woods of Wisconsin. When the conditions are right during a brief window of time each spring, the elusive mushroom emerges, inspiring countless foragers to set out in a challenging game of hide and seek. Those who find morels are few, but those that do are lucky Wisconsinites indeed. Here's what you need to know to improve your luck and make this delicacy part of your pantry.

When and Where to Hunt

Notoriously picky about temperature and moisture, morels tend to emerge in damp springs when the daytime temperature hovers in the 60s and nighttime temperatures stay above 40 degrees Fahrenheit. Their habitat of choice is far less predictable. When a morel patch is discovered, it is generally in a forested area—typically one without thick undergrowth (in fact, morel populations have been known to boom following a forest fire). But they're also known to inhabit tall grasses, old apple orchards, dried creek bottoms, and rivers' edges. Pine, white ash, aspen, and cottonwood trees are often considered morel hosts, as are dead and dying elm trees.

Identification

Morels are part of the foolproof four—mushrooms that look so distinctive, they're easy to identify (puffballs, shaggy mane, and chanterelles are the other three). A morel's most distinct feature is its narrow, waffled, conelike top. This ridged, honeycombed cap merges right into its smooth white stem, rather than folding under like a skirt. The true test, however, is what is—or isn't—within. If you cut a morel vertically, it will be hollow inside.

Harvesting

Break off or cut the morel at ground level, making sure not to disturb its rooted stem. Conventional wisdom warns against over-harvesting any one patch in order to ensure future growth in that spot. Gently shake or brush off as much dirt as possible, then drop it into a mesh carrying bag (many people use the sacks onions are sold in), which allows the mushrooms to breathe without becoming moist but also enable the fungi to scatter its spores and propagate future patches as you move through the woods.

Drying and Storing

Back at home, sort through your collected mushrooms, tossing any that are dry or slimy. If you're not able to eat them within five days, don't wash them. Simply thread a needle and string through them, leaving space for airflow between each mushroom, and hang them in a dry area (but not in direct sunlight) for several days. Once they are dried crisp, store them in an airtight jar in a cool, dark cupboard. When you're ready to eat them, you can reconstitute the dried morels in hot broth, water, or wine, which will then be infused with the morels' flavor—a great base for a sauce.

Cleaning and Preparing for Cooking

If you're able to eat your found morels within a few days, store them in a paper bag in the refrigerator. When you're ready to cook them, gently swish them in a large bowl filled with cool water and two to three tablespoons of fine salt, then rinse them with unsalted cool water. Pat them dry with a paper towel, then cook as you would any other mushroom: sautéed in butter or rolled in seasoned flour and fried in oil are two favorite ways Wisconsinites love to serve this subtle yet meaty-tasting mushroom.

❋ ❋ ❋ ❋

- *The scientific name for morels is* Morchella.

- *Muscoda calls itself the "Morel Capital of Wisconsin" and holds a morel festival every year.*

Fast Facts

- Wisconsin used to have a marshal who, if he were living today, probably could have played in the NBA. At 7'6", Anders "Big Gust" Anderson was the law in Grantsburg from 1901 to 1926. The towering Swede was well liked in town and figured prominently in the local community center.

- The Minnesota Twins once had a mascot named Twinkie the Loon. Brewer fans in particular were rough on Twinkie, pushing him, showering him with beer, and even once biting the costume's beak. As one wearer of the Twinkie costume noted, you know Wisconsinites really dislike you when they throw drinkable beer at you.

- The impressive thing about 1930s–40s Packer end Don Hutson isn't the 18 NFL receiving records he held at retirement, though that's definitely admirable. What's more impressive is that to this day, he still *holds* some of those records.

- Pat Summerall, the legendary broadcaster, learned the hard way about Packer fullback Jim Taylor's post-game refreshments after Super Bowl I. The locker room was like a sauna, and Taylor offered Summerall a drink from his Coke can—which contained straight bourbon. Coughing and hacking, Summerall almost couldn't go on camera.

- Hall of Fame Chicago fullback Bronko Nagurski once mistook a brick wall for a Packer tackler. Slamming his way through defenders and into the end zone after three frustrating stops, Nagurski bounced off a goalpost and hit the wall. After the incident, Bronko commented something to the effect of, "But tell 'em to watch that last guy, he hits pretty hard."

- In 1975, Brewer Gorman Thomas had a bad series in Boston. Very bad. After striking out eight consecutive times, he finally broke the streak. He wished he hadn't, because he hit into a double play. The Red Sox fans gave Thomas a standing ovation for the DP ball.

Groundhog Day: Badger State Edition

❊ ❊ ❊ ❊

Move over Punxsutawney Phil, Sun Prairie is Jimmy the Groundhog's turf.

Wisconsin's Weatherhog

Jerry Hahn of Sun Prairie possesses a fabulous miniature meteorologist, Jimmy the Groundhog. He's the centerpiece of the community's annual Groundhog Day celebration. The event includes the official "prognostication," entertainment, booths with activities, and a community pancake breakfast. It's usually held at Cannery Square Plaza, near a chainsaw-carved sculpture of Jimmy. Most important of all, when it comes to predicting spring, organizers claim their groundhog has an 80-percent accuracy rate.

Contrary to myth, Jimmy and his peers do not sleep solidly throughout the winter. Hahn and his family take care of Jimmy all year, and during the warmer months between spring and fall, you can visit the groundhog in the petting zoo at their orchard, Jerry's Apples and Farm Produce. As Groundhog Day draws near, Hahn brings Jimmy—officially Jimmy the Ninth—to area schools, for children to meet and pet.

A Meteorological Tradition

The Groundhog Day tradition seems to have been brought to America by German immigrants, and the first reference in print in the United States dates to 1841. Sun Prairie residents had been noting predictions of groundhogs in the wild since at least the 1880s, but it wasn't until 1948 that they formed the Sun Prairie Groundhog Club. The local postmaster began issuing annual commemorative postcards, and in 1950, a live groundhog was added to the festivities.

In 1952, Sun Prairie had two official groundhogs who were made royalty: Sir No-Talk-In-Sleep and Miss Sleep-All-Winter. They had a marriage ceremony that included a maid of honor, best man, ring bearer, and flower girl. The county clerk even issued a marriage license. A year later, their son was christened Prince Dauphine. He was albino and, after his parents abdicated, he became "King of the World's Groundhogs." Or so they said in Sun Prairie.

Meet Jimmy

Hahn found the current Jimmy in 2000, on nearby Highway 19. "He was just a little guy and he was trying to cross the road," he says. "Evidently he had got nicked by a car. He was standing up on his back legs with his paws up like he was praying, right in the center of the road."

Hahn stopped traffic and rescued the groundhog. "We got him all fixed up and we've just been buddies ever since." Jimmy spends nights in the family laundry room and days in their sunroom, apparently showing no fear of the shadows cast there.

Many other proud North American communities have adopted groundhogs who make their own "official" weather predictions. They include New York's Staten Island Chuck, Ontario's Wiarton Willie, Atlanta's General Beauregard Lee, and even Pardon Me Pete of Tampa, Florida, where a shadow and six more weeks of winter doesn't seem like it would matter in the slightest.

And, of course, in Pennsylvania, there's Jimmy's nemesis, Punxsutawney Phil. In the 1950s, a newspaper war erupted, with the Punxsutawney newspaper referring to Sun Prairie as a "remote two-cow village buried somewhere in the wilderness." While Dane County residents may have taken comfort in the fact that they had far, far more than two cows, the debate spilled over onto the floor of Congress and was even recorded in the Congressional Record.

The Midwest's best revenge may finally have come in 1993, with the Bill Murray movie *Groundhog Day*. Though it was set in Punxsutawney, it was actually filmed in a place not far from Wisconsin, picturesque Woodstock, Illinois.

Home Sweet Home: Miller Park

✳ ✳ ✳ ✳

Way back in the 1980s, Brewers owner Bud Selig started to lobby for a new ballpark in Milwaukee. After its approval, it took four and a half years to build. But as anyone who has seen a baseball game at Miller Park would tell you, it was well worth the wait.

Baseball's First Hurrah

Before Miller Park, there was County Stadium. An unexciting, unimaginative steel and concrete structure, County Stadium opened in 1953. It was built on the site of a garbage dump—and that pretty much says it all. Capacity was originally 28,111, but an upper deck was added in its second year to increase seating to 43,340. The most exciting aspect of County Stadium was that its very first tenant was the city's first Major League baseball team—the Milwaukee Braves.

The Braves never had a losing season in Milwaukee, so attendance skyrocketed the first few years. But when attendance began to sag, Braves owners started looking for a bigger television market for the team. They got their wish, and by the 1966 season, the Braves were gone. Milwaukee would go five years without baseball.

At least County Stadium didn't sit empty after the move. Beginning in 1953, it was also the part-time home of the NFL's Green Bay Packers, who played half their home games in Milwaukee. The arrangement lasted 41 years before they pulled out for good after 1994.

The Brewers Are Coming!

In 1970, Bud Selig found a new team for Milwaukee. He bought the Seattle Pilots, brought them to Wisconsin, and renamed them. The Milwaukee Brewers were born. A few important changes were made right away—a beer barrel, chalet, and slide for the new mascot, Bernie Brewer, were added. In 1974, the press box was renovated and a new scoreboard was installed. But by the mid-1980s, Selig realized that a new stadium would be one way to generate additional revenues. It took a decade to gather the support, but finally after the last game of the 1996 season, a groundbreaking ceremony was held and work began on a brand new home for Brewers baseball.

Construction took place in the parking lot behind center field, and it was exciting. Fans were able to watch their team in action at County Stadium even as they saw the progress of their team's future home. In 1999, Miller Brewing Company bought the naming rights and the stadium got a new name: Miller Park. The project was expected to be complete by April 2000, but things didn't turn out that way.

Tragedy Descends on Miller Park

A construction project the size of Miller Park involved a lot of planning, a lot of teamwork, and a lot of people. Things were going smoothly until it all came tumbling down in July 1999—literally. Two cranes were in use at the time, and the larger one had been nicknamed "Big Blue" (due, of course, to its massive size and bright blue color). In fact, it was the largest crane in North America.

Three ironworkers were in Big Blue's basket waiting to secure a giant piece of the roof into place when the unthinkable happened, and Big Blue collapsed. In mere seconds, it crumpled and fell into the bowl of the building, killing the three workers, scattering debris, and leaving massive damage in its wake. The unfinished Miller Park began to crumble.

It was a day of devastation. When all was said and done, there was $100 million in damage. And the opening day of the new stadium was moved back a year to 2001.

Worth the Wait

Something should be said here about the stadium itself. Miller Park is, to put it simply, a beautiful structure. It is made of red brick with arched windows and striking lines. There is a clock tower atop the main entrance, and just outside you'll find statues of former Milwaukee baseball greats. Inside, Bernie Brewer has a new place of honor near left field. And then there's the roof. Weighing 12,000 tons, its seven panels come together in a unique fan-shape design that can be opened or closed in just ten minutes. Ten minutes! The roof is 175 feet above the field and gets a lot of use during those unpredictable Wisconsin spring and fall seasons. Surprisingly, Miller Park's climate control system is able to keep the temperature inside the massive space as much as 30 degrees warmer than the outside air on cold nights.

The total cost to build Miller Park came in at $400 million—including $50 million for the roof alone. The state-of-the-art facility seats 43,000, with 3,500 club seats, 66 luxury suites, and a number of one-dollar Uecker Seats, named for broadcaster Bob Uecker. Situated in the upper deck, their inexpensive price comes thanks to an obstructed view from a roof overhang. Fans can dine at T.G.I. Friday's restaurant, a Mercedes-Benz Field Haus, the Metavante Club, or grab an old favorite from County Stadium days—a Dog-in-the-Sauce.

The greatly anticipated opening was all it was cracked up to be. On April 6, 2001, the Brewers played their first game in the new stadium against the Cincinnati Reds. A ceremonial pitch was thrown out by President George W. Bush, a big baseball fan. And the 48 by 37 foot video screen came to life as soon as Brewer pitcher Jeff D'Amico fired his first official pitch—a strike to batter Barry Larkin. A new era had begun.

Fast Facts

- *Famed Rebel spy Belle Boyd died in what is now Wisconsin Dells in 1900. The Rebel battle flag still decorates her gravesite. Virginian women visiting the well-tended grave in the 1950s were so moved that they erected a monument in Richmond honoring the 36th Wisconsin Infantry's Civil War dead.*

- *There was a reason they called Rep. John Potter of Milwaukee "Bowie Knife" Potter. In one famous 1860 incident, noisy Virginia congressman Roger Pryor challenged Potter to a duel. Potter accepted and chose the weapons and rules. They would stand four feet apart and battle with bowie knives. Pryor immediately rethought the entire notion.*

- *Perhaps the first Lambeau Leap involved Packer halfback Johnny "Blood" McNally and the real Curly Lambeau. Denied a loan by Lambeau, the spendthrift McNally climbed to a hotel roof, leapt eight feet to a ledge, and then jumped down to Lambeau's balcony. Alarmed, Curly relented and gave Johnny the money.*

- *If you see the original Wisconsin Constitution manuscript for sale online, don't buy it. No one knows what happened to the real thing, but it vanished more than a century ago.*

- *Wisconsinites skirted the Prohibition amendment in large numbers. In 1926, for example, a referendum supported legalizing beer with 2.75 percent alcohol. Also, in 1929, Wisconsin voted to stop prosecuting any Prohibition violators.*

- *The Madison area was well known for numerous Native American burial grounds. When surveyors tried to lay out the territorial capital in 1837, they encountered a strange phenomenon: Their compasses kept failing, making it difficult to survey the area.*

- *We know human tenancy in North America dates back 13,000 years because a museum volunteer took a closer look at a mammoth bone from a Kenosha-area farmer's field and found butchering marks. Before that, New Mexico's Clovis settlement (11,500 years old) held the claim for oldest habitation.*

Wisconsin Capitol Stands Above the Rest

✳ ✳ ✳ ✳

Sometimes Madisonians take it for granted, but the Wisconsin State Capitol building is truly a masterpiece. Situated between Madison's two largest lakes—Monona and Mendota—the building is the focal point of "the Square" of streets surrounding it. The beautiful granite dome, just three feet shorter than our nation's capitol building, rises proudly above the other buildings in town. And Madison's rolling hills make it possible to catch a glimpse of this majestic building from miles away in every direction.

Did You Know?

The first capitol building was quite different than today's. Made of prefabricated wood, it had no heat or water—and it was located in Belmont, the city chosen to be the capital of the Wisconsin Territory. The Wisconsin legislature met there for the first time on October 25, 1836. One of their first tasks was to choose a more permanent capital, and after much debate, Madison was selected.

The second capitol building was built in 1838 from locally cut oak and stone from Maple Bluff, along Lake Mendota. It cost $60,000 to build. Wisconsin became a state in 1848, making this building a state capitol!

A larger building was deemed necessary, and a new capitol was built on the same site, in

1863. The larger size, coupled with inflation, brought the price tag to $900,000. Fire broke out on February 26, 1904. Caused by a gas jet that ignited a newly varnished ceiling, the blaze spread quickly. Fire-fighters used the university's reservoir that normally supplied water to the building, but tragically, it was empty, forcing them to switch to city water. By then the fire had spread uncontrollably, and even with manpower and equipment brought in from Milwaukee, the building couldn't be saved. The north wing was all that was left standing.

A new building was commissioned, and it was completed in 1917, at a cost of $7.25 million. This is the building that still stands in Madison today.

People have argued for decades about the name of the statue that rises above the dome. It is named simply *Wisconsin*. It is made of gilded bronze and was created by Daniel Chester French of New York in 1920 for $20,325. Its head is adorned with a helmet featuring the state animal—a badger—on the top. In the statue's left hand there is a globe with an eagle on it. The right arm is outstretched—a gesture meant to symbolize the state motto, which is "Forward." Some people believe that the statue is called "Forward." While that isn't true, it is the name of an entirely different statue positioned elsewhere on the capitol grounds. Here are some other interesting facts about the iconic building:

- Wisconsin's capitol is the first ever to be built on an isthmus.

- How tall is it? From the ground to the tip of the statue perched atop the dome, the height is 284 feet, 5 inches.

- Each of the capitol's four wings is 125 feet wide and 187 feet long.

- Wisconsin's capitol dome is the only granite dome in the United States. It was constructed of white granite from Vermont and is considered the largest granite dome in the world.

- There were a total of 43 varieties of stone from around the world used within the building. It would take a pretty close look, but some of the stones used in the capitol's construction contain fossils. Check it out—one of the most visible is in the stairwell of the north wing. Look for the fourth step from the bottom of the Grand Staircase. You can see a starfish fossil on the far left side.

- In 1990, a state law was enacted preventing any building within a one-mile radius of the capitol from rising taller than the base of the columns that surround the dome.

- A mural painted by artist Edwin Blashfield covers the ceiling of the capitol rotunda. It is entitled *Resources of Wisconsin*. Another mural by Blashfield, found in the Assembly Chambers, illustrates Wisconsin's past, present, and future.

- The capitol was made a National Landmark in 2001.

- Wisconsin's Assembly Chamber was the site of the first electric voting machine in the world, all the way back in 1917. It sported a pretty high price tag for the times—$11,600.

- A renovation project was undertaken in 1988 and completed in 2002. The cost of the renovation came close to $150 million. The renovation became an opportunity to keep the building modern in terms of convenience, while restoring the look of the original structure.

- In 1925, the first Christmas pageant was staged at the capitol. It has been held every year since then, except during part of the renovation in 1997 and 1998.

- The capitol has 705 rooms.

- Birds don't nest in the capitol's ornate decorations because they are covered with wire mesh.

- Old Abe, an eagle adopted by Wisconsin's 8th Infantry (who lived in the capitol basement), died and was stuffed and put on display in 1881.

- Want a workout? Try climbing the capitol's 2,782 steps.

- There are 1,608 doors located throughout the capitol.

- You don't have to get elected to visit the Wisconsin State Capitol building. It opens its arms—and some of its many doors—and offers free tours to visitors.

Timeline

(Continued from p. 176)

July 1947
Wisconsin son and diplomat George Kennan first promotes his policy of Communist "containment" in an article titled "The Sources of Soviet Conduct," published in *Foreign Affairs* magazine.

1948
Milwaukee attorneys Elmer Winter and Aaron Scheinfeld found Manpower Inc. after a failed search for a last-minute staff addition. The company grows to become the foremost name in employment services, with more than 4,000 offices in 82 countries.

March 18, 1953
The Boston Braves baseball franchise announces that it will move to Milwaukee.

1954
Congress votes to withdraw government protection of Wisconsin's Menomonee peoples. This protection had been guaranteed to Menomonee leaders in 1854, when they agreed to relinquish control over the vast majority of their ancestral lands.

March 11, 1954
A U.S. Army report detailing efforts by attorney Roy Cohn and U.S. senator Joseph McCarthy (R-WI) to organize special treatment for Army Private G. David Schine is leaked to the press.

October 10, 1957
The Milwaukee Braves shut out the New York Yankees 5–0 in the seventh game of the World Series.

November 16, 1957
Police investigating the disappearance of a local woman enter the Plainfield shed of handyman Ed Gein and discover a house of horrors. Gein, a murderer and grave robber, will serve as inspiration for the characters in cinematic horror classics including *Psycho, The Texas Chain Saw Massacre,* and *The Silence of the Lambs.*

1960s
Congress institutes price supports for milk known as the Eau Claire Rule. By determining that Eau Claire, Wisconsin, is the center of American milk production, Congress decrees that dairy farmers are eligible for varying bonuses, depending on their location relative to the Wisconsin city.

January 22, 1964
The world's largest cheese is manufactured in Wisconsin for display in the Wisconsin pavilion at the New York World's Fair. The cheese weighs nearly 35,000 pounds and was made with 170,000 quarts of milk.

1966
The Smith family donates their lavish Milwaukee home, Villa Terrace, to Milwaukee County to serve as a museum of the decorative arts.

January 15, 1967
The Green Bay Packers defeat the Kansas City Chiefs 35–10 in Los Angeles to win the first Super Bowl.

(Continued on p. 236)

Vince Lombardi, Football Hero

❄ ❄ ❄ ❄

A lot of little boys want to grow up to be football stars. It's not really clear whether young Vince Lombardi felt that way, but what we do know is this: Lombardi grew up to make football stars, and his success with the Green Bay Packers is legendary.

A Coach Is Born

Born in Brooklyn, New York, in 1913, Lombardi studied for the priesthood for two years before he transferred to St. Francis Preparatory High School. He transferred his energy into sports and soon became a fullback on the football team.

Lombardi then enrolled at Fordham University. He played one year on the freshman team before his coach took notice and moved him to the varsity squad, where as a guard he became part of an offensive line known as "The Seven Blocks of Granite."

After graduation, Lombardi turned to coaching. His first steps down that path were modest—but exhausting. He coached football, basketball, and baseball at Cecilia High School in Englewood, New Jersey, while also teaching Latin, algebra, physics, and chemistry. He did all of this for $1,700 a year.

When his alma mater came calling in 1947, Lombardi answered. And just like when he was a student, he spent a year with the Fordham freshman team before moving on to the varsity squad. After that, he got a job working with the defensive line at West Point Academy, which he did for five years before heading to the pros. In 1954, Lombardi took an assistant coaching job with the New York Giants, and his defensive strategy helped turn the team into champions within a few years.

The Beginning of a Golden Era

Then, in 1958, Lombardi took the position of head coach with the Green Bay Packers. In the season before Lombardi arrived, Green Bay had won just a single game. One can only imagine the skeptical looks from players and personnel at the first team meeting when he told them that if they followed his rules, they could be a championship team. Yet, no one was doubtful when those words came true.

Lombardi was a force to be reckoned with. His confidence and enthusiasm won him both the coaching job in '59 and the general manger position. He wasted no time, winning Coach of the Year honors and leading the Packers to a 7–5 season in his first year. The next year, the Packers reached the NFL championship game (this was before the Super Bowl) but lost to the Eagles. But in 1961, Lombardi's Packers beat the Giants for the NFL championship—the seventh for Green Bay and the first for Lombardi.

In his nine years with the Packers, Lombardi amassed numerous wins, records, and honors, including historic victories at Super Bowls I and II. He was named NFL Man of the Decade, won six division titles, and five NFL titles with the Packers. And he'll always be remembered for coaching the Packers to a win in the famous Ice Bowl of 1967 against the Dallas Cowboys in sub-zero weather.

The Lombardi Sweep

Lombardi's drive to win was as strong as his work ethic, and he excelled at motivating his players. His offense employed methodical, no-frills plays, but these tactics worked so well that other teams soon adopted them. Lombardi retired from coaching after the 1967 season but remained with the Packers as general manager for the 1968 season. In 1969, he returned to coach the Washington Redskins to their first winning season in 14 years.

Sadly, this would be his last football season, as he was diagnosed with intestinal cancer. He died on September 3, 1970, and more than 3,500 came to pay their respects at his funeral. Jim Taylor, one of Lombardi's players, put it best when he said, "All he wants from you is perfection." That's all he gave in return.

Talkin' Wisconsin

"Fifty states and four continents later, I still call Madison home. I love to travel. I love returning home. Madison has the balance of important things just about right."

—*From* Madison *by Zane Williams*

"There is health in leisurely journeys taken in Wisconsin. The bold headlands left by the glaciers, the hundreds of talkative streams, little and big, along the way, the bluish eyelets of water peeking from beneath green plumed pines in northern Wisconsin, all give inspiration to life and compensation for any discomforts. Beauty abounds in Wisconsin."

—*From* Alluring Wisconsin *by Fred L. Holmes*

"I never saw a country that changed so rapidly, and because I had not expected it everything I saw brought a delight. The air was rich with butter-colored sunlight, not fuzzy, but crisp and clear so that every frost-gay was set off, the rising hills were not compounded, but alone and separate. It was a magic day. The land dripped with richness, the fat cows and pigs gleaming against the green, and in smaller holdings, corn standing in little tents as corn should, and pumpkins all about."

—*From* Travels with Charley *by John Steinbeck*

"The rough-hewn and rustic character, the proximity to the natural world, the absence of distraction and the absolute sense of freedom in its vastness—perceived or real, this is the stuff of Northern Wisconsin's soul, the essence of its allure. Here, time stretches the usual bounds. The days seem longer, the nights more peaceful, moments less fleeting."

—*Kate Bast, from the introduction to* Spirit of the North, a Photographic Journey Through Northern Wisconsin *by Richard Hamilton Smith*

"People who drink light 'beer' don't like the taste of beer; they just like to pee a lot."

—*Capital Brewery, Middleton, WI*

Notable Wisconsin Scalawags

❋ ❋ ❋ ❋

The best, the brightest . . . boring! Do-gooders may be heroes, but let's face it: rascals are more fun. Fortunately, for every lovely La Follette, Ringling, or Orson Welles, Wisconsin has an entry in its Hall of Shame. Here are some of the state's most entertaining scalawags.

John Schrank

Today, Schrank is a minor footnote in history, but if not for a pair of spectacles he would surely be better remembered. He tried to assassinate Theodore Roosevelt when the former president made a campaign stop in Milwaukee on October 14, 1912, just three weeks before the election.

Roosevelt was leaving his hotel when Schrank fired a pistol from inside his coat. Wounded, pale, and nearly inaudible, Roosevelt went on to his scheduled appearance and, incredibly, gave a 90-minute speech, during which he referred to Schrank as "that poor creature." Roosevelt was hospitalized immediately afterward. The bullet had "traversed the tissue of the chest 4 inches," reported *The Milwaukee Journal*. It traveled first through the president's spectacles case, lodging so close to vital organs that doctors thought it would be too dangerous to take out. In fact, it was never removed.

Roosevelt later lost the election to Woodrow Wilson. Schrank was committed to the Northern Hospital for the Insane near Oshkosh after he told police that the ghost of President William McKinley had told him to commit his crime. Eventually, the would-be assassin tired of constant questioning and said, "I have nothing to say." He died of bronchial pneumonia at Wisconsin's Central State Hospital, in Waupun, in 1943.

Jennie Justo

"The Queen of the Bootleggers" was popular in the press, beloved by the public, and pursued by G-men. Justo's family came to Wisconsin from the east coast, allegedly fleeing gang warfare and assassination. Besides producing booze, they set up several illegal Madison bars, or "speakeasies," during Prohibition. The press loved the idea of a woman gangster, and by all accounts, Justo was quite charming.

Despite her reputation as a ladylike Robin Hood for liquor lovers, at least as reported at the time in *Esquire* magazine, Justo was arrested by the FBI in 1932. She received two federal sentences and went to prison. After her release, Justo returned to Madison and, in 1939, opened a popular steakhouse that today survives as Smoky's Club on University Avenue. In later years, she flatly refused to speak of her past career. Justo died in 1991.

Eleazar Williams

This Green Bay resident enjoyed fame in the 1850s. He claimed he was Louis XVII, the rightful king of France! Williams was born in 1787 in New York and raised among the Oneida St. Regis peoples. During the War of 1812, he served as an American spy. After that he became a missionary. In 1821, the War Department sent him to Green Bay to negotiate land deals with Native Americans.

A few years after Williams' birth, in 1793, French revolutionaries beheaded the king and queen, Louis XVI and Marie Antoinette. Their son died two years later in the Bastille. Or did he? Rumors held that he had been spirited to America.

Williams wove the tale of his life together with that of the royal heir and believed the story. He also claimed that in 1841, surviving French royalty had asked him to relinquish any claim to the throne. It's possible—since the city was visited that year by France's Prince de Joinville, son of King Louis Philippe. Williams refused the prince's alleged request and retained his royal rights. "Though I am in poverty and exile, I will not sacrifice my honor," he said.

For the next few years, he was celebrated, first as royalty and then as a joke. He died in 1858, in a chateau built by his supporters.

Vorsicht! Fliegende Kraut!
(Beware! Flying Cabbage!)

✽ ✽ ✽ ✽

Heads fly, but they don't roll, in Shiocton each autumn at the World Championship Cabbage Chuck, a fund-raiser for a local church that pays homage to the cabbage-growing community.

The Shiocton area is known for its cabbage, albeit in a more refined form: sauerkraut, or kraut for short, which is finely shredded, fermented cabbage. Zesty, tangy sauerkraut was a favorite of the German immigrants who originally settled the area. In nearby Bear Creek is the Great Lakes Kraut Company, which dates back to 1900 and is the world's largest sauerkraut plant, processing more than 170,000 tons of raw cabbage each year. That's a lot of kraut!

Cabbage Chuck entrants come in two varieties: those using an air cannon to launch the leafy greens into orbit, and those who go medieval using a trebuchet to catapult their heads of cabbage.

From the firing line, entrants launch their cabbages into the air, seeing whose contraption can send the cabbage careening the farthest. As Shiocton isn't far from Green Bay, home of the Packers, team pride runs rampant. An outhouse painted purple and labeled "Vikings Draft Room" (for one of the Pack's main NFL rivals) is a hot target for flying cabbages.

The record cabbage chuck has remained intact since the event began in 2006—unlike the hundreds of heads of cabbage that have been sacrificed in the name of food fun. That record is a whopping 1,171 feet, courtesy of a cabbage shot from an air cannon built by Pat Peeters of Bear Creek. That should be good enough for Guinness, as there's no cabbage-throwing record on the books.

Still, there's a challenge to tracking the distance these heads fly. They tend to disintegrate as they move through the air, essentially changing from cabbage to coleslaw in a matter of seconds.

Quiz

So you think you know all about the Badger State?
Then try the Wisconsin Cultural Literacy Quiz!

1. Silent movie comic Ford Sterling, a native of La Crosse, provided which element of Charlie Chaplin's distinctive "tramp" costume?

a) Bowler hat
b) Oversize shoes
c) Cane
d) Baggy pants

2. Who lives within 500 miles of Wisconsin?

a) $\frac{1}{20}$ of all Americans
b) $\frac{1}{10}$ of all Americans
c) $\frac{1}{4}$ of all Americans
d) $\frac{1}{3}$ of all Americans.

3. Wisconsin has more than 2,000 miles of hiking trails and more than 20,000 miles of trails for _____.

a) snowmobiling
b) cross-country skiing
c) inline skating
d) mountain biking

4. How many Native American reservations are in Wisconsin?

a) 0
b) 11
c) 65
d) 102

5. Lon Chaney, the actor famous for his iconic roles in *The Phantom of the Opera* and *The Hunchback of Notre Dame,* made his last silent film, *Thunder,* in what city?

a) Milwaukee
b) Kenosha
c) Green Bay
d) Monroe

6. Late bloomers, take heart! Laura Ingalls Wilder didn't write her first book, *Little House in the Big Woods,* set near her native Pepin, until she was what age?

a) 26
b) 50
c) 65
d) 77

Answers: 1. b; 2. d; 3. a; 4. b; 5. c; 6. c

Taste of Wisconsin

Hearty Fare

Wisconsin epitomizes the meat-and-potatoes Midwest cliché while reigning proudly as America's undisputed Dairy King. After all, Two Rivers is known as the site of the first ice cream sundae. Malted milk was invented in Racine. And of course cheese curds are bites of beer-battered heaven. However, many of Wisconsin's enduring culinary traditions stemmed from its early pioneers.

Like the greater United States in general, Wisconsin is comprised of a hodgepodge of cultures from around the globe. Its first settlers brought along their own customs, especially in the kitchen. Take a German base, add a measure of Irish and a dash of Polish, fold in several other ethnicities, and you have the Wisconsin Melting Pot: a brew of delicious, and often interesting, fare that keeps on cookin'.

Das Food

What do you call a grumpy German?... A Sour Kraut! By 1900, about a million Germans hung their hats in Wisconsin. Roughly a third of the state was either German-born or of direct German descent. Therefore, Wisconsin inherited recipes for German chocolate and beer along with bratwurst, schnitzel, krautwickel, kassler rippchen, and strudel. And, of course, sauerkraut! The largest sauerkraut plant in the world shreds its cabbage in Bear Creek.

Limburger: Just for the Stink of It

When talking about the Dairy State, perhaps it would be more appropriate to call it a cultural Fondue Pot rather than a Melting Pot. After all, it's hard to talk about historic Wisconsin foods without mentioning cheese!

The world can thank the Germans for the invention of Limburger cheese, known to be the most olfactory-challenging of all cheeses. However, it was a couple of Swiss gentlemen who championed the putrid nostril offender in Wisconsin. Green County became known as a Limburger haven, starting with Rudolph Benkert, who cured the first Limburger in his home cellar in 1867. Soon after, Nicholas Gerber opened Green County's first Limburger factory. The cheese caught on like pungent wildfire when taverns all over southern Wisconsin and beyond began offering an inexplicably popular combo of Limburger and beer. When Prohibition closed saloons down, Limburger sales took a nosedive. So without lots and lots of beer, the taste of this smelly cheese is less appealing? As of press time, the Chalet Cheese Cooperative in Monroe is the nation's only remaining producer of Limburger cheese!

Irish Influx

The mid-19th century saw a surge of Irish immigration, largely due to the Great Irish Potato Famine. In fact, roughly half of all English-speaking (as opposed to German-speaking) Wisconsinites born in the second half of the century shared Irish

lineage. Amongst the fertile fields of Wisconsin, theses lads and lasses were free to harvest relatively cheap potato crops and introduce the state to their homespun concoctions such as shepherd's pie.

Pole Position

Over the last 200 years, more than 200,000 immigrants of Polish origin have polkaed their way into Wisconsin. About half of those settlers planted their roots in urban or industrial areas. Others chose small cities, and about a third selected farmland. Those rural residents and city folk alike have cultivated their own foodie rituals, inspired by back home. Poland's cuisine has a lot in common with that of its German neighbors. The Poles put their distinctive twists on pierogi and potato dumplings, along with various hearty stews and baked fish dishes.

Mining Their Own Business

Southeastern Wisconsin experienced a British invasion in the early 19th century. Prosperous lead mining in Mineral Point attracted new settlers, particularly from Cornwall, England. A hundred years later, the mining boom had come and gone, and the settlement of Cornish-style stone cottages was a virtual ghost town. Cornish immigrants Robert Neal and Edgar Hellum vowed to revive their people's land and homes, and they called their first restoration Pendarvis. Key to preserving their heritage was the promotion of authentic Cornish food. Neal and Hellum opened the Pendarvis House Restaurant, specializing in Cornish cuisine such as pasties. Pasties are wrapped pastries with a filling such as sliced beef, potato, and onion. Around 1970, the restaurant became a Wisconsin Historic Site.

Up and Comers

Wisconsin's Hmong people are less well known than its European settlers, but they are a culinary culture force in their own right. In ancient China, the Hmong people lived in remote mountain villages and learned to be self-reliant and frugal farmers. They developed simple flavors based on rice and available vegetables. Over the years, the Hmong immigrated to Thailand and Vietnam and incorporated food elements of those countries into their cooking. The result is unique dishes ranging from boiled pork soup to papaya salad and, of course, plenty of entrees utilizing lots and lots of rice. Sweet rice, sticky rice, long grain rice...depending on the meal, the Hmong find an appropriate rice counterpart.

❋ ❋ ❋ ❋

- *Eat like an Egyptian: In Beaver Dam, the pyramid-shape Pyramid Supper Club will immerse you in Egyptian kitsch. Knock back a Royal Nile Cocktail, start with a Scarab Salad, and munch your Cleopatra Burger.*

- *Since the town of Seymour grilled the largest hamburger in history (8,266 pounds), it's only fitting that they built a monument to the achievement atop the grill they used. Also, if you go to their annual Burger Fest, make sure you take a ride on the ketchup slide.*

- *If you want lumberjack-style eating, go to Minocqua. Paul Bunyan Meals has no private seating; it's school cafeteria style, with whatever they're serving presented in all-you-can-eat bowls. Menus? Unnecessary! Have it their way!*

Baraboo's Space-Time Blast-pad

✳ ✳ ✳ ✳

Standing 50 feet tall and sprawling over 10 acres, a massive assemblage meant to hurl adventurers through time and space lurks just 5 miles south of Baraboo on Highway 12. Its creator calls himself Dr. Evermor, and he has named his ongoing project the Forevertron.

Born Thomas Every in 1938, Dr. Evermor is a Wisconsin native who began welding salvaged machine and factory parts into creatures and faux devices in the early 1980s. Evermor had spent decades accumulating rescued treasures—including an Apollo space mission decontamination chamber—through his scrap and demolition business and finally decided to "recycle" them in order to create something astounding and new.

Even without any artistic training, Every possessed a knack for seeing the hidden potential of his treasures. A metal coil could be transformed into a bird's neck, or a bent pipe might form a spider's leg. Soon, oversized bugs and beasts and small, rusty environments began to surround the central "launch" sculpture, which looks like a huge apparatus from the mind of Jules Verne. This centerpiece culminates in an egg-shape glass space capsule that Evermor says he will use to shoot himself into another universe. It is supported and suspended by a tangle of other purpose-driven sculptures, ranging from an observation deck to a dehydration chamber meant to turn Evermor into a strip of dried human jerky for his voyage.

At 320 tons, the Forevertron is the world's biggest scrap metal sculpture and is unique because Evermor uses no specially fabricated parts. His work has inspired a legion of metal sculptors in Wisconsin and around the world, but no one else comes close in size or scope. And the Forevertron has not finished reaching for the stars.

"I've got a new project I call 'The Energy Spot of the World,'" he said in a recent interview. "It will be like looking at the Nazca lines in Peru. I got the attitude that I can keep building, building, building."

From the Badger State to Tinsel Town

❋ ❋ ❋ ❋

Is it something in the water? Or perhaps in the cheese? Whatever Wisconsin's secret might be, this state has played a part in the start of some of America's favorite television and silver screen stars.

Peter Weller

Born in Stevens Point in 1947, Weller was the titular brain surgeon, rock musician, and alien-fighting character in the 1984 cult sci-fi film *The Adventures of Buckaroo Banzai*. Later, the actor played Alex Murphy, the fatally wounded cop who is brought back to life as RoboCop in the 1987 Oscar-nominated film of the same name.

Carole Landis

She appeared in nearly 50 films from 1937 to 1948—among them *A Star is Born*—but the beautiful Landis wasn't taken seriously as an actress (among her nicknames: "The Chest" and "The Blonde Bomber") and was mostly left to bit parts and B movies. Five failed marriages and an affair with the married Rex Harrison didn't bolster her image, but Landis ultimately achieved a place in Hollywood lore with a final dramatic act. In 1948, at age 29, Landis committed suicide. She is said to be the inspiration for Jennifer North, the fragile character in Jacqueline Susann's 1966 bestseller *Valley of the Dolls*.

Arnold Schwarzenegger

The action film star and politician graduated with a bachelor of arts degree in business and international economics from the University of Wisconsin in Superior in 1979. However, the Austrian-born Schwarzenegger didn't go far from his adopted Southern California to get his degree. He earned it by taking correspondence courses.

You Can Thank Wisconsin

The Long, Hard Road to the Common Typewriter

Christopher Latham Sholes didn't set out to invent a typewriter. Inside Milwaukee's Kleinsteuber Machine Shop in the winter of 1867, Sholes tried to invent a device to print consecutive numbers on paper—for creating book pages, tickets, or bank notes.

Another tinkerer in the shop suggested to Sholes that a machine printing letters and words might be better. After reading a *Scientific American* article about such a device, Sholes, an ex-newspaperman, was intrigued. With the help of two other inventors, Sholes began building his own word machine.

A Rough Start

By fall, Sholes' machine was complete, but not perfect. Resting on a kitchen table, the device was the size of a small piano and styled like one, with two rows of ebony and ivory keys moved by wires. It could only print capital letters on tissue-thin paper. Also, the paper faced downward, meaning the typist could not see them as they were being typed. Undaunted, the men began a letter-writing campaign to potential investors.

One letter recipient was an old newspaper colleague of Sholes' named James Densmore. He was itching to invest, and without ever seeing the machine, offered the three inventors $200 each, plus funding for manufacturing in exchange for interest in the enterprise. The next spring, Densmore first saw the machine. Sholes also had a simpler, smaller second version. Pleased, Densmore secured a patent for each. He made 15 of the new version and tried selling them. However, the machines were not a hit. Densmore prodded the inventors to keep tinkering.

Initially, they attacked the challenge with vigor. Together the trio toiled to simplify the machine so that it could be manufactured quickly and cheaply. Densmore also begged them to devise a design that allowed for paper of regular thickness rather than tissue.

Enough, Already!

By 1869, Sholes' companions tired of the toiling. They sold their rights to the original patent to Densmore and left Sholes to work alone. That year, Sholes, who was tiring of the invention himself, typed a note to Densmore. "I am satisfied," he said. "The machine is now done." On heavy cardstock he added a smug note scrawled in pencil: "Is this paper thick enough?"

However, in response to criticisms of the new version, Densmore demanded that Sholes make further improvements. Sholes protested at each request, but Densmore pressed Sholes to toil on. Over the next few years he made several versions of his machine, but none caught on.

Giving Up

Densmore wouldn't quit. In a last-ditch effort in 1872, Densmore built his own manufacturing outfit on a spit of land wedged between the Milwaukee River and the Rock River Canal. He warned Sholes not to give up his shares, but Sholes sold them to Densmore and other parties. Initially, it looked as if Sholes' pessimism was justified. The improvised factory was failing and Densmore was spending more to manufacture the machines than he was earning as profit.

An old friend suggested Densmore show the machine to E. Remington and Sons, a maker of firearms, sewing machines, and farm equipment in Ilion, New York. In 1873, Densmore took the machine to Remington's headquarters and made the only deal he could: After working out a way to be paid, he would allow Remington to mass-produce the machines.

Remington began to produce his typewriters, yet it was a decade before Densmore began earning returns on his investment. As for Sholes, he considered the Remington Typewriter an insult. He disowned his part in its creation and declared it too complicated and cumbersome, even the portions of its design he himself had created.

It wasn't until the end of his life that Sholes was ready to take his rightful place in history. In one of his last letters, he wrote, "Whatever I may have felt in the early days of the value of the typewriter, it is obviously a blessing to mankind, and especially to womankind. I am glad I had something to do with it. I built wiser than I knew, and the world has the benefit of it."

Welcome, Extraterrestrials

✳ ✳ ✳ ✳

A visitor to Poland, Wisconsin, from this planet or any other, can't miss the converted grain silo with its friendly welcome to extraterrestrials—a sign reading, "We're not the only ones."

At first glance, it might seem strange to be driving through the Wisconsin countryside and come across a tower roughly 40 feet tall that opens into a docking platform for unidentified flying objects. But in a state where you can also find Martian cheese castles and alien museums, a UFO landing port actually makes perfect sense!

UFOs do seem to like Wisconsin. With an openness to alien encounters, and the do-it-yourself practicality of a true Wisconsinite, Bob Tohak took it upon himself to create his own alien welcome center. Not one to wait for the government to build a top-secret facility, he built a UFO launchpad on his property in 1992. Constructed of metal headboards, the pad is mounted on a former grain silo and is illuminated by blue flashing lights. It has become a magnet for those seeking strange sights in the Wisconsin countryside and has made the list of the weirdest roadside stops in the country.

It might be easy to laugh off Mr. Tohak's project as an eccentricity, but just an hour south of Poland, in the city of Sheboygan, a group of investors and researchers plan to build a functioning spaceport on the city's lakefront. The project has already been approved for government funding. As it turns out, the city's location next to a large body of water, its low population, and its lack of air traffic make it an ideal place for launching spacecraft. If its dream is realized, Sheboygan could become a hotbed of space tourism—one more reason for the aliens to stop by Mr. Tohak's launchpad.

Brewing Great Ideas: Beer in Wisconsin

❋ ❋ ❋ ❋

You already knew that beer is a part of Wisconsin's heritage. Almost everyone has seen Miller commercials on TV, but Wisconsin also has many small independent craft breweries and brewpubs.

The Beer Capital of the World

Breweries have been a part of Wisconsin as long as dairy farming. German immigrants brought their brewing knowledge with them as they settled in Wisconsin in the 1830s. By the turn of the century, most towns had breweries of their own.

Owens Brewery—founded in 1840 in Milwaukee—was the first commercial brewery in the state. By 1860 there were 200 breweries in Wisconsin, with 40 of them in Milwaukee alone. With skilled German workers, plentiful lumber, and Lake Michigan to provide both ice and transportation, Milwaukee quickly became a beer giant.

Protestants, Temperance, and Prohibition

Not everyone agreed that beer was such a fine influence. Some Wisconsin settlers were from New England, a hotbed of puritanical belief. They were not, as a rule, inclined to chug a beer. In fact, they lobbied for temperance as early as the 1850s. The battle continued, mostly deadlocked, until Prohibition was enacted in 1919.

Some of the state's breweries survived by producing near beer— beer with little or no alcohol content. Others made malt syrup, soda, and ice cream. Some simply closed down. By 1933, the nation had enough and with the 21st Amendment, Prohibition was repealed.

Wisconsin breweries have seen a lot of changes in brewing methods, consumption, and even advertising since the early days. Some have closed or consolidated and some have grown. And one has a major league ballpark named after it—Miller Park.

The Beer That Made Milwaukee Famous

Joseph Schlitz established his brewery in 1856, but it was the 1871 Chicago Fire that first boosted sales. With breweries in that city out of commission, Schlitz sold hundreds of barrels of his beer to Chicagoans.

Blatz: Milwaukee's Finest Beer

Blatz Beer was founded in 1846 as City Brewery, becoming Blatz Beer in 1851. It was the first Milwaukee beer with an international distribution. It is now sold as a craft-style beer.

Pabst Blue Ribbon

Pabst made its name in Milwaukee in 1864 and earned its popular nickname (Pabst Blue Ribbon) in 1876 when the company won several awards for its beer. After a period of slipping sales, an underground ad campaign has made it popular again.

The $1,000 Beer

Gettelman Beer of Milwaukee had more than a slogan, they had a challenge. Back in 1891, the company offered $1,000 to anyone who could prove that Gettelman was made from anything other than pure malt and hops. The prize went unclaimed for 80 years until the company officially closed in 1971.

Leinie's Makes Its Mark

Jacob Leinenkugel and John Miller founded a brewery in Chippewa Falls in 1867. The company existed for almost a century with its original brew. In the 1970s, it introduced a light beer and has since added several other successful beers.

Shhh ... Slow Down ... Heileman's Aging Here

So reads a billboard near the G. Heileman Brewing Co. in La Crosse. The company, which was in business from 1858 until 1996, is best known for Heileman's Old Style and Special Export. Today, these beers are brewed by the Pabst Brewing Company.

Good Point

The Stevens Point Brewery holds the title of fifth-oldest privately owned brewery in the United States. Founded by Frank Wahle and George Ruder in 1857, the company provided beer to Union troops during the Civil War. In 2002, the brewery also started producing premium sodas.

Microbreweries on the Rise

Sprecher Brewing Company is considered a microbrewery due to its small size compared to the brewing giants. It was founded by Randal Sprecher in 1985, in Milwaukee, and is known for its regional beer, old-world brewing methods, and specialty sodas.

The New Glarus Brewing Company is a relative newcomer, opening its doors in 1993. A small craft brewery, it is the first to have a female founder. Deborah Carey and her husband Dan produce several brands and distribute only in Wisconsin.

It's Miller Time

Frederick Miller began his Plank Road Brewery in 1855, with yeast he brought with him from Europe. Coors Brewing was founded about 20 years later in Colorado by Adolph Coors, who stowed away in a ship in order to live out his dream of brewing beer in America. The two companies merged in 2007, and together they are a leader in the industry, keeping Wisconsin beer on the map.

Fast Facts

- One of Wisconsin's early trials and tribulations was "prairie itch," an aggravating ailment caused by tiny parasites. Most common in wet farmland, the little varmints did their work mainly on the neck, shoulders, and genitals of people of both sexes.

- Instead of complaining about postal workers, the people in Elk Mound took a more positive tack. Just outside town is a memorial to "the deceased rural letter carriers of Dunn County." Odd, because there is no record of mass mailman deaths in the area.

- A fair number of people come to Muskego in search of Haunchyville, the legendary city of little people. It doesn't exist, and most people have the sense to realize it, but the curious come anyway. Many of them get arrested for trespassing and are fined— a helpful revenue source for Muskego.

- Angostura bitters are 90 proof and taste so nasty that they aren't subject to liquor tax (the theory being no one could pound enough shots to become drunk). On Washington Island, though, it's traditional to take straight bitters shots. Take the ferry there and try it!

- The first Milwaukee telephone operators were telegraph messenger boys. They turned out to be a pack of troublemakers prone to abuse eager callers with coarse insults. After enough customers complained, the Wisconsin Telephone Company replaced the yahoos with women, and civility soon reigned.

- South of Marshfield along Highway 13, you can view a blue Chevrolet on top of a silo. If that does not fascinate you, continue north to Marshfield itself, where you can feast your eyes on the world's largest round barn.

- In a snowy 1984 battle in Denver, the Packers fumbled on their first two plays from scrimmage. Not in the same series, though; both were returned for touchdowns by Bronco defenders. When Denver's offense first took the field, the Broncos already had a 14–0 lead.

Ludicrous Laws

Wisconsin, if nothing else, is a state of laws. The state simply loves to legislate. The license plates may read "America's Dairyland," but in fact it is America's Weird Law Land. But if you want some really odd and unusual laws, you have to look to the municipalities around the state.

Brookfield

- It is forbidden to get a tattoo except for medical purposes.
- It is also unlawful to use anyone's phone but your own when making prank phone calls.

Green Bay

- Bicycle tricks are forbidden.

Hudson

- Between May 1 and October 1, screens must be on all windows.
- And while you're putting up those screens, stay away from the neighbor's garbage! It's illegal to place litter in someone else's trash without express permission.

Kenosha

- Try to look bored! A law prohibits men from being "aroused" in public.

La Crosse

- It is illegal to display unclothed mannequins in store windows.
- It must be a land of felicitous rodents; by law, you may not "worry a squirrel."
- On Third Street, it's against the law to tie up your horse.
- Playing checkers in public is outlawed.
- You may not sell, raffle, or barter baby chicks. There goes the weekend!

Madison

- Members of the city council may not do business with taverns. They can, however, own them.

Milwaukee

- Put that flute and drum away! It is illegal to play them on Milwaukee streets. Trombones, tubas, and steam calliopes apparently remain legal.

- You can't park a car for more than two hours unless a horse is tied to it.

- It is perfectly legal to buy a disassembled automatic machine gun, but it is illegal to purchase or use sparklers.

Onalaska

- Fortune-telling is prohibited.

- So is throwing snowballs.

- So are alcoholic beverages during picnics in cemeteries.

Racine

- Missiles may not be shot at parade participants.

- When visiting Racine, always make sure to have a fire extinguisher handy, because it's illegal to wake a sleeping fireman.

- Women are forbidden from walking on public streets at night without being accompanied by a man.

Sheboygan

- Only police officers may shoot birds in the city.

- And let your imagination roam: No person may water his or her lawn in such a way as to annoy his or her neighbor.

St. Croix

- In public, it is illegal for women to wear anything red.

Sun Prairie

- Nuclear weapons may not be manufactured within city limits.

- Don't bring your cat to any cemetery in town. They're forbidden to enter.

Tomah

- Those who have imbibed alcohol may not participate in public dances.

West Salem

- Watch your mouth! Swearing is forbidden by law in public places.

Summerwind:
Wisconsin's Most Haunted House

❋ ❋ ❋ ❋

On the shores of West Bay Lake, in northeastern Wisconsin, are the ruins of a once-grand mansion known as Summerwind. The house is long gone, but the memories remain—as do ghostly legends.

A Frightening Beginning

Summerwind was built by Robert P. Lamont in 1916 as a summer home. It provided a quiet place for Lamont to escape the pressures of life in Washington, D.C., where he worked in politics, later serving as the secretary of commerce under President Herbert Hoover.

But life was not always sublime at Summerwind. Those who claim ghost stories of the house were "created" later on forget the tale of Lamont's spirit encounter. According to legend, Lamont fired a pistol at a ghost inside the house, and bullet holes remained in the basement door for years as evidence of this encounter. After Lamont's death in 1948, the house was sold several times, and nothing out of the ordinary occurred for years.

Insanity and Spirits

Arnold and Ginger Hinshaw and their six children moved into Summerwind in the early 1970s. They stayed for only six months, but it was an eventful time. As soon as they moved in, the Hinshaws saw strange things in the house. Vague shapes and shadows moved down the hallways. Voices mumbled in dark, empty rooms but stopped when the rooms were entered. More alarming was the apparition of a woman who was often seen floating past the French doors off of the dining room.

The family wondered if they were imagining things, but events convinced them otherwise. Appliances, a hot-water heater, and a water pump mysteriously broke down and then started working again before a repairperson was called. Windows and doors opened on their own. One particular window raised and lowered itself at all hours. Out of desperation, Arnold drove a heavy nail through the window casing and it finally stayed closed.

One morning, Arnold walked out to his car to leave for work and the vehicle suddenly burst into flames. No one was near it at the time. Of course, it's unknown whether the source of the fire was supernatural in origin or not, but no cause was ever found.

Despite the strange events, the Hinshaws wanted to make the best of their house, so they hired workers to make renovations. Crews would often skip work, claiming illness. Some told Ginger they avoided Summerwind because of its haunted reputation. The Hinshaws eventually gave up and tried to do the work themselves.

One day, while painting a bedroom closet, Arnold pulled out a shoe drawer from the back of the closet and noticed a large, dark space behind it. He wedged himself into the narrow opening and looked around with a flashlight. Suddenly, he jumped back, scrambling away from the opening—there was a body in the wall!

Thinking that it was an animal, Arnold tried to get a better look, but he couldn't fit into the space. So he asked his daughter Mary to take a better look. She crawled into the space with a flashlight and screamed—it was a human corpse! Hinshaw claimed they found a skull with strands of dark hair still attached and several long bones.

For whatever reason, the Hinshaws never contacted the authorities. They decided to leave the body where it was, not thinking that the hidden remains might be the cause of supernatural activity in the house. Things then took a turn for the worse at Summerwind.

Arnold began staying up late, madly playing an organ the Hinshaws had purchased when they moved in. His playing became a frenzied mix of notes that seemed to make no sense and grew louder as the night wore on. Arnold claimed voices in his head demanded he play. He would often stay up until dawn, frightening his family so badly that they huddled together in a bedroom, cowering in fear. Soon after, Arnold apparently suffered a nervous breakdown, and Ginger attempted suicide around the same time. Were the strange stories of Summerwind merely the result of two disturbed minds? But what about the children who also reported ghostly encounters?

Return to Summerwind

The Hinshaws eventually divorced after Arnold was sent away for treatment. Ginger later remarried and settled into a new, peaceful life but was shocked a few years later when her father, Raymond Bober, announced he was going to buy Summerwind. Bober planned to turn the mansion into a restaurant and an inn.

Ginger was horrified at her father's plan and begged him not to buy the property. His mind was made up—he knew the house was haunted and claimed that he knew the identity of its ghost. Bober said the ghost was Jonathan Carver, an 18th-century explorer who was searching for a deed that was given to him by the Sioux nation— allegedly giving him rights to the northern two-thirds of Wisconsin. Carver believed the deed was in a box, sealed into the foundation. Bober claimed that Carver had asked for his help in finding it.

The story goes that shortly after Bober bought the house, he, his son Karl, Ginger, and her new husband, George Olsen, spent a day exploring the house. After Ginger told them about the bones, they opened the hidden chamber to search for the remains, but they were gone. Where had the corpse gone? Had it ever been there at all?

History Lost

Bober's plans did not go smoothly. Workers refused to stay on the job, complaining of tools disappearing and feeling as though they were being watched. The project went over budget and was eventually abandoned. However, Bober did not give up on finding Jonathan Carver's deed. He spent many days searching, chipping away at the foundation. To this day, the mysterious deed has never been found.

The house was abandoned in the early 1980s and fell deeper into ruin. In 1986, investors reportedly purchased the house, hoping to revive Bober's idea of a restaurant, but Summerwind was struck by lightning two years later and it burned to the ground. Today, only the foundation, the stone chimneys, and perhaps the ghosts remain.

Wisconsin Olympic Athletes Are Golden

❋ ❋ ❋ ❋

Wisconsin hasn't hosted the Olympic Games, but that doesn't mean it hasn't produced its share of Olympic athletes. Do you remember these Olympians from Wisconsin?

- **Suzy Favor-Hamilton (Stevens Point) Track 1992, 1998, 2000:** Suzy is the only American woman to have the fastest seasonal time in the world in the 1,500-meter race. She is also a seven-time U.S. national champion. Suzy competed in three Olympic Games but did not place. She is now a motivational speaker, based in Madison.
- **Matt Tegenkamp (Madison) Track 2008:** UW track star Matt Tegenkamp ran the fastest mile in Wisconsin history. He ran the 5,000-meter race in Beijing but did not win a medal.
- **Peter Mueller (Madison and Mequon) Speed Skating 1976, 1980:** Peter won gold in the 1976 Olympics and went on to coach Olympic skaters Dan Jansen and Bonnie Blair.
- **Eric Heiden (Madison) Speed Skating 1976, 1980:** Eric was considered the king of speed skating during the 1980 Olympics at Lake Placid. He won five individual gold medals—the most ever at one Olympics. Eric later graduated from medical school and became an orthopedic surgeon. He went back to the Olympics in 2002 and 2006 as the speed skating team doctor.
- **Beth Heiden (Madison) Speed Skating 1976, 1980:** Beth (who is Eric Heiden's sister) won bronze in the 3,000 meters at the 1980 Olympics. She also placed seventh in the 500- and 1,500-meter races and fifth in the 1,000 meters. After placing first in all four races in the 1979 World Championships, Beth was expected to repeat in Lake Placid, but an ankle injury marred her success. Today, she is active in cross-country skiing competitions.

'Sconsin Scandals

✻ ✻ ✻ ✻

Over the years, many a Wisconsin politician has been caught being naughty. From drunken driving and assault to lots of campaign violations, Wisconsin has a sordid history of lawmakers being bad.

The Great Caucus Scandal

Corruption. Misconduct. Falsification. Extortion. The biggest political scandal in Wisconsin history went down in 2001. Madison's Capitol Hill made embarrassing national headlines when five bigwig lawmakers were brought up on multiple criminal felony charges. The case was cracked open by *Wisconsin State Journal* investigative journalist Dee J. Hall. The ace reporter's suspicions were substantiated when a key former Republican Assembly caucus staffer finally agreed to blow the whistle. Brian Burke (D-Milwaukee), Senate Majority Leader Chuck Chvala (D-Madison), Assembly Majority Leader Steven Foti (R-Oconomowoc), Assistant Assembly Majority Leader Bonnie Ladwig (R-Mount Pleasant), and Assembly Speaker Scott Jensen (R-Waukesha) all pleaded guilty or were convicted of several counts of campaign violations. Apparently, illegal campaigning is one thing state Democrats and Republicans could agree upon.

Repeat Offender

Representative David Plombon's long entanglement with Johnny Law started in 1994. He was in a car with his estranged wife and assaulted her. He pleaded no contest to disorderly conduct and received a year of probation. That same year, his driver's license was revoked after an OWI (operating while intoxicated). Months later, this busy lawbreaker was caught green-handed and arrested for possession of marijuana. The following year, he landed a spot in prison for violating conditions of his probation. He served 12 days.

I Saw that Parking Spot First!

Road-raging Representative Robert Behnke pleaded no contest to disorderly conduct in 1982. Why the disorder? A heated argument over a State Capitol parking space! He was fined $25 plus $13 for court fees. For Behnke, 1982 was a banner year. He was also accused of second-degree sexual assault. That case was dismissed when the alleged victim was deemed an incompetent witness.

Wily Wally

In 1980, Representative Walter Ward pleaded guilty to two election law violations for misuse of campaign funds and was sentenced to jail. By the next year, the shameful bad boy was convicted of misdemeanor and felony sexual assault stemming from an incident with a legislative aide. He was sentenced to four years of incarceration. To no one's surprise but his own, Wally was not reelected.

If He Builds It …

Senator Bruce Peloquin was charged with a mysterious misdemeanor theft in 1978. What did he allegedly try to steal? Bricks! However, he was subsequently found to be not guilty of the crime.

Bad Credit

Misusing credit cards must have been popular in 1978. Representatives R. Michael Ferrall and Joseph Looby, along with Senator Henry Dorman, were all charged with their own dubious charges.

Ethically Challenged

A recent scandal concerns Wisconsin Supreme Court Justice Annette Ziegler. During her stint in the Washington County Circuit Court, she ruled in multiple cases involving West Bend Savings Bank. The problem was that she failed to disclose a pesky conflict of interest: Her husband was a paid director on the bank's board.

You Can Thank Wisconsin

Great Wisconsin Inventions

Two ways the Badger State has made the average American's life even better.

Babcock's Butterfat Tester

Fatty milk is better milk—or at least it was in the 1880's. Problem was, without a way to test milk's fat content, Wisconsin's burgeoning dairy industry had no way to regulate quality. Enter Stephen M. Babcock. In 1890, the University of Wisconsin professor created the Babcock bottle and tester. To a specially made longneck bottle filled with milk, Babcock added a bit of sulphuric acid, and then placed the bottle in a hand-cranked spinning machine. The acid would dissolve everything but the fat, and the centrifugal force would push butterfat into the graduated neck of the bottle, where it could be reliably measured. This invention made it possible for farmers to selectively breed their best dairy producers and also made it impossible for farmers to cheat buyers with watered-down milk.

Outboard Motor

Legend has it that Milwaukee's Ole Evinrude, an eccentric machinist who built his own horseless carriages, decided in 1906 to build a motor for a boat after rowing five miles to fetch ice cream for his ladylove, Bess Cary. Outboard motors weren't unheard of in those days, but his ideas—vertical crankshaft, horizontal flywheels, and bevel gears—were. By 1911, Evinrude had patented his marine propulsion system. His motors were so successful that in 1914, he sold his interests in the company so he could take a round-the-nation vacation with Bess—by then his wife—and their son, Ralph. Five years later, Evinrude returned to his former company and offered them a new outboard motor design. The new owner snubbed Evinrude's offer, so Evinrude formed his own company. By 1929, he'd taken over the market and reacquired his former company. The merged companies became the Outboard Marine Corporation, which still leads the outboard motor industry today.

Aztalan: A Prehistoric Puzzle

❋ ❋ ❋ ❋

A millennium ago, Wisconsin ruled the north.

A Mysterious Site

Aztalan is a fortified settlement of mysterious outsiders who worshiped the sun. The Middle Mississippian culture erected stepped pyramids, may have practiced cannibalism, and enjoyed coast-to-coast trade. Some have linked the Mississippians to the Aztecs and even to the legendary city of Atlantis. All that is truly certain is that they lived at Aztalan for 150 years. Then they disappeared.

Aztalan, near present-day Lake Mills, is now a state park and, in fact, a National Historic Landmark. Still, what happened at Aztalan and the truth about the people who lived there are among the greatest archaeological puzzles in the world.

Aztalan is ancient. During the period when it was settled, sometime between A.D. 1050 and 1100, gunpowder was invented in China. Macbeth ruled Scotland. The Orthodox and Roman Catholic churches split. In America, across the Mississippi from St. Louis in what is now Illinois, there was a strange, 2,000-acre city of earthen pyramids later dubbed "Cahokia." Its population was roughly 20,000—more than London at that time.

Aztalan appears to be the northern outpost of the Cahokia peoples. Because of location, archaeologists call their civilization Middle Mississippian. They are distinct from the Woodland peoples, who were there first and remained afterward. The Mississippians were quite enamored with the sun, and at Cahokia, residents erected wooden solar observatories, similar to Britain's Stonehenge.

Like Cahokia, Aztalan was a truly weird place: 22 acres surrounded by a stockade with 32 watch towers, all made from heavy timbers and then covered with hard clay. Inside, pyramidal mounds stood as high as 16 feet. Outside the fortifications, crops were planted. According to Cahokia experts, the Mississippians are the ones who introduced corn to North America.

Today, Aztalan looks much different than it did at its peak. The mounds remain, and part of the stockade has been rebuilt. Also, the Friends of Aztalan group is trying to recreate antique agriculture with a small garden of gourds, squash, sunflowers, and an early type of corn, all planted just as the Mississippians would have.

In addition to vegetables, the Mississippian diet may have included some more interesting dishes—namely human flesh. At Cahokia there's evidence of human sacrifice, and since the time of Aztalan's discovery by whites in 1836, it has been thought that its residents practiced at least some sort of cannibalism. But science and interpretations change with time. There is speculation that the so-called "cannibalism" could have simply been a ceremonial or funerary practice that had nothing to do with eating human flesh.

Gone Without a Trace

Another puzzle is why the Mississippians suddenly vanished from the Midwest sometime between A.D. 1200 and 1300. Author Frank Joseph has taken the folklore of three continents and made a case linking Atlantis, Aztalan, and the Aztecs in his books, *The Lost Pyramids of Rock Lake* and *Atlantis in Wisconsin*. Joseph's theory is that the people of Atlantis founded Cahokia and Aztalan, mined copper, cast it into ingots, and shipped it back, fueling Europe's Bronze Age. After a cataclysm destroyed their Mediterranean island empire, leaderless survivors in the Wisconsin settlement migrated south. They created a new Aztalan in Mexico and became the Aztecs.

The Aztecs themselves referred to their far-away, long-ago homeland—wherever it was—as "Aztlan." However, scholars deny that residents of Aztalan ever used that name. It was merely a fanciful label applied by European settlers.

Joseph's evidence is circumstantial but intriguing. One of the great mysteries of Europe's Bronze Age is where all the necessary copper came from (bronze is made of copper and tin). Known low-grade deposits in Great Britain and Spain would have been quickly exhausted. Yet Lake Superior's shores have, and had, the only known workable virgin, native copper deposits in the world.

The Mississippians certainly knew that—they mined Michigan's Upper Peninsula. Meanwhile, according to legend, Atlantis was reigning supreme, enjoying great wealth derived from its trade throughout the known world of precious metals, especially copper. The Lake Superior mines closed precisely when Europe's Bronze Age ended. Coincidentally, or perhaps not, it was at this time that Atlantis supposedly sank and disappeared forever.

Many more answers about the Mississippian culture are yet be found. According to the Cahokia Mounds Museum Society, archaeologists have explored only 1 percent of the site. Could the decisive link to Atlantis or the Aztecs still be buried beneath the grounds of Cahokia or Aztalan? Only time will tell.

❋ ❋ ❋ ❋

- *As the name suggests, Mississippian culture spanned the length of the Mississippi River, including areas in what are now the states of Mississippi, Georgia, Alabama, Missouri, Arkansas, Illinois, Indiana, Kentucky, Ohio, Wisconsin, and Minnesota.*

- *It must have been desirable real estate! While Aztalan is usually considered to be a Mississippian settlement, there are many artifacts at the site from other groups of people that predate their arrival.*

- *For many years before it was studied and preserved, the area of Aztalan was plowed for farming; pottery and other artifacts were carted away by souvenir hunters.*

- *Aztalan became a National Historic Landmark in 1964 and was added to the National Register of Historic Places in 1966.*

- *There is speculation that some of the mounds at Aztalan could have been used for astronomical purposes.*

- *It is believed that Aztalan was a planned community with spaces for the general public, ceremonial locations, residential areas, and sections designated for elite individuals.*

- *Based on the artifacts unearthed at Aztalan, it appears that the people living there were skilled at farming, hunting, and fishing.*

A Striking Pastime:
The Badger Bowling Obsession

* * * *

*Almost everyone has done it—or at least you've thought about it.
Maybe they've even daydreamed about doing it with a coworker, or
even a complete stranger. Rest assured, there's no shame in pursuing
this fantasy in Wisconsin—everyone is welcome to go bowling!*

Bowling is the sport of the common man and woman and is as much
a part of the Wisconsin cultural landscape as beer, cheese, and bratwurst. But this is no new obsession.

Over the millennia there have been many games similar to
bowling. The ancient Egyptians played something very much like it;
Moses' pharaoh may well have had a gilded bowling shirt. In colonial
times, the little men played ninepin while lulling Rip Van Winkle
into a two-decade sleep. That game was played on an alley consisting
of a single plank. The modern game grew directly from that humble
pursuit, thanks to the ingenuity of German immigrants.

"It was part of their religious culture. They used to have it at
church festivals centuries ago," says Milwaukee bowling historian
Doug Schmidt, author of *They Came to Bowl.*

As Germans started landing in New York in the 1800s, they
quickly set up bowling clubs. Eventually, these immigrants started
making their way to the Midwest, and bowling followed them. Tavern owners, among others, began installing bowling lanes.

Originally, it was a game of ninepin set up in a diamond formation. Gambling was a popular feature, and as a result the game was
outlawed. The immigrants added another pin, changed the formation to a triangle, and satisfied the courts that it was a different
game. Modern bowling was born—almost.

Go Play Outside!

As strange as it may sound today, bowling was originally outdoor fun, played in the sun. In the 1850s, "the only bowlers were Germans and the only alleys were crude ones at the picnic groves and other German resorts," wrote historian Andrew Rohm in 1904. In Milwaukee, in the late 1800s, brewers Frederick Pabst and Frederick Miller each opened their own private pleasure parks and pavilions. There, the German biergarten tradition incorporated their favorite game. Gradually, for year-round enjoyment, bowling moved inside.

Almost every small Wisconsin town once had a bowling alley, or at least a couple of lanes inside a lodge hall. Sometimes, as with Fountain City on Wisconsin's western edge, there was even an alley inside city hall. In Madison, the university's Memorial Union had a basement alley. Today, it's still a strong sport on campus. In 2009, the University of Wisconsin-Madison men's bowling team won its fourth consecutive Wisconsin Collegiate Bowling Conference championship. And Milwaukee could be called the capital of bowling—it's home to the United States Bowling Congress.

Wisconsin is also home to such legendary bowlers such as Connie Schwoegler, who, in 1948, invented the "fingertip grip." In 1930, Wisconsinite Jennie Hoverson became the first woman to bowl a perfect game in the history of league bowling. Her recognition came much later, however.

"Apparently, back in the days when she was bowling, nobody thought much of submitting award applications," says Schmidt, "so her game was never submitted for sanctioning." A *Wisconsin State Journal* sportswriter, Joe Dommershausen, lobbied for ten years to get the Women's International Bowling Congress to finally recognize Hoverson.

Something for Everyone

For much of its American history, bowling was a northern pastime. Besides sexism, nationally there was worse bowling bigotry. African Americans were not allowed into sanctioned league bowling until 1951, four years after Jackie Robinson broke the color barrier in baseball.

While that fact shames league bowling of the era, in the 1940s, African Americans were already enjoying the game in Milwaukee. They had come to the area in search of factory jobs and found themselves near taverns with bowling alleys. They assimilated into the game, and many African Americans enjoyed the sport and became well-known bowlers. As Wisconsin grew, social networks formed around the game—people who worked together bowled together.

Today, bowling's best features remain as satisfying as ever: The cost is low, the rules are simple, and the bowling alley provides all of the equipment. Then there's the satisfying, almost-musical crash of the maplewood pins. And what other sport has ten second chances? There's also the camaraderie, or, in other words, waiting.

"The big advantage is that it's a team sport that promotes social interaction," says Schmidt. With other games, such as football or baseball, "you're either out on the field or on the sidelines, where in bowling you're sitting around connecting with each other while you're waiting for your turn."

Keep the Good Times Rolling

In Wisconsin, as in the rest of the north, bowling tends to peak over the winter months, as people seek indoor recreation. In warmer parts of the country it's enjoyed equally all year. Even so, bowling is not as popular as it once was.

There are more activities than ever for young people and, as in baseball, experts argue that changes to the game and equipment have artificially inflated scores compared to years past. However, there are some signs of a comeback for bowling. Thanks to the cult movie *The Big Lebowski,* for many people bowling is hip. Also, there are trendy clubs, like one in north shore Milwaukee, where the elite meet to enjoy the menu of exotic martinis—and to bowl.

Young people are attracted to new multi-activity entertainment centers that offer video games and food in addition bowling. More and more high schools are also taking it up as an organized sport and even awarding varsity letters for it. The advantage, for young and old, is that you don't have to be the biggest and strongest to make the team.

Fast Facts

- *Early Wisconsin territorial law was based on Michigan law, but no written copy existed for a couple of years. This confounded the territorial legislators, who had some minor interest in reading and referencing the laws they'd been passing. In 1839, the territory finally obtained printed copies.*

- *When the state prepared its official map in 1967, it omitted Winneconne (population 2,401). Deeply affronted, Winneconne statespersons sent Governor Warren Knowles a declaration of secession and set up a toll bridge. Not wanting war with scrappy Winneconne, Knowles restored it to the map.*

- *Whitewater has such a history of hauntings that it used to have a Spiritualist college, founded by Morris Pratt in 1889. The modest medium named it the Morris Pratt Institute. In 1946, the Institute moved to Wauwatosa, where it's still in business.*

- *There's certainly no shortage of cows in the Wisconsin country-side. New Glarus, however, has a downtown full of them—lovingly decorated by the town's artistic community. Bonus tidbit: A resident of New Glarus is called a Glarner.*

- *The Hillsboro & North Eastern Railroad, plying 5.37 miles between Union Center and Hillsboro, genially advertised itself as the World's Smallest Railroad. It ran from 1903 to about 1975.*

- *What do the Milwaukee Badgers, Racine Legion, and Kenosha Maroons have in common? They were all NFL teams in the 1920s.*

- *People mostly know Paul Robeson today as an African American entertainer and social activist. Few know that in the early 1920s, he was an end for the Milwaukee Badgers—a professional football team remembered for its large (in its day) number of black players.*

- *Convalescing after Second Bull Run (1862), Wisconsinite Colonel Lysander Cutler hobbled on canes to pay respect to Secretary of War Edwin M. Stanton. Stanton rudely ordered Cutler back to his regiment. Cutler said, "If I had not been shot and a fool, I would never have come here. Good day, Mr. Secretary."*

How to Talk Wisconsin

✽ ✽ ✽ ✽

If you're traveling Wisconsin and become lost, good luck! You may not be in a foreign land, but you still don't speak the language, at least when it comes to finding your way around. Here's a brief rundown of some of the Badger State's fitful geographical pronunciations.

It's Hard Being the New Kid

Wisconsin casts a strange mist over even the most common names, as Kathryn Lake discovered. The East Coast native and radio personality served at Madison's WORT, WMAD, and WTDY, and later at Chicago's WGN. But despite her broadcasting skills, she first had to learn that natives pronounce it "wis-GON-sin" and "MWAW-kee."

"Once I mastered those, I felt like I was finally at home," she recalls.

Public affairs specialist Cathy Fox, at northern Wisconsin's Chequamegon-Nicolet U.S. National Forest, has heard everything. The forest's mere name strikes fear in the hearts of non-locals. Fox recalls a phone call from one such hapless tourist from California. "He said, 'I need to update some information on Ch-Ch-Ch'—I said, 'Give it a try!'"

Rule Number 1: Wisconsin place names sometimes feature a silent "Q." The correct pronunciation of Chequamegon is SHAW-em-gun. The strangest Fox has heard is check-wa-ME-gun. That was the phonetically correct person, she says, awarding an A for effort.

Wisconsin is designed to embarrass. For example, which "ough" sound should one make when pronouncing the city 20 miles to Madison's southwest? Attempting to alternately parallel "rough," "through," and "thought," it could be called Stuffton, Stewton, or Stawton. But don't ask for directions to any of those places, because they don't exist. Stoughton is called "STOW-tun."

Or take the Strange Case of Muscoda, which you might expect to be mus-KOE-duh. There is hope that the Grand Unification Theory of the Universe, when completed, will explain why it's actually pronounced MUSS-kuh-day.

Similarly, take Theresa and Rio, two Wisconsin villages. You would think that no names could be easier to pronounce. You would be wrong. It's tuh-RESS-uh. Rio rhymes mysteriously with EYE-Oh. Following this linguistic pattern, the capital city should be called MADE-ice-own.

This siren's song of familiar, look-alike words has long baffled spelling-bee contestants and visitors both foreign and domestic. After mighty labors, school children finally manage to wrap their tongues around the name of President Thomas Jefferson's home. That's pronounced mont-uh-CHELL-oh. But Wisconsin's own Monticello is pronounced mont-uh-SELL-oh.

Germanic travelers from old BerLIN must surely be surprised by Wisconsin's New BERlin. Still, 'tis not the Teutonic tongue that tangles most. France may have ceded the Wisconsin territory to Great Britain in 1763, but they left behind the city whose name would be pronounced "bell-WAH" in the old country. If you call it that when asking for directions, you'll never find your way to Beloit (bell-OYT).

The city of Tomahawk sounds as you might expect, but its shorter near-twin, the City of Tomah, does not. It's TOE-muh. And traveling musicians are welcome to take their bows and play viola in Viola, even if they pronounce the town's name as they would their instrument. Yet, the beginning of the town's name is pronounced the same as the word "violet."

Perhaps that's the best way to approach Wisconsin's names, as a kind of strange music—that the young people listen to and which you will never understand. Composers know that different meters playing at the same time is called a hemiola. Try dancing a waltz played to a polka. On the other hand, don't; they'll cut you off at the bar. But this musical stagger effect is like speaking on the wrong syllables. In the music of Wisconsin place names, there is likewise a repeated preference for unexpected word parts.

One example is Gillett, which is JILL-it. Another is Boaz, which is not "boze," but BO-az. Still, how can one follow rules when there are so many exceptions? It's not Muh-ZAHM-uh-nee, WAW-puk-aw or Bos-KOE-buhl. Third, second, and first syllables are each favored, in order, in Mazomanie, Waupaca, and Boscobel: may-zoh-MAY-nee, Wah-PACK-uh, and BOSS-kuh-bell.

Perhaps we should not hear music in Wisconsin place names after all but instead look to museum galleries. Paintings that fool the eye are called *trompe l'oeil*, a French phrase that means just that. Similarly, it's the ear, not the eye, which is fooled by the county and village of Trempealeau, or trem-pill-OH. Even Napoleon would be lost in that west-central Wisconsin region, because proper Parisians know that the "correct" pronunciation should be truhmp-LOW. Similarly, Marie Antoinette, while eating cake, would have taken the "sheen" sound that ends Prairie du Chien and made it a good French "shyen." Off with her head!

And then there's that tribute to the conservation of vowels: Oconomowoc. It could be a phonics test, with its perfectly alternating hard and soft Os. The Wisconsin Historical Society says it's a corruption of "Coo-no-mo-wauk," a Pottawatomie term that refers to a waterfall nearby. As the story goes (and it's only a story), tired pioneers arrived at the waters and punned the name from "I can no mo' walk."

With so much lingual confusion, the meaning and original pronunciation of "Wisconsin" could have been lost in the sands of time. Sadly, there is no truth to the theory that it means "land of no toll roads." Actual Native American translations include "river of red stone," "gathering of waters," and "river of the great rock." The Wisconsin Historical Society says it's the English spelling of a French version of an Indian word. French explorer Jacques Marquette, garbled it from the get-go in 1673, when he spelled it both "Meskousing" and "Miskous." Just think, had this name stuck, the state song could be "On, Miskous!"

🍽 Taste of Wisconsin

Test your knowledge of Wisconsin's most delicious, calcium-rich facts and stats.

1. Wisconsin's mild and sweet Trumpeter Meadow cheese is a pasta filata (stretchy) cheese named in honor of:

a) Famous jazz musician Fred Radke, former lead trumpeter with the Glen Miller Orchestra, who proclaimed that Wisconsin cheese was the best part of playing jazz clubs in Milwaukee.

b) The endangered trumpeter swans that frequent the marshes and meadows in northwest Wisconsin.

c) The squeaky noise that the cheese, which is crafted primarily in the meadow country of northwest Wisconsin, makes when stretched.

d) An annual outdoor marching band festival.

2. In 2007, 34.8 percent of the cheese produced in Wisconsin was this kind:

a) Cheddar
b) Monterey Jack
c) Colby
d) Mozzarella

3. What year did Mrs. Anne Pickett, using milk from her neighbor's cows, establish the state's first cheese factory?

a) 1841
b) 1845
c) 1858
d) 1861

4. Early Wisconsinites crafted cheese from their excess dairy milk because it offered more portability, longer shelf life, and high concentrations of fat, protein, calcium, and this mineral:

a) magnesium
b) phosphorus
c) sodium
d) zinc

5. Wisconsin produces more cheese than any other state—2.5 billion pounds annually in 2007. Which state is second?

a) Vermont
b) Idaho
c) California
d) Oregon

6. Who was the first Wisconsinite to market cheese outside state lines in 1858? Hint: this Wisconsinite was also was the first to obtain a cheese vat.

a) Mrs. Anne Pickett
b) Hiram Smith
c) John J. Smith
d) P. T. Barnum

7. How much of the milk produced by Wisconsin's more than 1 million dairy cows is devoted to cheese production?

a) 68 percent
b) 75 percent
c) 87 percent
d) 90 percent

8. Which of the following cheeses were invented in Wisconsin?

a) Brick
b) Colby
c) American
d) Both a and b

9. What test did Stephen Babcock develop at the University of Wisconsin in 1890 that allowed dairy farmers to detect which cows produced the richest milk? Hint: It's still used today.

a) the milk-riche test
b) the lacto-riche test
c) the milkfat test
d) the milkshake index

10. At last count, Americans consume about 32.5 pounds of cheese per person. Which two countries consume—at about 50 pounds per person—the most?

a) Mexico and Brazil
b) France and Greece
c) Austria and Germany
d) Kenya and China

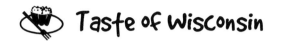

Taste of Wisconsin

Extra Cheddar, Please: More Cheese Facts

- The Sargento Cheese Company in Plymouth introduced packaged shredded cheese in 1958. In 1986, the company went even further to ensure the "spread of the shred" by introducing the resealable plastic bag for its cheeses.

- Until 2002, cheddar was the second-most-popular cheese in the United States (after processed American), but the country's passion for pizza has bumped it to number three after mozzarella.

- The production of cheddar involves "cheddaring"—the repeated cutting and piling of curds to create a firm cheese.

- "Squeaky curds" refers to fresh young cheddar in its natural shape, before it's pressed into a block and aged. Fresh curds are considered a delicacy—and they make a squeaking sound when you eat them.

- Cheddar cheese is naturally white or pale yellow. These days, much of it is dyed orange with seeds from the annatto plant, whereas early cheese makers used carrot juice and marigold petals.

- Originally, cheese was dyed to prevent seasonal color variations. Traditional cheddars had a natural orange color derived from the carotene-rich grass cows ate during spring and summer. In winter, cows ate dry feed, and the resulting cheese was white. Consumers had the misperception that orange cheese was more nutritious, so cheese makers began uniformly coloring their cheeses a "healthful" shade of orange.

- As dry feed has become more commonly used year-round, dyeing now depends on regional preferences and traditions. Cheddars from Wisconsin are usually dyed orange, while New England and Canadian cheddars are typically left white.

- Prior to 1850, nearly all cheese made in the United States was cheddar.

Timeline

(Continued from p. 194)

July 30, 1967
Four die in a Milwaukee race riot on a day that President Johnson had declared a National Day of Prayer.

October 18, 1967
Forty-seven are injured when violence erupts during a student protest against Dow Chemical in Madison.

December 10, 1967
Otis Redding and six others are killed when the singer's plane crashes in Lake Monona. His recently recorded single "(Sittin' On) The Dock of the Bay" becomes a massive posthumous hit.

January 14, 1968
Legendary coach Vince Lombardi leads the Green Bay Packers to victory over the Oakland Raiders in Super Bowl II. This will be Lombardi's last game at the helm of the Green Bay Packers. He resigns his post on February 1.

March 18, 1968
The Producers is released, featuring Milwaukee native Gene Wilder in his first leading role in a major screenplay. The role will lead to an Academy Award nomination for Wilder.

April 2, 1968
Perennial presidential candidate Eugene McCarthy wins the Wisconsin primary.

1970
The Seattle Pilots baseball franchise relocates to Milwaukee and is renamed the Brewers.

April 22, 1970
The first Earth Day, the brainchild of Wisconsin Senator Gaylord Nelson, is celebrated nationwide.

August 24, 1970
Robert Fassnacht is killed when antiwar protestors detonate a bomb inside the Army Math Research Center at the University of Wisconsin-Madison.

1971
The *Rouse Simmons* wreck is discovered off Two Rivers in 165 feet of water. Its hold still contains the skeletal remains of the 10,000 Christmas trees it was carrying when it sank in 1912.

1972
Milwaukee-born William Rehnquist is named a Justice on the United States Supreme Court. He will become Chief Justice 14 years later, in 1986.

1976
Shirley Abrahamson is named to the Wisconsin Supreme Court, becoming the first woman to serve on the state's highest court.

1985
The American Girl doll company is founded in Madison by educator and publisher Pleasant Rowland. She sells the company to Mattel in 1990, for $700 million.

September 6, 1985
An Atlanta-bound Midwest Express DC-9 crashes on takeoff from Milwaukee's Mitchell Field. All 31 passengers and crew are killed.

(Continued on p. 271)

Badger Legacies:
University of Wisconsin Traditions

❊ ❊ ❊ ❊

Fires and canes, parades and caps, "Varsity" and football games;
traditions at the University of Wisconsin-Madison are annually
passed from the oldest alumnus to the youngest freshman.

If It Works, Keep It

Although many people might think that beloved UW traditions have
been around forever, most are fairly recent. For example, the first
Homecoming celebration wasn't held until 1911, and in the decades
that followed, "traditions" were conceived on the spot. Many are still
around today, but others—some exciting, some violent, some just
plain weird—would be unrecognizable to all but the oldest alumni.

The origins of some customs are lost in the past. Take, for
instance, the seated figure of Abraham Lincoln in front of Bascom
Hall. The statue, dedicated in 1909, is said to stand up every time a
virgin coed passes by. No one can prove that Abe has ever stood up,
but on the other hand, no one can prove that he hasn't, either.

For many years, an annual parade has been held during Homecoming and has itself been an inspiration for many other traditions.
The parade features the costumed mascot, Bucky Badger (introduced at Homecoming in 1949), and floats decorated by Greek
houses, residence halls, and student organizations.

Remnants of the Past

A few of the earliest traditions have survived largely unchanged.
"On, Wisconsin!" for example, might have been played at the first
UW Homecoming, though returning alumni may not have known

the words—the song was only three years old. At that first Home-coming, a crowd of 3,000 gathered to hear speeches and watch a mock alumni football game during halftime.

During halftime the next year, and every year since, Law School seniors have taken the field. They charge the north goalpost, where they try to throw their canes up and over, and then catch them. Those making the catch, tradition says, will win their first case.

From 1925 to 1948 it was a far more elaborate ritual, with law students carrying their canes constantly for a full two weeks before the game. Finally, they would formally parade from the corner of Park Street and University Avenue to the game at today's Camp Randall (dedicated at Homecoming 1917).

If the Hat Fits

Freshmen before the 1940s had a special reason to cherish Home-coming, as it meant that they could stop wearing their dark green caps. Beginning in 1901, this rule was just one of several degradations imposed by older classmates. For example, freshmen had to salute upperclassmen—all of them—constantly.

Freshmen who failed to wear their caps were usually thrown into Lake Mendota, believe it or not, by vote of the student senate. In 1912, one convicted capless freshman pleaded that he was in ill health and could not stand the drubbing. The official UW student clinic backed up his claim—but agreed to set a later date for the dunking, as soon as the student regained his health.

At first, caps had to be worn from October until Thanksgiving, and from Easter to commencement, but later they had to be worn only from the beginning of school until Homecoming, when the caps were thrown into another Homecoming tradition—a huge bonfire.

The bonfires were raucous affairs through the 1920s and '30s. In 1940, 25 unruly revelers were arrested and kept in jail overnight. A year later the bonfire was so big, and the 15,000 students so violent, that firefighters were called to put out the blaze. Police shot tear gas to disperse the crowd. As the mob dispersed, windows of businesses were broken and cars were overturned. Efforts were made to tone down the event, unsuccessfully, and the last bonfire was lit in 1946.

Hey, That Looks Good!

Many cherished UW customs were actually taken from other schools. The idea of making freshmen wear caps was borrowed from "Cornell, Columbia, and a number of other larger universities," according to one student paper, *The Daily Cardinal,* in 1901.

While Badgers have sung "Varsity" since 1898, they've waved their arms to it only since 1924, when band director Ray Dvorak lifted the concept from the University of Pennsylvania. The tradition of the "You've Said It All" song was taken from a Budweiser commercial in 1978. The business of law students' canes was borrowed, with elaboration, from Harvard.

Football games are another hotbed of tradition, but when UW celebrated its first Homecoming, it had been playing intercollegiate football for only 22 years, since 1889. There had scarcely been time enough for student fads to mature into honored customs. And students wanted traditions, even instant ones.

For example, the freshmen beanies were brought to the UW, *The Daily Cardinal* reported at the time, only because upperclassmen specifically were "desirous of giving Wisconsin a worthy set of traditions." (Also, they probably wanted those freshmen salutes.) And so, faced with a hunger for traditions, students borrowed them or invented them from scratch.

Cheerleaders, Skyrockets, and Sexism!

Today cheerleading is a complex affair, but it started out much more simply. As the name suggests, it only involved cheering—and it started close to Madison. In 1898, the first cheerleader led the first cheer at a University of Minnesota football game. The cheering fad soon spread next door to Wisconsin.

For decades, cheerleading was admittedly sexist—that is, only *men* were allowed. During the 1920s, women were allowed because so few athletic activities were open to them. Wisconsin was famous for a peculiar jazz age cheer called the "skyrocket." It went "Ssss-boom-ahh!" and was followed by a name or humorous remark. It eventually fell out of fashion but survives in the UW Marching Band; you'll often hear the cheer at its annual Varsity Band concert.

Fast Facts

- One unforgettable Badger was UW Heisman Trophy winner Alan "The Horse" Ameche of Kenosha, who played six years for the NFL's Baltimore Colts. It often took three defenders to drag Ameche down. Also, you may have heard of his cousin from Kenosha—actor Don Ameche.

- A gathering of Badger alumni (if all were living) could include historian Stephen Ambrose, former Second Lady Lynne Cheney, architect Frank Lloyd Wright (he received an honorary degree), astronaut Laurel Clark, air conditioning mogul Reuben Trane, adventure travel writer Tim Cahill, and Liberian President Ellen Johnson-Sirleaf.

- UW-Milwaukee alumni include integrated circuit inventor Jack Kilby, Internet pioneer Scott Yanoff, author Lynne Rae Perkins, former Peruvian President Alberto Fujimori, former Israeli Prime Minister Golda Meir, NASCAR legend Alan Kulwicki, and comic Frank Caliendo.

- Wisconsin icon "Crazylegs" Hirsch was too big a fan favorite on the Los Angeles Rams. He announced his retirement before a 1954 home game against Green Bay, and the Rams fans mobbed him for souvenirs afterward—stripping him to his hip pad girdle.

- Before John Muir came to study at UW-Madison, he invented a device that would have helped lots of students: an alarm clock that raised one side of his bed, dumping Muir onto the floor. The machine also lit a lamp so he could see once he was awake.

- In 1900, the annual tuition at UW-Madison was $20.

- Dating back to 1890, the oldest Division 1 football rivalry pits the University of Wisconsin against the University of Minnesota. Since 1948, the winner of each year's match-up gets a unique trophy—Paul Bunyan's Axe—that has the scores of every game written on its handle.

- The University of Wisconsin first admitted female students in 1863.

Wisconsin's Subterranean Secrets

✾ ✾ ✾ ✾

*Wisconsin is famous for its well-tended roads and highways,
but hidden from public view lies a less visible web: the labyrinth
of underground passages built by businesses, the military, and
bootleggers throughout the state's colorful history.*

Historic Hideaways

One of Wisconsin's oldest tunnels still in existence was built by abolitionist Joseph Goodrich. He constructed a unique, hexagonal inn in Milton in 1844. In addition, he added a tunnel that led from the Milton House's grout basement to a small log cabin in the backyard. It became a regular stop on the Underground Railroad, which was the route followed by escaped slaves that secretly helped them travel to safe locations.

In Fond du Lac, Mayor Isaac Brown had an eight-sided, grout and stucco place built in 1856. Like the Milton House, the Octagon House also hid a tunnel. The 14-foot passage led to a shed, which may also have served Underground Railroad passengers.

Oshkosh's Secret City

Some Wisconsin tunnels were built as a bow to the state's climate, allowing shoppers to move easily from store to store during winter months in the days before modern snow removal equipment was available. The city of Oshkosh boasts a very well-documented underground downtown, which was at one time a kind of subterranean shopping mall.

Many businesses operated in basements that were accessed by outside stairways and were connected to other merchants by passageways under the street-level sidewalks. These "hollow sidewalks" dating from the 1860s are now closed, but evidence of them still exists in the prismatic glass "windows" and iron trapdoors set into the upper sidewalks.

The most famous tunnel in Oshkosh led across downtown's Monument Square from the Athearn Hotel (now demolished) to the magnificent Grand Opera House. The tunnel was probably built in the early 1900s, and local legend says actors, showgirls, and whiskey-toting gangsters all made use of it. Oshkosh historian Julie Krysiak Johnson even wrote a book about it, called *Oshkosh Down Under.*

Tunnel Trespassers of Madison

In the days when institutions were heated by large steam plants, gigantic tunnel systems often housed the pipes and furnaces. Today, hundreds of students still tread over an array of steam tunnels under the University of Wisconsin-Madison's historic Bascom Hill. The tunnels splay outward to the Memorial Library and other buildings.

These tunnels are perhaps best known for their legendary resident, Tunnel Bob, a tall, haggard man who walked their mazelike length for many years. Some who saw Tunnel Bob reported he had ghastly scars from burns caused by the steam vents. Although the tunnels are strictly closed to visitors, Tunnel Bob proved impossible to oust, and the maintenance staff eventually began to tolerate his presence. Reputedly, they even paid him for changing lightbulbs in hard-to-reach places.

Oddly enough, Madison claims another Tunnel Bob. The second Bob belongs to Madison East High School. The school's newspaper has printed stories about a homeless man or drifter who was seen in the school's subterranean steam tunnels. Others say he still lives there—as some students claim to have glimpsed his ghost in the school's shadowy corners.

The Bong Boondoggle

The Richard Bong State Recreation Area in Kenosha County is a marshy, 4,515-acre tract of land originally developed in the mid-1950s as a base for the U.S. Air Force. It is named for World War II flying ace Major Richard Ira Bong. It was intended as a strategic point of defense against air attacks aimed at Milwaukee and Chicago. But construction stopped in 1959, before the base ever came into full use, leaving a partially graded 12,900-foot runway and a maze of underground tunnels and sewers.

The tunnels were a spot for partying area teenagers as late as the 1970s, and still exist, although they are now sealed. They gained a local reputation as a center of criminal, ghostly, and cult activity, and one Burlington paranormal group has also reported numerous UFO and ghostly light sightings in the skies above them.

Gangsters Underground

Famed Chicago gangster Al Capone kept hideouts in almost every corner of Wisconsin, if all such rumors are to be believed. A good example is Burlington, on the western edge of Racine County. The city became a hotbed of "speakeasies," or illicit taverns, during the Prohibition era of the 1920s and early '30s. Many residents believe underground tunnels connected these businesses so that liquor could be transported without being seen by the authorities, and so the criminals could move easily between them.

One speakeasy, located on Milwaukee Avenue where Coach's Sports Bar and Grill now stands, had no fewer than three tunnels leading from its basement. Other Burlington locations served by bootleg liquor tunnels include the First Banking Center on Highway 11 and what is now a parking lot next to Reineman's True Value Hardware on Milwaukee Avenue. That tunnel was reportedly large enough to hold its own bowling lanes!

Capone may have also crisscrossed his property, which covered more than 400 acres at Couderay, near Hurley. His Wisconsin retreat sported 18-inch-thick walls, gun turrets, an eight-car garage with gun portals, and secret underground passages. Still known by its gangster-era name, "The Hideout," the two-story stone lodge may have had tunnels leading from the home's basement to other buildings on the grounds, though the truth about such tunnels has not been verified.

Talkin' Wisconsin

"Washington, D.C., is to lying what Wisconsin is to cheese."
—*Dennis Miller*

"Weirdness is not my game. I'm just a square boy from Wisconsin."
—*Willem Dafoe*

"A man who lives in Milwaukee is judged by the beer he drinks."
—*Philip Hamburger in* An American Notebook

"The greatest escape I ever made was when I left Appleton, Wisconsin."
—*Harry Houdini*

"Everything considered, it's really something that you can't really explain how excited guys are. Even guys who aren't from Wisconsin, they want to see how the Packers fans are and the tradition of Lambeau Field."
—*Jake Dowell, hockey player and Wisconsin native*

"We were just in Milwaukee. If we had to list our top five states, Wisconsin would have to be one of them. We're actually bigger in the North than we are in the South. You northern folks really have a hankerin' for what we do."
—*Richard Young of country-rock band the Kentucky Headhunters*

"There's something about this place, about Madison and Wisconsin and the Midwest, that's really comforting."
—*Jane Kaczmarek, actress and Wisconsin native*

"It's a dream come true. Coming from Wisconsin, playing for the Badgers, especially in the NCAA championship, there's nothing better than that."
—*Josh Engel, member of University of Wisconsin's 2006 NCAA Champion hockey team*

"The thing about Wisconsin, you've got to beat them. They're not going to beat themselves. They're not going to give you the ball. They're not going to do stupid things."
—*Joe Paterno, Penn State University football coach*

It's a Logger's Life for Me

❋ ❋ ❋ ❋

The lumber trade may be more efficient, economical, and environmentally conscious today than it was in the past, but few industries evoke the mystique and nostalgia that comes when we think of the lumberjacks of old. And Wisconsin was a major contributor to that image—and to making logging what it is today.

The True Life of a Tall Tale

If you've heard the tales of Paul Bunyan, you know what it was like to be a lumberjack in the 19th century. Well, okay, maybe it wasn't quite like that. Stories of the larger-than-life lumberjack were told around the campfires, and while some people claimed to have actually met the man of the legend, most just enjoyed the image of the giant and his blue ox, Babe. Paul Bunyan was said to have made camp in the northwoods of Wisconsin, about 45 miles west of Rhinelander. In tall tales, he was credited with endless feats of bravery, strength, and skill, including the digging out of Lake Superior.

Some of the stories originated as pure fun. Others were mostly fun for the seasoned lumberjacks who told them in order to test the gullibility of their rookie counterparts. And some may have been told (and fabricated) to enhance the image of the logger's life in the northwoods—and the danger awaiting those who dared to choose that profession.

In the Beginning

When pioneers began to settle in Wisconsin, the dense forests were cleared to make room for cabins and outbuildings—and also to supply the building material. As more people gravitated to an area, towns sprung up, and with them, the need for logs. After all, no town would be complete in those days without a general store, jail, and schoolhouse. And don't forget the two most important meeting places—the church and the saloon. Naturally, they were all made out of wood.

Like farming, logging started out on a small scale, with settlers cutting down what they needed for themselves and their community. But by the 1840s, logging was an industry and Wisconsin was in a prime location to take advantage of that. Remember, author Laura Ingalls Wilder started her life—and book series—not on the prairie, but in the "big woods" of Wisconsin.

The agriculture boom was also a boon to the lumber industry. They worked hand in hand, with farmers providing food for the lumbermen and sawmill workers as well as their horses and oxen. Logging, in turn, brought the railroads in, cleared new land for settlements, and provided winter work for farmers.

As anyone who has spent a summer vacation in the lush pine forests of Wisconsin knows, trees are thick and plentiful. As you travel north, the air dips a few degrees and the sweet scent of pine fills the air. Imagine what it was like 150 or 200 years ago when high-grade pine accounted for 130 billion board feet—and that doesn't even include acres and acres of cedar, spruce, hemlock, and other hardwoods that were also harvested in the territory.

Making a Living of Logging

Lumber companies snatched up forestland, and trees were cut down, then sawed into logs and sent downriver—or loaded onto railroad cars—to newly created sawmills. By 1840, there were 124 sawmills in Wisconsin. Twenty-five years later, there were five times that many, and logging had become a $4.3 million industry. But even that was a paltry sum compared to the $60 million generated by lumber in 1890, and the $28 billion Wisconsin's forestry industry nets today.

Fall and winter were the prime seasons for logging, with groups of 50 to

150 men setting up camp throughout the north. While some of the workers were farmers looking for seasonal work, many were professionals who were experts at their craft. Today almost all are Certified Master Loggers who are trained not only in logging, but also in environmental issues surrounding the industry, such as water, wildlife, and forest conservation.

Just about half the land in Wisconsin is forestland—containing a whopping 16 million acres of trees. By the end of the 19th century, the pine forests were being depleted with no effort to replace the felled trees. Today, as people have become more and more conscious of "going green," the lumber industry has also changed to reflect that attitude. Now, nearly every part of a harvested tree is used. Logs are made into both lumber and paper products. Smaller pieces are glued together, and particleboard is created from wood shavings. Wood chips form the wood siding that you see on houses, and even the bark is burned to run machines.

Goin' Back in Time

The days of the old-fashioned lumberjack are gone, but you can step back into that world today when you visit Scheer's Lumberjack Show, which takes place in both Hayward and Woodruff. The show entertains and fascinates the audience with competitions in many of the skills needed by the old-time loggers. Champion lumberjacks (who are more sportsmen than timber workers) compete in climbing poles, sawing wood, and, of course, log rolling. They demonstrate springboard chopping where they notch a tree and then insert a small platform that they climb to reach the top. And don't forget the speed carving and log jousting events.

Logging today is an up-to-date model of efficiency and a thriving business for Wisconsin, but the lumberjack show will take you back in time—to the days when Paul Bunyan was king.

❋ ❋ ❋ ❋

• *Eau Claire is one of many cities in the United States that claims to be the home of Paul Bunyan.*

The Clairvoyant Crime-Buster

❊ ❊ ❊ ❊

Before there were TV shows like Ghost Whisperer *and* Medium, *which make the idea of solving crimes through ESP seem almost commonplace, there was Arthur Price Roberts, Wisconsin's psychic detective. His work was accomplished in the early 1900s, when high-tech aids like electronic surveillance and DNA identification were still only far-fetched dreams. In those days, police needed psychics to break many cases.*

He Saw Dead People

A modest man born in Wales in 1866, Roberts avoided a formal education because he thought too much learning could stifle his unusual abilities. He moved to Milwaukee as a young man. There, ironically, Roberts, who never learned to read, was nicknamed "Doc."

One of his earliest well-known cases involved a baffling missing person incident in Peshtigo, a small town northwest of Milwaukee. A man named Duncan McGregor had suddenly gone missing in July 1905, leaving no clue as to his whereabouts. Police searched for him for months, and finally his desperate wife decided to go to the psychic detective who had already made a name for himself in Milwaukee. She didn't even have to explain the situation to Roberts; he knew immediately upon meeting her who she was.

Roberts meditated on the vanished husband, then sadly had to tell Mrs. McGregor that he'd been murdered and that his body was in the Peshtigo River, caught near the bottom in a pile of timber. Roberts proved correct in every detail.

Mystery of the Mad Bombers

Roberts solved numerous documented cases. He helped a Chicago man find his brother who had traveled to Albuquerque and had not been heard from for months; Roberts predicted that the brother's body would be found in a certain spot in Devil's Canyon, and it was.

After coming up with new evidence for an 11th hour pardon, "Doc" Roberts saved a Chicago man named Ignatz Potz, who had been condemned to die for a murder he didn't commit. But his biggest and most famous coup came in 1935 when he correctly predicted that the city of Milwaukee would be hit by six large dynamite explosions, losing a town hall, banks, and police stations. People snickered; such destruction was unheard of in Milwaukee. Roberts made his prediction on October 18 of that year. In little more than a week, the Milwaukee area entered a time of terror.

First, a town hall in the outlying community of Shorewood was blasted, killing two children and wounding many other people. A few weeks later, the mad bombers hit two banks and two police stations. Federal agents descended upon the city, and several local officers were assigned to work solely on solving the bombings. Finally, the police went to Roberts to learn what was coming next. Roberts told them one more blast was in the works, that it would be south of the Menomonee River, and that it would be the last. Police took him at his word and blanketed the area with officers and sharpshooters.

And sure enough, on November 4, a garage in the predicted area was blown to smithereens in an explosion that could be heard as far as eight miles away. The two terrorists, young men 18 and 21 years old, had been hard at work in the shed assembling 50 pounds of dynamite when their plan literally backfired. Few people argued with Roberts's abilities after that.

His Final Fortune

Roberts's eeriest prediction, however, may have been that of his own death. In November 1939, he told a group of assembled friends that he would be leaving this world on January 2, 1940. And he did, passing quietly in his own home on that exact date. Many of his most amazing accomplishments will probably never be known, because a lot of his work was done secretly for various law enforcement agencies. But "Doc" Roberts had an undeniable gift, and he died secure in the knowledge that he had used it to help others as best he could.

From the Badger State to Tinsel Town

✳ ✳ ✳ ✳

Is it something in the water? Or perhaps in the cheese? Whatever Wisconsin's secret might be, this state has played a part in the start of some of America's favorite television and silver screen stars.

Don Ameche

This star was born in Kenosha in 1908. Following his starring role as the title character in 1939's *The Story of Alexander Graham Bell,* folks began referring to the telephone as the "Ameche." By 1946, he was half of the combative comedic couple on *The Bickersons,* a groundbreaking radio show. Younger audiences may best remember him for his film roles, such as Mortimer Duke in 1983's *Trading Places* and Art Selwyn in 1985's *Cocoon,* for which he received an Academy Award for Best Supporting Actor. He died in 1993.

Spencer Tracy

With nine Best Actor Academy Award nods and two wins throughout the course of a 78-film career that began in 1930 and lasted until his death in 1967, Spencer Tracy was undoubtedly a Hollywood darling. Tracy was born in Milwaukee in 1900 and returned there often when he wanted to escape Hollywood's spotlight.

Orson Welles

The son of a gifted concert pianist and wealthy inventor, Kenosha's Welles (1915–1985) proved a precocious child, excelling in music, art, and even magic. By age 16, Welles had set out to make his mark in the dramatic arts. Within three years, he'd entered stage, film, and radio, and by 1941 he'd co-written, directed, and starred in *Citizen Kane,* considered by many to be one of the greatest films of all time.

Badger Ingenuity:
Damming the Red River

❋ ❋ ❋ ❋

*In 1864, during the Civil War, a combination of homegrown
Wisconsin ingenuity and sheer brawn saved the day for Union
soldiers stuck in an embarrassing jam on Louisiana's Red River.*

Mind Over Matter

Great battles are decided in many different ways. Acts of bravery
and courage under fire often determine the outcome of armed
conflict. Other struggles end in defeat through the folly or indecision
of a commander. Only 14 people were given the official Thanks of
Congress for their services to the Union during the Civil War, and
all but one—Lieutenant Colonel Joseph Bailey of Wisconsin—were
commanders in the armed forces. As the chief engineer of the 19th
Corps, Bailey saved a Union gunboat fleet trapped on Louisiana's
Red River in May 1864 using a single formidable weapon—his brain.

Revered River

The Red River, a tributary of the Mississippi, was highly prized by
Union forces as a channel by which to capture Shreveport and establish its control over northern Louisiana. The plan was that Shreveport and the surrounding area would then serve as a springboard
for launching excursions into Texas and Arkansas. In April 1864,
General Nathaniel Banks led a Union force of 32,000 soldiers and
13 gunboats, including 6 formidable ironclads, northward up the
Red River.

Stuck in the Mud

A series of skirmishes with a determined Confederate opposition slowed the Union advance. At Alexandria, Confederate defenders had been busy digging channels to divert the river. They succeeded in lowering the water level to a depth of less than four feet, which created quite a problem for the Northern fleet. The smallest Union gunboats required seven feet of water to travel, and the larger craft needed a depth of more than ten feet.

The Union advance was stalled. The gunboats were at risk of becoming stranded on the river as the waters continued to recede, which would make them sitting ducks for either capture or destruction by Confederate artillery. On May 1, Chief Engineer Bailey was authorized to take any actions necessary to free the boats and permit the advance to continue. To the amazement and consternation of the Union leadership, he resolved to build a dam.

Dam It All

Bailey had worked in the Wisconsin woods in his youth, and he sought out lumbering experience among the approximately 3,500 soldiers he had at his disposal. He then directed the felling of hundreds of trees in the Red River's adjacent forests and had the cut timber fashioned into cribbing. Other soldiers were detailed to gather rock and earth to fill the cribbing that would be used in the makeshift dam. All the while, Bailey's lumberjacks and laborers were subject to continuous Confederate sniper fire.

To complete the dam, Bailey intended to have four barges deliberately overloaded and sunk midstream above the rapids. He would then connect the cribs to the barges, creating two 300-foot wing dams jutting into the river from each bank. This backup would force the water level up to a point at which the gunboats could maneuver down the river. The remaining open water in the middle of the river would form an ingenious spillway through which the gunboats could pass over the rapids.

Cleverness Lauded

In just ten days, the dam was built. The Red River water level rose to almost 13 feet because of Bailey's dam, which allowed the gunboats safe passage into navigable water. The last boat passed over just as the dam itself was breaking due to the water pressure in the river. In his report to the War Department, General Banks lauded Chief Engineer Bailey as the person who both saved a Union fleet worth more than $2 million (a value of approximately $200 million today) and permitted the Red River Campaign to continue.

❋ ❋ ❋ ❋

- *During the Civil War, the Iron Brigade's proud Badgers wore a black campaign hat similar to an Aussie hat (with one side turned up) as a distinctive emblem. It was one of the most dreaded sights for Confederate soldiers, who knew that these Yanks had never run from a fight.*

- *To replenish the Iron Brigade's appalling Gettysburg losses, the generals assigned to it a mutinous Pennsylvania conscript regiment, the 167th. The mutiny ended when Colonel Rufus Dawes ordered the 6th Wisconsin to form line, load, and aim at the Easterners. Fortunately, the command of "Fire" was not necessary.*

- *The 32nd Infantry Division of the Wisconsin National Guard, known as Les Terribles (a French compliment for its World War I valor) and the "Red Arrow" Division (for its patch). It helped invade New Guinea and the Philippines in World War II and its soldiers earned eleven Medals of Honor in that conflict.*

- *World War II was tough on Janesville. Ninety-four Janesville men, all of Company A of the 192nd Tank Battalion, became prisoners at Bataan in 1942. Because of the Bataan Death March and a brutal POW camp regime, barely a third ever saw home again.*

Backwoods Butcher: Ed Gein

✳ ✳ ✳ ✳

To find the story of one of the most gruesome killers in American history, you don't have to look far from Wisconsin. The terrifying tale of Ed Gein unfolded in the town of Plainfield.

Ed Gein was the son of an overbearing mother who taught him that sex was sinful. When she died in 1945, he was a 39-year-old bachelor living alone in a rundown farmhouse in rural Plainfield. After his mother's death, he developed a morbid fascination with the medical atrocities performed by the Nazis during World War II. This fascination led him to dig up female corpses from cemeteries, take them home, and perform his own experiments on them, such as removing the skin from the body and draping it over a tailor's dummy. He was also fascinated with female genitalia, which he would fondle and, on occasion, stuff into women's panties and wear around the house.

He soon tired of decomposing corpses and set out in search of fresher bodies. Most of his victims were women around his mother's age. He went a step too far, however, when he abducted the mother of local sheriff's deputy Frank Worden. Learning that his missing mother had been seen with Gein on the day of her disappearance, Worden went to the Gein house to question the recluse. What he found there defied belief. Human heads sat as prize trophies in the living room along with a belt made from human nipples and a chair completely upholstered in human skin. But for Worden, the worst sight was in the woodshed. Strung up by the feet was the headless body of his mother. Her torso had been slit open, and her heart was found on a plate in the dining room.

Gein confessed but couldn't recall how many people he'd killed. He told detectives that he liked to dress up in the carved-out torsos of his victims and pretend to be his mother. He spent ten years in an insane asylum before he was judged fit to stand trial. He was found guilty, but criminally insane, and died in 1984, at age 77.

Fast Facts

- On February 8, 1858, the U.S. House of Representatives became Fisticuff Central. Rep. John Potter (R-Milwaukee) supplied the climax by yanking off a Southern representative's toupee. Potter put up a good fight before being overwhelmed by his foe's compatriots.

- President Calvin Coolidge spent the summer of 1928 in Wisconsin. He wanted to fish, and he picked the area near Superior. During Silent Cal's sojourn, Superior Central High School served as headquarters for the presidential retinue.

- Mental hospitals were a rough gig in the old days, as a visit to Winnebago Mental Health Institute's museum in Oshkosh will attest. It displays large amounts of non-food items ingested by inmates, weapons they made, and straitjackets, among other old-school oddities.

- A key pioneer in horror writing and publishing was August Derleth (1909–1971) of Sauk City. During his life, he ended up publishing more than 90 books. Notably, he was the first to publish genre titan H. P. Lovecraft, later famous for his Cthulhu mythos—to which Derleth contributed writing as well.

- The La Crosse pray-a-thon has continued uninterrupted since August 1, 1878, when the local Franciscan Sisters of Perpetual Adoration started praying in shifts, two at a time, 24 hours a day.

- Boyceville native Andy Pafko's memorable baseball career had one painful moment. In 1949, while playing for the Chicago Cubs against the St. Louis Cardinals, Pafko somersaulted to catch a liner. No catch, said the ump. Andy argued so heatedly he forgot the ball was still in play—while the tying and winning runs scored.

- Mitchell Red Cloud Jr., a member of the Ho-Chunk nation from Hatfield, won the Medal of Honor (posthumously) for his actions on November 5, 1950, along the Chongchon River in Korea. After giving early warning of a heavy Chinese assault, Red Cloud's fatal courage under fire saved his company from likely annihilation.

Major Richard I. Bong: America's "Ace of Aces"

✽ ✽ ✽ ✽

Calvin Coolidge, wet laundry, and a plane named Marge *helped create America's highest-scoring ace of all time.*

The scene was a farm on the outskirts of Poplar. The year was 1928, and the event was the daily flyover by a plane carrying mail to President Calvin Coolidge's summer home in Superior. An eight-year-old boy watched with rapt fascination as the plane passed directly over his house. Even at that tender age, Richard Bong knew he wanted to be a pilot. He grew up a typical American boy of the period—fishing, sports, church, and chores—but he never lost his dream of flying. While attending Superior State Teacher's College, Bong became a certified pilot through the government-sponsored Civilian Pilot Training Program and soon afterward joined the Army Air Corps. He never looked back.

A Promising Recruit

Bong's instructors, including future presidential candidate Barry Goldwater, noticed the young man's natural abilities as a pilot. However, Bong's penchant for antics while stationed at Hamilton Field near San Francisco raised the indignation of his commanding officer, Major General George C. Kenney. He'd been willing to tolerate Bong's loops around the Golden Gate Bridge and low-level flights through the city's business district but reached his breaking point when a woman called the base to complain that one of the pilots had flown so low over her house that all the laundry had blown off her line. Bong was ordered to go to the woman's house and hang whatever laundry needed to be dried.

In October, 1942, Bong was assigned to the 9th Fighter Squadron in the Southwest Pacific. He soon began racking up kills in his P-38 Lightning, which he named *Marge* after his fiancée. He developed a unique dogfighting technique in which he would swoop down on enemy planes and engage them at extremely close range. By January 1943, he was an ace (five kills), and on April 2, 1944, he shot down his 27th aircraft, surpassing Eddie Rickenbacker's World War I record. He was sent home on leave but returned in time for the South Pacific campaign, in which his tally reached 40 confirmed kills. General Douglas MacArthur personally awarded Bong the Congressional Medal of Honor, claiming that the pilot had "ruled the air from New Guinea to the Philippines." General Kenney pulled Bong out of combat and sent him home with orders to marry Marge and start a family. In the meantime, his services promoting war bonds were in constant demand.

At home, Bong was a hero. The international press covered his wedding, and his accomplishments continued to be celebrated. However, he wanted to be a test pilot. Soon after their wedding, Dick and Marge moved to Dayton, Ohio, where new jet aircraft were being tested at Wright Field. On the day that the atomic bomb was dropped on Hiroshima, Bong was tragically killed testing a Lockheed P-80 Shooting Star jet plane. He was just 24 years old.

❋ ❋ ❋ ❋

- *The area that became the Richard Bong State Recreation Area in Kansasville was once destined to be a fighter jet base until the plug was pulled on the project. The state purchased the land in 1974, and it became Wisconsin's first recreation area—offering outdoor activities not available in state or national parks.*

- *The Richard I. Bong Veterans Historical Center opened in Superior in 2002. It features a P-38 Lightning aircraft restored to look like Bong's original* Marge—*complete with a portrait of his sweetheart on the plane's nose.*

Wisconsin Olympic Athletes Are Golden

❊ ❊ ❊ ❊

Wisconsin hasn't hosted the Olympic Games, but that doesn't mean it hasn't produced its share of Olympic athletes. Do you remember these Olympians from Wisconsin?

- **Mark Johnson (Madison) Ice Hockey 1980:** Mark led the youthful USA hockey team to a 1980 gold medal, with 11 points over the course of the Olympics. He went on to play in the NHL and was an assistant hockey coach for UW Madison men's hockey before accepting a job as the UW women's head hockey coach.

- **Bob Suter (Madison) Ice Hockey 1980:** Bob Suter was a defenseman on the 1980 USA team that beat the Russians and won the gold. He is the father of two hockey players and owns Gold Medal Sports in Madison.

- **Honorary Wisconsinites:** In addition to homegrown hockey talents, we wouldn't want to forget the other University of Wisconsin hockey players that competed in the Olympics:

  Chris Chelios (silver 2002)

  Gary Suter (silver 2002)

  Mike Richter (silver 2002)

  Barry Richter (1994)

  Tony Granato (1988)

Also, 2008 made 11 straight Olympic games for Badger rowers. That group includes:

Stewart MacDonald, Bob Espeseth, Carie Graves, Neil Haleen, Peggy McCarthy, Tim Michelsen, Jackie Zoch, Chris Cruz, Kris Thorsness, Chari Towne, Cindy Eckert, Sarah Gengler, Mara Keggi, Dave Kromtovich, Kim Santiago, Mark Berkner, Yasmin Farooq, Eric Mueller, Tori Folk, Micah Boyd, and Beau Hoopman.

Taste of Wisconsin

The Seven Wonders of Wisconsin cuisine are beer, cheese, and brats, brats, brats, brats, and brats. Whether at festivals, picnics, tailgating, or in the backyard, the Badger State has a love affair with the bratwurst.

The Sausage of Champions

If you are what you eat, Wisconsinites are bratwurst. And they eat lots of brats. For example, every year, during a single Memorial Day weekend, residents of the capital city, Madison, eat around 20 miles of brats at the World's Largest Brat Fest. That's roughly 200,000 sausages.

Wisconsin loves brats, even if no one is too certain what they are. "Translated, a bratwurst means a sausage to be fried," says Debra Usinger, director of retail operations and corporate services for the 129-year-old Usinger's Famous Sausage, based in Milwaukee. And she should know, since she's also a great-granddaughter of the founder.

The grilled brat served as a sandwich, Usinger says, is a distinctly American creation. In Germany, the sausages are browned in a pan and served on a plate, with nary a bun in sight. The spirit if not the intent of old-style Germanic cooking style is preserved in the Sheboygan area, where the act of grilling brats on a barbecue is still called a "brat fry." And the history of the brat goes back farther than that.

Did bratwurst fill the bellies of the builders of the pyramids? Not quite, but Ancient Egypt is where the first sausage was born. Even 4,000-plus years ago, it was immigrant food. The constant movement of nomads and roaming armies brought sausages up to Europe through the Mediterranean. Long after Alexander the Great, after all, Napoleon said that an army travels on its stomach. What travel food is more convenient than sausage?

"You couldn't bring steak with you, but you could take sausages that were smoked and dried," says Usinger. "It was portable."

As sausages spread, their flavors changed. "You might have a region that did not have a particular spice that was available in another region," she says. New tastes were incorporated as sausages traveled the globe.

The bratwurst itself became a distinct member of the sausage family in Germany. In Nuremberg, a restaurant named Zum Goldenen Stern calls itself "the world's oldest bratwurst kitchen." Because the restaurant dates back to 1419, few dispute its claim.

In Germany, and especially Austria, a primary recipe developed for what came to be called the bratwurst: a mild, seasoned sausage consisting of pork, salt, pepper, nutmeg, mace, and other spices. Some were prepared with veal. Using rare cuts of meat was not the bratwurst's original reason for being. It was just the opposite.

"Sometimes less palatable parts were used," says Usinger. "Nobody wanted to waste anything because nobody could *afford* to waste anything." The parts were ground up. But how did they keep it all in one piece? Enter digestion—a pig or sheep's digestion, rather, and not your own. Sausages are contained in casings made from the cleansed parts of the animal intestines used for digestion, not for waste. This was an ideal solution because it was an otherwise unusable part of the animal.

In these modern times, you can find brats made from beef, chicken, turkey, spinach, tofu, and other ingredients. "People are very creative with newer trends," says Usinger. "That's what I like about sausage. You can be creative in so many different ways."

As for brat preparation, before grilling them Usinger recommends bringing water to a boil. Put in the brats, and turn off the heat. Keep the pot covered. Continued boiling may burst the casing, shriveling the brats; the meat will be exposed, and the brats will over-

cook. On the other hand, her brother Fritz, the company's president, just plops them on the grill. But when it comes to boiling in beer, the Usinger siblings agree that it's a bad brat idea. Beer can impart a bitter taste, changing the spicing profile of the brat.

If you don't pre-cook your brats, you should ideally grill them about 25 to

30 minutes, turning often to keep the casing from splitting. Keeping the juices inside retains flavor. Don't cook brats like steak, searing the outside. When they're firm to the touch and reach about 180 degrees internal temperature, they're done.

Some people even use brats as ingredients in other dishes, slicing them for soups and salads, or removing the casings to use them as loose sausage. Some even make brat patties—sausage burgers!

If you happen to be in the area on Memorial Day, you can take part in the annual World's Largest Brat Fest in Madison. Billed as "the biggest picnic on the planet," the weekend features volunteers attempting to set new world records—by serving brats to raise funds for more than 70 groups and charities. Brat Fest started in 1982 as a customer appreciation day at Madison's Hilldale Shopping Center. Sentry Foods owner Tom Metcalfe set out one 19-inch grill, one table, and three chairs. Things have changed somewhat.

Festivities have moved to the Dane County Fairgrounds, at the Alliant Energy Center, and a 19-inch grill isn't big enough to serve the necessary 88 brats every minute of the four-day festival. The event is now sponsored by Johnsonville, which donates most of the brats and also provides a gargantuan grill: 53,000 pounds, 6 feet in diameter, 20 feet tall, and 65 feet long. It has the capacity to serve about 2,500 brat-lovers per hour.

❀ ❀ ❀ ❀

- *Sheboygan has held its Brat Days festival annually since 1978, though the roots of the event go as far back as 1953. Brat Days features a bratwurst eating contest and the four-mile Brat Trot run and walk. You may not want to compete in both events—it wouldn't be wise to join the run after gorging on brats!*

- *In 2004, the people of Campbellsport grilled and served a 48-foot-long bratwurst made from 25 pounds of pork. Topped with nearly 25 pounds of ketchup and mustard, more than a pound of onion, and four gallons of relish, it was cut into 160 pieces and sold to benefit the fire department.*

Werewolves in Wisconsin?

❋ ❋ ❋ ❋

Do you believe in werewolves? If you head out to southeastern Wisconsin, you might just meet one face-to-fang.

Meeting the Beast

The first recorded sighting of the Beast came in 1936, long before it even had a name. Security guard Mark Schackelman was walking the grounds of a convent near Jefferson shortly before midnight when he saw a strange creature digging on top of a Native American burial mound. As Schackelman got closer, the creature ran off into the darkness. The scene repeated itself the following night, but this time, the creature stood up on its hind legs, growled at the shocked security guard, and simply walked away.

Encounters like this have continued through the years. Most people describe the creature as six to eight feet tall. It gets around on all fours but can also walk on two feet. Its entire body is covered with fur (similar to Bigfoot), but this Beast also has clawed hands, the head of a wolf, and bright yellow eyes. With a description like that, it's easy to see why some people believe that the creature is a werewolf. But several people have seen the Beast in broad daylight.

The Beast Gets a Name

In the early 1990s, an outbreak of Beast sightings in southeastern Wisconsin—specifically, along an isolated stretch of Bray Road, just outside the town of Elkhorn—led a local reporter to dub the creature "The Beast of Bray Road."

Today, the Beast continues to linger around southeastern Wisconsin, but it's seldom seen on Bray Road anymore. It was, however, spotted in Madison in 2004. So if you're ever driving through the area, keep an eye out for what might be lurking around the bend.

A Tangy Tourist Attraction: The Mustard Museum

❋ ❋ ❋ ❋

In a world of idiosyncratic people and places, Barry Levenson and the Mustard Museum just may be the spice of your life.

Triumph in the Face of Defeat

Their story begins on the early morning of October 28, 1986. The Boston Red Sox had just lost the World Series to the New York Mets, and just hours after the devastating undoing, despondent Red Sox fan Barry Levenson traipsed through an all-night grocery soul-searching for a clearer understanding of life. Crushed by his team's seventh game squander, Barry sought comfort in the condiment corridor. He waltzed by the pickles, the ketchups, the relishes, the horseradishes, and the mayos. When he hovered over the mustards, he heard a powerful voice: "If you collect us, they will come."

At the time of this zestfully zany epiphany, the Massachusetts native served as Assistant Attorney General for the State of Wisconsin. Five years later, his mustard collection had grown so large that it warranted a bigger spotlight. So Levenson fully heeded that voice and devoted his attention full-time to the great golden hue, quitting law to start a museum with room enough to display the 1,000 jars he had already amassed.

Since then, tens of thousands of faithful minions and curiosity hounds have come to the Mount Horeb Mustard Museum, which opened April 6, 1992. Even after years of talking mustard, Levenson has not lost his interest in discussing the pungent paste's history, origins, varieties, and virtues, jawing at a pace approaching the speed of light.

The Wide World of Condiments

The Mount Horeb Mustard Museum represents the whole world of mustard powders and plants, from Azerbaijan to Zimbabwe, and quite a few places in between. Slovenian, South African, Italian, Scottish, Welsh, Russian, and Japanese mustards receive special attention, and Wisconsin mustards are spotlighted as well.

The museum houses more than 5,000 mustards and hundreds of items of mustard memorabilia, including mustard and hot dog art, literature, apparel, toys, coffee mugs, billboards, gift boxes, dispensers, model trucks, and souvenir buses and railroad cars. Mustard gift boxes are available to suit any occasion, and the tasting area allows visitors to sample local, regional, and exotic mustard sources.

Gourmet mustard patrons learn just how versatile, practical, and diverse mustard is—the museum teaches that there are more savory mustards than just the standard yellow variety. Thousands of hot pepper, garlic, herb, maple walnut, spicy apricot, black truffle, champagne, organic, dill, Dijon, and fruit variations await discovery.

Cutting the Mustard

About 35,000 visitors a year from across the globe come to the museum in search of insight. It has been featured on *The Oprah Winfrey Show,* HGTV's *The Good Life,* and the Food Network.

Nevertheless, for Levenson, who has even authored a children's book entitled *Mustard on a Pickle,* no praise is too lavish for one of the world's most ancient spices and oldest known condiments, dating back to at least 3000 B.C. when it was harvested in India. Today, Levenson says that about 700 million pounds of mustard are consumed worldwide each year, and that the U.S. uses more mustard than any other country.

But what if his beloved Red Sox hadn't lost the World Series to the Mets in October 1986? Would he have started collecting mustards that night—or ever? Would he have been so depressed as to wander the aisles of an all-night supermarket, ripe for that profound voice lurking in the condiment aisle? Would the mustards sometime after have cried out so resonantly? The world may never know.

Fast Facts

- The Air Force Academy's first Medal of Honor winner was Captain Lance Sijan of Milwaukee. He was awarded for his valor after his F-4 fighter/bomber was shot down on November 9, 1967, near Hoa Lo, Vietnam. The USAF now bestows the Sijan Award upon airmen who demonstrate exemplary leadership.

- At least no one was killed in Wisconsin's Walleye War, a 1988–1991 conflict over Ojibwa off-reservation fishing rights in the state. There were, however, some fisticuffs and unpleasant language. The Ojibwa won, more or less, as the courts upheld their treaty rights and the protests died down.

- Today's NBA Atlanta Hawks had a short stint as the Milwaukee Hawks between 1951 and 1955. They had relocated from Moline, Illinois, and had four lamentable seasons in Wisconsin, finishing 17–49, 27–44, 21–51, and 26–46. Only when they left for St. Louis did the Hawks finally leave the league cellar.

- On one day in 1957, the County Stadium faithful were treated to the sight of an opposing manager (former Braves skipper Bobby Bragan) protesting his ejection by trying to pass an orange drink around the umpiring crew. No one wanted any, but they still wanted Bragan to hit the showers.

- Johnny "Blood" McNally, a 1930s Packer great, did goofy things. In one contest against the Giants, Packers QB Red Dunn handed off to McNally. With nothing but daylight in front of him, McNally threw a lateral straight back to Dunn, who got clobbered for a five-yard loss.

- Perhaps McNally's craziest feat was his train-catching escapade. Rising late after a long evening with an ardent female fan, McNally missed the Packers' train. No problem: He sped ahead and parked his car on the tracks. Luckily, the train was able to stop in time.

- Houdini wasn't the only Wisconsinite escape artist. Ben Bergor (1893–1981) of Madison wowed crowds for two generations. There's still a Ben Bergor Magic Club in Madison.

Quiz

So you think you know all about the Badger State?
Then try this Wisconsin Cultural Literacy Quiz!

1. Gutzon Borglum sculpted (with a lot of help) the figures on Mount Rushmore. What outdoor figure did he sculpt for Madison?

a) *Forward*
b) *Wisconsin*
c) The Abraham Lincoln statue at UW-Madison
d) The bust of Governor William Dempster Hoard

2. Which films were shot in Madison?

a) *I Love Trouble*
b) *Back to School*
c) *For Keeps*
d) All of the above

3. Why is UW-Madison's Chadbourne Hall dorm an embarrassment to former UW President Paul Chadbourne?

a) He disliked the building's architecture.
b) It is home to a notoriously foul composting facility.
c) It is a women's dorm, and he opposed admitting women to the school.
d) His home had to be knocked down in order to build it.

4. How did Pabst Blue Ribbon get its name?

a) It was brewed in Milwaukee, and the Milwaukee River is sometimes referred to as "The Blue Ribbon."
b) The Pabst family's thoroughbred racehorses all wore blue ribbons.
c) Blue cloth ribbons originally decorated each bottle of beer.
d) It won first prize (a blue ribbon) at the 1893 Chicago World's Fair.

5. UW-Madison football Badger and Heisman Trophy winner Alan Ameche went by what nickname?

a) "The Horse"
b) "Old Reliable"
c) "Superman"
d) "Mr. Endurance"

Answers: 1. d; 2. d; 3. c; 4. d; 5. a

266

The Real Indiana Jones

✳ ✳ ✳ ✳

Indiana Jones may have roamed the globe, battling Germans and digging up deserts while saving religious relics and drop-dead beauties with equal aplomb, but in the end he came home to Wisconsin. The real Indiana Jones, that is: Roy Chapman Andrews.

This Story Should Be a Movie!

Real-life paleontologists largely agree that Andrews was the inspiration for Dr. Henry "Indiana" Jones Jr. While that has never been confirmed by movie producer George Lucas, the six-foot-tall Andrews wore a holstered revolver and a wide-brimmed hat during his own escapades. He served as a spy in World War I, faced death at least ten times, and was incorrectly reported deceased at least once.

"If you want to argue that he fails to resemble Indiana Jones, throw in the fact that he hated snakes, and think again," says Ann Bausum, author and one of the founders of the Beloit-based Roy Chapman Andrews Society. Her book, *Dragon Bones and Dinosaur Eggs*, published in 2000 by the National Geographic Society, examines Andrews's real-life exploits.

Andrews was an explorer and archaeologist, but also much more. He was a globetrotting adventurer and one-time director of the American Museum of Natural History in New York. He was born and is buried in Beloit. He never located the Holy Grail or the Lost Ark, as did his fictional counterpart, but he discovered something perhaps just as exciting. He found out how dinosaurs were born.

"Roy Chapman Andrews is best known as the man who discovered fossil dinosaur eggs in Mongolia's Gobi Desert," *Time* magazine reported in 1940. "Before that, no one knew whether dinosaurs laid eggs or bore their young alive. Andrews has done a great deal of other scientific junketing, slaking an insatiable curiosity which he has had ever since he was a Wisconsin boy."

A Boy from Beloit

Born in Beloit in 1884, Andrews trained himself as a naturalist. As a boy, he hunted in woods nearby and learned taxidermy. He attended Beloit College and received a bachelor's degree in English. Later, he would use his education to write more than 20 books. *Discover* magazine named Andrews's *Under a Lucky Star* as one of the 25 greatest science books of all time.

In 1906, Andrews went to New York. He tried to get an interview at the American Museum of Natural History and was almost turned away, but the enterprising Andrews asked, "You have to have somebody to scrub floors, don't you?" He was hired as a janitor. Soon afterward, he joined the museum's collecting staff and earned a master's degree in "mammalogy" from Columbia University. In 1909, he became a collector for the museum and began crossing the globe.

Andrews journeyed to the East Indies, gathering specimens. In about 1920, his travels took him to China on a series of trips. A single Andrews expedition resembled an invading army. His crew traveled in specially built Dodge touring cars with a train of 75 supply-laden camels. For a 1923 expedition, he shipped back two tons of fossils and wound up on the cover of *Time* for his efforts.

In a 1923 article, *Time* reported, "Mr. Andrews owes his position as leader of the Asiatic expedition to a unique combination of scientific authority and practical resourcefulness in big game hunting and open-air life. He is as thoroughly at home in these as the late Theodore Roosevelt."

Just like those of his cinematic counterpart, Andrews's expeditions had to contend with outrageous obstacles like raiders, sandstorms, and packs of wild dogs—not to mention snakes. During one particularly bad night in the Gobi Desert, his expedition killed 47 vipers.

And his reptile problems didn't end when he left the Gobi, either. "Several times he has been on death's brink," *Time* reported.

While he was on expedition in Borneo, a boy "yanked him out of range of a huge python which was about to drop on the explorer from a tree."

In 1934, Andrews became director of the American Museum of Natural History, where he once scrubbed the floors. After that, he was mostly forgotten. He was not an embarrassment, exactly, but a reminder of a time when scientists also had to be showmen to gain attention. At the time Andrews entered the field of natural history, there were few special areas of study and scientific academia was still organizing into various formalized disciplines. Meanwhile, explorer-adventurers, often with little education, were going out and getting the actual work done.

Still, Andrews's education and sound scientific practice kept him above the fray. At that time, to be a successful scientist, he had to be a promoter. For example, Andrews's first expedition to Mongolia cost $250,000, and he raised all of it from donations. Thanks to Andrews, science also opened up to corporate sponsorship—a development that made many scientific breakthroughs possible.

In 1942, Andrews left his position at the museum and retired to Colebrook, Connecticut, later moving to Carmel, California. He died in 1960 and, per his request, his cremated remains were buried in Beloit. Today, the memory of Roy Chapman Andrews is alive in his many books, and perhaps in the exploits of Indiana Jones, his fictional twin. Lately, he's getting a little attention again from his former employers, too.

A 2007 IMAX movie, *Dinosaurs Alive!*, features footage of Andrews in the field, and the Roy Chapman Andrews Society offers prestigious annual awards to the top modern explorers, such as oceanographer Robert Ballard, discoverer of the wreck of the R.M.S. *Titanic*, and entomologist-ecologist Mark Moffett. The scientists partner with educators in Andrews's native Beloit to reach out to schoolchildren—and possibly inspire the next globetrotting Wisconsinite explorer.

As Andrews said, "Always there has been an adventure just around the corner—and the world is still full of corners!"

You Can Thank Wisconsin

Great Wisconsin Inventions

Some ways the Badger State made the average American's life even better.

Vitamin D

Harry Steenbock didn't invent vitamin D, but in 1923, the University of Wisconsin-Madison professor figured out that exposing food to ultraviolet radiation increased its vitamin D content. Rather than receive a big payday from the Quaker Oats Company, which wanted the technology to fortify breakfast cereal, Steenbock helped create the first university technology transfer office, the Wisconsin Alumni Research Foundation (WARF). It was a nonprofit organization that ensured university research profits would go toward funding future research. WARF's first action was selling the license for Steenbock's technology to Quaker Oats and various pharmaceutical companies, which netted WARF roughly $8 million by 1945.

The Snowmobile

Joseph Bombardier of Quebec is often considered the father of the modern snowmobile, and rightly so: His endless track vehicle, patented in the United States in 1962, was the first commercially successful model in the nation. However, in 1927, Carl J. Eliason of Sayner received a patent for an oft-forgotten precursor called the snow machine—essentially a toboggan with a seat and a motor. Eliason couldn't find commercial success and ended his endeavor in 1953. Nevertheless, his final K series is credited with influencing companies like Polaris and Arctic Cat.

The Automobile (Kind of...)

Although his name is not usually mentioned along with early automobile pioneers, in 1871, Racine's John Wesley Carhart invented and perfected an oscillating valve for a steam engine, which he used to power a buggy he called the Spark. Though the contraption was deemed too noisy to be practical—local legend says the noise spooked a neighbor's horse, indirectly causing its death and prompting neighbors to demand that Carhart dismantle his invention—it was recognized years later by the American Manufacturers' Association as a forerunner of the automobile.

Timeline

(Continued from p. 236)

1988
Construction on the Bradley Center, the $90 million home of the Milwaukee Bucks and Marquette University basketball teams, is completed.

July 22, 1991
Jeffrey Dahmer, a serial killer who preys on young men and teenagers, is arrested. A search of his Milwaukee apartment turns up vats of gory evidence linking him to many of the 15 murders of which he is ultimately convicted.

March 1993
An outbreak of cryptosporidium bacteria in Milwaukee's drinking water supply kills more than 100 people and sickens some 400,000.

November 1998
Democrat Tammy Baldwin is elected to the U.S. House of Representatives, serving Wisconsin's 2nd District. She is the first woman to represent Wisconsin, and the first openly gay woman to serve in Congress.

1998
University of Wisconsin research scientist Dr. James Thomson successfully cultivates human embryonic stem cells in a laboratory setting.

1999
Wisconsin dairy farmers circumvent laws prohibiting the sale of unpasteurized milk by instituting a cow-sharing program.

January 1, 2000
Wisconsin is victorious in the first Rose Bowl of the new millennium, beating Stanford by a score of 17–9.

2001
The Milwaukee Art Museum unveils its $121 million addition and renovation.

September 6, 2001
Milwaukee native Scott Stoll begins a three-year, 25,000-mile circumnavigation of the globe by bicycle.

July 9, 2002
Milwaukee hosts Major League Baseball's All-Star Game. The matchup ends on a frustrating note when both teams run out of pitchers in the 11th inning, leaving the game in a 7–7 deadlock.

July 15, 2002
Thirty-four train cars of a 107-car Canadian freight train jump the tracks and catch fire near Allenton.

January 2, 2004
John Norquist, the four-term Milwaukee mayor who served most of his last term being dogged by a sex scandal, is replaced by Marvin Pratt.

July 12, 2008
Harley-Davidson's $75 million museum in downtown Milwaukee opens to the public.

March 18, 2009
UW-Madison's women's hockey team beats Mercyhurst College 5–0 for their third NCAA championship title.

A Tale of Two Cinemas

❈ ❈ ❈ ❈

In this era of super-size multiplexes and stadium seating, most classic movie houses have disappeared. In the early 20th century, when screens were silver, there were close to 100 motion picture theaters in Milwaukee. Today, only a handful of those remain, most notably the Oriental Theater and the Times Cinema.

The grandiose Oriental Theater on Milwaukee's east side is a real neighborhood gem. It was built on the site of the former Farwell Station horse, mule, and streetcar barn. Designed by local architects Alex Bauer and Gustave A. Dick, the building was decidedly East Indian-inspired, *not* Asian, despite the theater's name. The ornate palace included two minaret towers, three beautiful stained-glass chandeliers, eight porcelain lions, dozens of lavish draperies, close to 100 elephants, and six huge gilded Buddhas with illuminated eyes.

Bleak House

In conjunction with the original Oriental Theater was Bensinger's Recreation, owned by Moses Annenberg. The life of Moses Annenberg would make good fodder for a movie! In true rags to riches form, Moses emigrated from East Prussia penniless. Fast forward 40 years, and Moses was a multimillionaire in Milwaukee operating more than 40 businesses and running a publishing empire to rival William Randolph Hearst, who he happened to previously work for in Chicago. However, Moses's financial success was plagued with stories of run-ins with Chicago gangsters, and by the 1940s, Moses and his son Walter were indicted in the biggest tax evasion case in U.S. history. Moses agreed to a plea in exchange for getting charges dropped against his son. Moses served a couple years in a federal penitentiary and never recovered. He died in 1942, and ownership of his businesses, as well as his IRS debts, transferred to Walter.

The Oriental Theater and Bensginer's Recreation were sold to the Orto Theater Group in 1946. As for the Annenberg family's cinematic happy ending, Walter Annenberg went on to create *TV Guide* and *Seventeen* magazines and eventually surpassed his disgraced father's publishing success. He also racked up impressive political and philanthropic achievements. Walter served as the American Ambassador to Britain during the Nixon administration and became a close friend of Ronald Reagan during his presidency. Over time, Annenberg donated more than two billion dollars to museums and educational institutions.

American Notes

At its grand opening in 1927, the Oriental Theater screened *Ben-Hur*. Since then, the theater has thrived and evolved. In the 1970s and '80s, the Oriental showcased musical acts such as R.E.M., Iggy Pop, Blondie, and Tears for Fears. One evening, the Pretenders were slated to perform but their opening act canceled. The band invited three street performers to fill in. That turned out to be the big break for Milwaukee's own Violent Femmes.

Music remains closely affiliated with this treasured theater as it houses the largest theater pipe organ in the United States, and the third largest in the world! The Kimball Theatre Pipe Organ still entertains the audience in the main theater every Saturday before the 7:00 P.M. show.

The Oriental also holds the world record for longest running of *The Rocky Horror Picture Show,* with its midnight screenings since 1978. Delighted moviegoers still flock to the Oriental in costume ready to shout and sing along with the movie, augmented by live performers.

Our Mutual Friend

Perhaps taking a cue from the Oriental, another classic Milwaukee theater has incorporated live performances into some of its shows. The Times Cinema, located on Vliet Street in the historic Washington Heights neighborhood, is the only theater in Milwaukee to feature a non-Rocky Horror shadow cast, namely the Warped Cast. Assistant Director Joanna Amos spent years dodging rice for *The Rocky Horror Picture Show*, but she has "Time Warp"-ed over to the Times Cinema. There she leads a talented crew through live midnight performance revivals of campy classics such as *Clue*. The Warped Cast has put their stamp on *Little Shop of Horrors, Cannibal: The Musical*, and *Willy Wonka and the Chocolate Factory*. In the process, they have added to the rich saga of this beloved cinema.

Great Expectations

Designed by architect Paul Bennett, the Times auditorium was built right into a garage. It opened on June 12, 1935. Ben Marcus, the movie mogul behind the Marcus Corporation, partnered with a Mr. Smirnoff and acquired the Times in 1940. At that time, it became an S & M Theater. Not *that* kind of S & M theater! Named after their respective initials, it operated under their ownership for 45 years.

Over the years, the Times has undergone many updates while staying true to its original art deco spirit. When it opened, the Times became Milwaukee's first and only Translux Theater—meaning, it played films from an innovative, mirrored rear-projection system hidden behind the screen. With the introduction of CinemaScope technology in the 1950s, the projection booth moved to the back. Seating capacity expanded to 448, yet the Times has steadfastly remained a single screen theater.

The Best of Times, the Worst of Times

Former Times manager Cory Jacobson fondly recalls patrons from all over Milwaukee lined up around the block every day for 18 weeks when the theater exclusively showed *The Big Chill*. But as years went on, things slowed down and ticket sales declined. In 2007, theater historian and writer Larry Widen purchased the struggling theater. As both a movie buff and a member of the Wisconsin State Historical Society, Widen is committed to preserving this viable theater and screening an eclectic mix of art films, blockbusters, Hollywood classics, and modern flicks, in addition to staging live acts including the Warped Cast and the Philip Walker Blues Band.

Index

❋ ❋ ❋ ❋

A

A. Piker Clerk, 170
Aaron, Hank, 97
Abdul-Jabbar, Kareem, 151–52
Abolitionists, 52, 241
Abrahamson, Shirley, 236
Adventures in Time, 111
Adventures of Buckaroo Banzai, 206
Ainsworth, Ellen, 132
Alcindor, Lew (Kareem Abdul-Jabbar),
     151–52
Alex Jordan Creative Center, 142
Aliens in America, 66
Al Johnson's Swedish Restaurant &
     Butik, 155–56
Allenton, 271
Ameche, Alan "The Horse," 240
Ameche, Don, 240, 250
American Birkebeiner, 40–41
American Dreamer, 65
American Girl doll company, 236
Ames, Aldrich "Rick," 154
Amityville Horror, The, 101
Amos, Joanna, 274
Anderson, Anders "Big Gust," 184
Anderson, Carl, 172
Andrews, Roy Chapman, 267–69
Animal symbols and mascots, 19–20,
     27–29. *See also* Wildlife.
Annenberg, Moses, 272
Annenberg, Walter, 272–73
Answering machines, 95
Appleton, 103, 109–10
Apps, Jerry, 63, 162
Arndt, Charles, 36
Arndt, Richard, 97
Arthur Anderson, 164
Aswang: The Unearthing, 101
Atlantis in Wisconsin (Joseph), 224
Automobile forerunner, 270
Aztalan State Park, 49, 223–25

B

Babcock, Stephen, 147, 222
Babiarz, Stacey, 153
Badger Four-Wheel Drive Auto
     Company, 153
Badgers (mascot, symbol), 19, 27–29
Baile, Joseph, 251–53
Baldwin, Tammy, 57, 271
Baraboo, 10–11, 205
Barnum, Phineas Taylor, 121
Barnum & Bailey Circus, 11, 176
Baseball
     American League, 146
     announcers, 82–83
     ballparks, 187–89, 210
     Girls' Professional League, 132
     history, 107–8, 236, 271
     players, 15, 30, 96–97, 169, 184, 255
     team moves, 194, 236
     team owners, 124
     Twins' mascot, 184
     World Series, 194
Basilica of St. Josaphat, 26
Basketball, 151–52, 265, 271
Bauer, Alex, 272
Bausum, Ann, 267
Bay View tragedy, 53–55
Bear Creek, 200, 202
Bears, 85
Beast of Bray Road, 262
Beast of Bray Road, The, 101
Beaumont, William, 36
Beaver Dam, 102, 204
Beaver Island, 18
Beck, Carl, 179
Beer, 12, 210–12
Beer Run, Riverwest, 173
Behnke, Robert, 221
Belleville, 62
Belmont, 191
Beloit, 231
Bembenek, Laurie "Bambi," 115–16

Benkert, Rudolph, 203
Bennett, Paul, 274
Benson's Holiday Hideaway, 62
Berkner, Mark, 258
Berners, Edward, 121, 167
Besserdich, William, 153
Bickersons, The, 250
Big Chill, The, 274
Black Hawk War, 36
Black Sheep, 143
Blair, Bonnie, 77, 79
Blatz Beer, 211
Blood Harvest, 101
Blood Hook, 101
Blue Mounds, 125–27
Boaz, 231
Bober, Raymond, 218
Bong, Richard I., 56, 242, 256–57
Boogeyman, The: The Devonsville
    Terror, 101
Boscobel, 232
Boulder Junction, 73
Bowling, 226–28
Boyd, Belle, 190
Boyd, Micah, 258
Bradley Center, 271
Bragan, Bobby, 265
Brat Days, 261
Bratwurst, 259–61
Braun, Ryan, 96
Bremer, Arthur, 169
Brew Crew (2008), 96
Breweries, 12, 210–12
Bride Wars, 143
Bridge Wars, 128–29
Briggs, Clare, 170–71
Brigham, George, 169
British immigrants, 203–4
Brodhead, 111
Brookfield, 214
Brown, Isaac, 241
Bruno, Ralph, 60–61
Bubblers, 44
Bucket Bagger, 153
Bucky Badger, 27–29
Buhl, Bob, 15
Bunyan, Paul, 245
Burger Fest, 204
Burke, Brian, 220

Burlington, 70, 155, 243
Burnette, James, 91
Burrows, Robert, 91
Bush, George W., 189
Butter, vs. margarine, 133–35, 175
Butterfat tester, 222

C
Cabbage Chuck, World
    Championship, 200
Cahill, Tim, 240
Cahokia, 223–25
Campbellsport, 261
Canals, 91
Capital Brewery, 197
Capone, Al, 118, 243
Capone, Ralph "Bottles," 118–19
Capture of Bigfoot, The, 102
Carey, Deborah, 212
Carhart, John Wesley, 270
Cartoonists, 170–72, 176
Carver, Jonathan, 218
Catt, Carrie Chapman, 57, 132
Cave of the Mounds, 125–27
Cave paintings, 36
Celebrities. *See specific names.*
Cemetery, Confederate, 154
Chalet Cheese Cooperative, 203
Cheese
    cheddar, 235
    as dairy industry niche, 148
    facts about, 149, 150
    laws, 175
    Limburger, 175, 202–3
    quiz, 233–34
    world's largest, 194
Cheese curds, 202
Cheese Days celebration, 150
Cheesehead hats, 60–61
Chelios, Chris, 258
Cheney, Martha (Mamah) Borthwick,
    93, 146
Chequamegon-Nicolet U.S. National
    Forest, 230
Chicago Fire, 88
Chicken-plucking record, 176
Chippewa, Lake, 72
Chippewa Falls, 66, 211
Chvala, Chuck, 220

Circuses, 10–11, 176
Circus World Museum, 11
Citizen Kane, 176, 250
City Brewery, 12, 211
Civil War, 111, 124, 190, 212, 229, 251–53
Clephan, James O., 208
Clinton, 74
Clintonville, 52
Coach's Sports Bar and Grill, 243
Cocoon, 250
Cohn, Roy, 194
Coins, 21, 169
Colborn, Jim, 30
Cold War, 154
Communist "containment," 194
Confederate Rest, 154
Conrad, Connie, 27
Constitution (state), 190
Coolidge, Calvin, 255
Cornucopia Yacht Club, 52
Couderay, 243
Cougars, 86
Cow Chip Throw, 67
Cows, 15, 19, 149, 150
Coyotes, 87
Cranberries, 13–14
Crazylegs, 33
Creature That Ate Sheboygan, The, 45
Cruz, Chris, 258
Cultural influences, 202–4
Cultural Literacy Quizzes, 31, 104, 201, 266
Cutler, Lysander, 229
Cyprus disaster, 146

D
Dafoe, Willem, 76, 103, 244
Daggett, Henry, 146
Dahmer, Jeffrey, 159–61, 271
Dairy industry, 133–35, 147–49, 194, 222, 271
Daly, Tyne, 124
Damien: Omen II, 102
Davis, Jefferson, 154
Death penalty, 36
Deer Shelter Rock, 140–42
Densmore, James, 207–8
Derleth, August, 255

Devine, Dan, 70
Dick, Gustave A., 272
Dillinger, John, 117–18
Dinosaurs Alive!, 269
Dixon, Jeane, 124
Dodge, Augustus, 70
Dodge, Henry, 70
Door County, 15
Dorman, Henry, 221
Dowell, Jake, 244
Dragon Bones and Dinosaur Eggs (Bausum), 267
Ducks (vehicles), 177–78
Duncan Yo-Yos, 30
Dungeons & Dragons, 111
Dun Rovin Lodge, 156

E
Eagle River, 71, 102
Earth Day, 236
East River, 102
Eau Claire Rule, 194
Eckert, Cindy, 258
Edmund Fitzgerald, 163–65
Elcho, 111, 119
Eliason, Carl J., 176, 270
Elkhorn, 262
Elk Mound, 213
Elmwood, 62
Elson, Edward Ben, 52
Engel, Josh, 244
Engelman, Marjorie, 45
Erin, 25–26
Eschborn, Archie, 51
Espeseth, Bob, 258
Every, Thomas (Dr. Evermor), 205
Evinrude, Ole, 222

F
Farley, Chris, 143
Farooq, Yasmin, 258
Fassnacht, Robert, 236
Favor-Hamilton, Suzy, 219
Ferrall, R. Michael, 221
Fever Lake, 102
Fielder, Prince, 96
Fingers, Rollie, 96
Fires, 88–90, 121, 176
Fish fries, 22–23

Fishing, 73, 166
Fitzrandolph, Casey, 79
Flags, 21, 45
Flintstones in Viva Rock Vegas, The, 143
Flu epidemic, 30
Foie gras, 37
Folk, Tori, 258
Fond du Lac, 241
Foods. *See also* Cheese.
   bratwurst, 259–61
   cranberries, 13–14
   cultural influences, 202–4
   fish, 22–23
   foie gras, 37
   ice cream sundaes, 167–68
   maple syrup, 42–43
   morel mushrooms, 182–83
   pasties, 80–81, 204
Football (college)
   Eastman insult to, 181
   players, 32–33, 45, 240
   rivalries, 240
   Rose Bowl, 91, 271
Football (NFL)
   coaches, 70, 144–45, 195–96, 236
   Ice Bowl, 144–45, 196
   Packers formation, 176
   Packers vs. Broncos (1984), 213
   players, 30, 111, 124, 169, 184, 190,
      229, 265
   stadiums, 187
   Super Bowl, 194, 236
   teams, 229
Forevertron, 205
Foti, Steven, 220
Fountain City, 70
Four-wheel drive, 153
Fox, Cathy, 230
Fox, Selena, 132
Fox River, 71
Franciscan Sisters of Perpetual
      Adoration, 255
Frankenstein: The True Story, 102

G
G. Heileman Brewing Company, 212
Galesville, 112–14
Gangsters, 117–19, 243
Garbage disposals, 95, 176

Garden of Eden, 112–14
Garner, John, 103
Gasoline Alley, 171–72, 176
Gavin, Gertrude Hill, 34–35
Gein, Ed, 102, 194, 254
Gengler, Sarah, 258
George Wendt Show, The, 65
Gerber, Nicholas, 203
German immigrants, 30, 202, 210
Gettelman Beer, 211
Gettysburg, Battle of, 111
Ghosts, 91, 154, 216–18, 243
Giant Spider Invasion, The, 102
Gideons, 114
Giffy, George, 167
Gillett, 231
Gleason, 102
Goldmember, 143
Goodrich, Joseph, 241
Graham, Heather, 76
Granato, Tony, 258
Grantsburg, 184
Graves, Carie, 258
Great Lakes, 71–73
Great Lakes Kraut Company, 200, 202
Great Lakes Shipwreck Historical
      Museum, 165
Green Bay, 214
Green Bay Packers. *See* Football (NFL).
Green County, 202–3
Grimes, Burleigh "Ol'
      Stubblebeard," 169
Grottkau, Paul, 53
Groundhog Day, 185–86
Groundhog Day (movie), 186
Gymnastics, 158

H
Hahn, Jerry, 185–86
Haleen, Neil, 258
Hall, Dee J., 220
Hallauer, George, 167
Hamburger, world's largest, 204
Hamm, Morgan, 158
Hamm, Paul, 158
Hammes, John W., 95, 176
Hankscraft Company, 124
Happy Days, 64
Hardwood Range, 52

Harley-Davidson motorcycles, 146, 271
Harley-Davidson Museum, 271
Harvey's Wallbangers, 96
Haunchyville, 213
Haunted houses, 216–18
Hausen, Ernest, 176
Hayward, 101, 156, 166
Heiden, Beth, 219
Heiden, Eric, 219
Heider, Dave and Valerie, 98–100
Heisman, John, 52
Hemings, Sally, 52
Henry, 172
Herschberger, Clarence, 45
Hickok, Lorena, 111
Hideout, The, 243
Hillsboro & North Eastern
    Railroad, 229
Hinshaw, Arnold and Ginger, 216–18
Hirsch, Elroy "Crazylegs," 32–33, 240
Hmong people, 204
Hodag, 130–31
Hogs, wild, 87
Holmes, Fred L., 197
Holy Hill, 25–26
Hoopman, Beau, 258
Horicon Marsh, 71
Horlick, James and William, 95
Houdini, Harry, 109–10, 121, 244
House on the Rock, 140–42
Hubbard, J. S., 180
Huckleby, Harlan, 44
Hudson, 214
Hurley, 119
Hutson, Don, 184

I
Ice Bowl, 144–45, 196
Ice cream sundae birthplace, 121,
    167–68, 202
Ice hockey, 258
Indiana Jones, 267–69
InSinkErator Manufacturing Company,
    95, 176
Inventions, 95, 153, 176, 207–9,
    222, 270
Irish immigrants, 203
Iron Cross Society, 15
Ithaca, New York, 168

J
Jacob Leinenkugel Brewing
    Company, 211
Jacobson, Cory, 274
Janesville, 253
Jansen, Dan, 79
Jefferson, Thomas, 52
Jensen, Scott, 220
Jim Beam Company, 166
Jimmy the Groundhog, 185–86
Joan of Arc chapel, 34–35
Johnson, Julie Krysiak, 242
Johnson, Mark, 258
Johnson-Sirleaf, Ellen, 240
Johnston, Kristen, 143
Jordan, Alex, Jr., 140–42
Jordan, Alex, Sr., 140
Joseph, Frank, 224
Joseph Schlitz Brewing Company, 211
Juneau, Solomon Laurent, 36, 121,
    128–29
Juneautown, 128–29
Justo, Jennie, 199

K
Kaczmarek, Jane, 244
Kaelin, Kato, 45
Kangaroo Panic, 70
Keeler, Leonarde, 176
Keggi, Mara, 258
Kennan, George, 194
Kennedy, Jack (diver), 51
Kenney, George C., 256, 257
Kenosha, 65, 91, 102, 190, 214
Kenosha Maroons, 229
Kenzie, W. D., 91
Kettle Moraine, 70, 154
Kilbourn, Byron, 128–29
Kilbourntown, 128–29
Kindergarten, 15
King, Frank, 171–72, 176
Kinney, Kathy, 76
Knowles, Warren, 229
Kohler Company, 44
Korean War, 255
Kraft, J. L., 150
Kromtovich, Dave, 258
Kuehne, "UFO Bob," 62
Kuenn, Harvey, 96

L

Labor unions, 53–55
LaBuche, Marianne, 132
La Crosse, 12, 212, 214
La Crosse Nursing Home, 154
La Crosse pray-a-thon, 255
Ladwig, Bonnie, 220
La Follette, Robert M., 58, 90, 146
Lake, Kathryn, 230
Lake Geneva, 102
Lake Mills, 49–51, 223
Lakes
  Chippewa, Lake, 72
  Great Lakes, 71–73
  Little Buttes des Morts Lake, 73
  Michigan, Lake, 71, 72, 73
  Pepin, Lake, 8–9
  Poygan Lake, 72
  Rock Lake, 49–51
  Wazee Lake, 73
  West Bay Lake, 216–18
Lambeau, Curly, 30, 190
Lamont, Robert P., 216
Landis, Carole, 206
LaserMonks, 114
Laverne & Shirley, 64–65
Laws, 135, 174–75, 214–15, 229
League of Their Own, A, 132
Legal decisions, 169. *See also* Laws
Legislature, territorial, 91
Leopold, Aldo, 46–47
LeTourneau, Jack, 51
Levenson, Barry, 263–64
Liars' Trail, 70
Liberace, Wladziu Valentino, 38–39
Life with Louie, 66
Lightning strikes, 169
Limburger cheese, 175, 202–3
Lincoln assassination, 91
Little Bohemia Lodge, 117–18
Little Buttes des Morts Lake, 73
Little House in the Big Woods (Wilder),
  8–9, 43, 162
Little House on the Prairie
  (TV series), 8–9
Little White Schoolhouse, 106, 121
Locust Street Festival of Music and
  Art, 173
Logging industry, 245–47

Lombardi, Vince, 144–45, 195–96, 236
Looby, Joseph, 221
Lost Pyramids of Rock Lake, The
  (Joseph), 224
Lumberjacks, 131, 245–47

M

MacArthur, Arthur, 154
MacArthur, Douglas, 56, 257
MacDonald, Stewart, 258
Madison, 65, 190, 191, 199, 214, 261
Madson, Mark "Mad Man of
  Wisconsin," 74–75
Mailman memorial, 213
Major League, 83
Mallon, Jim, 101
Malted milk, 95, 202
Manpower, Inc., 194
Maple syrup, 42–43
Marcus, Ben, 274
Margarine vs. butter, 133–35, 175
Marquette, Jacques, 25, 36
Marquette University, 34–35, 271
Marshfield, 213
Mathews, Eddie, 96
Mazomanie, 232
McArthur, Archibald, 70
McCaffary, John, 36
McCarthy, Eugene, 236
McCarthy, Joseph, 58, 68–69, 194
McCarthy, Peggy, 258
McCartney, Paul, 180–81
McGregor, Duncan, 248
McNally, Johnny "Blood," 190, 265
McSorley, Ernest, 163–64
M-Day, 157
Meet the Applegates, 102
Meir, Golda, 57, 132, 240
Memmel, Chelsie, 158
Mendota, Lake, 122–23
Menomonee River, 72–73
Merrill, 102
Michelsen, Tim, 258
Michigan, Lake, 71, 72, 73
Microbreweries, 212
Milk production, 194
Miller, Dennis, 244
Miller, Frederick, 212
Miller, John, 211

Miller Brewing Company, 188
Miller Park, 187–89, 210
Milquetoast, Casper, 171
Milton, 241
Milwaukee
    Beer Run, 173
    bombings, 249
    breweries, 211
    incorporation of, 129
    labor movement, 53–54
    laws, unusual, 215
    movies filmed in, 101
    movie theaters, 272–74
    pronunciation, 230
    restaurants, 155
    in television shows, 64–65
    water contamination, 271
Milwaukee Art Museum, 271
Milwaukee Badgers, 229
Milwaukee Bears, 107–8
Milwaukee Braves, 15, 96–97, 107–8,
    187, 194
Milwaukee Brewers, 30, 96, 107, 124,
    188–89, 236
Milwaukee Bucks, 151–52, 271
Milwaukee Hawks, 265
Mindwarp, 102
Mineral Point, 203–4
Minocqua, 204
Minute With Stan Hooper, A, 66
Mississippian culture, 223–25
Mitchell, Billy, 56
Mitscher, Marc "Pete," 45
Molitor, Paul, 96
Monster of Phantom Lake, The, 102
Montello, 169
Montgomery, Jim, 158
Monticello, 231
Moore, Gwen, 57
Moorehead, Agnes, 102
Morel mushrooms, 182–83
Mormonism, 16–18
Motorcycles, 146
Mount Horeb Mustard Museum,
    263–64
Movies, 101–3
Movie stars, 143, 206, 250
Movie theaters, 272–74
Mr. and Mrs., 171

Mueller, Eric, 258
Mueller, Peter, 219
Muir, John, 136–39, 162, 240
Mukwonago, 102
Murders, murderers
    Bembenek, Laurie "Bambi," 115–16
    Cheney, Mamah, 93, 146
    Dahmer, Jeffrey, 159–61, 271
    Fassnacht, Robert, 236
    Garner, John, 103
    Gein, Ed, 102, 194, 254
    Juneau, Solomon, 121
Muscoda, 231
Museums
    Circus World Museum, 11
    Great Lakes Shipwreck Historical
        Museum, 165
    Harley-Davidson, 271
    Little White Schoolhouse, 106
    Milwaukee Art Museum, 271
    Mount Horeb Mustard Museum,
        263–64
    National Fresh Water Fishing
        Hall of Fame, 166
    Outagamie Museum, 110
    Squirrel and Chipmunk
        Museum, 103
    Villa Terrace, 194
    Winnebago Mental Health
        Institute, 255
Mushrooms, morels, 182–83
Muskego, 213
Mustard on a Pickle (Levenson), 264

N
Nagurski, Bronko, 184
National Fresh Water Fishing
    Hall of Fame, 166
National Guard, 253
Native Americans
    burial grounds, 190
    fishing rights, 265
    Ho-Chunk people, 45, 255
    legends and lore, 25, 72–73, 98–100,
        131, 154
    Menomonee protection, 194
    traditional foods, 22, 42
    wars, 36, 121
Neal, Robert, 204

Neenah, 102
Nelson, "Baby Face," 117–18
Nelson, Gaylord, 236
Newall Hotel fire, 121
New Berlin, 103, 231
New Glarus, 229
New Glarus Brewing Company, 212
Nitschke, Ray, 169
Nohl, Max, 50
Norquist, John, 271

O

Oconomowoc, 232
"Oh, Wisconsin, Land of My
    Dreams," 120
O'Keeffe, Georgia, 146
Oleo Wars, 133–35, 175
Olympic athletes, 77, 79, 158, 219, 258
O'Malley, Ryan, 52
Omen III: The Final Conflict, 102
"On, Wisconsin!", 179–81, 237–38
Onalaska, 215
Oriental Theater, 272–73
Oscar Mayer Weinermobile, 48
Oshkosh, 102, 241–42
OshKosh B'Gosh clothing, 146
Oshkosh Down Under (Johnson), 242
Otto, Jim, 111
Outagamie Museum, 110
Outboard motors, 222
Owens Brewery, 210

P

Pabst Brewing Company, 211, 212
Pafko, Andy, 255
Pasties, 80–81, 204
Paterno, Joe, 244
Paul Bunyan Meals, 204
Peck, Roseline, 36
Peloquin, Bruce, 221
Pendarvis House Restaurant, 204
Pepin, 8–9
Pepin, Lake, 72
Perry, Julius, 53–55
Peshtigo, 88–90, 121, 248
Peshtigo Fire, 88–90, 121
Petenwell, Lake, 72
Pettit National Ice Center, 77–78
Picket Fences, 66

Pit, The, 102
Place name pronunciations, 230–32
Plainfield, 194
Plank Road Brewery, 212
Platte Mound, 157
Platteville, 157
Plombon, David, 220
Poland (city), 7, 209
Polish immigrants, 203
Political leaders. *See also* Republican
    Party.
    facts about, 70, 91, 124, 132, 154, 255
    Juneau, Solomon, 36, 121, 128–29
    La Follette, Robert M., 58, 90
    McCarthy, Joseph, 58, 68–69, 194
    quiz on, 58
    in timelines, 121, 146
Political scandals, 220–21, 271
Polygraph machine, 176
Pope, John Russell, 34
Port Washington, 65
Potter, John F., 121, 190, 255
Poygan Lake, 72
Prairie du Chien, 36, 232
Prairie du Sac, 67
Pratt, Marvin, 271
Pratt, Morris, 229
Presley, Elvis, 59
Producers, The, 236
Professional Dairy Producers of
    Wisconsin, 148
Prohibition, 190, 210, 243
Proxmire, William, 58
Pryor, Roger, 190
Psychics, 248–49
Psycho, 102, 194
Purdy, W. T., 179–81

Q

Quaker Oats Company, 270
Quizzes
    cheese, 233–34
    cranberries, 13–14
    cultural literacy, 31, 104, 201, 266
    political leaders, 58
    war heroes, 56
    women, famous, 57
Quotes, 24, 63, 120, 162, 197, 244

R

Racine, 95, 202, 215
Racine Legion, 229
Railroads, 121, 174, 229, 271
Rana, Legend of Shadow Lake, 103
Reaume, Charles, 169
Red Cloud, Mitchell, Jr., 255
Redding, Otis, 236
Red River damming, 251–53
Rehnquist, William, 58, 236
Republican Party, 105–6, 121. *See also*
    Political leaders.
Restaurants, 155–56, 204
Rhinelander, 52, 130–31
Richard Bong State Recreation Area,
    242–43, 257
Richard I. Bong Veterans Historical
    Center, 257
Richter, Barry, 258
Richter, Mike, 258
Ringling Brothers Circus, 10–11, 176
Rio, 231
Riots, 236, 238
Ripon, 105–6
Riverwest Beer Run, 173
Roberts, Arthur Price "Doc," 248–49
Robertson, Oscar, 151–52
Robeson, Paul, 229
RoboCop, 206
Rock Elm crater, 36
Rock Lake, 49–51
Rock Lake Research Society, 51
Rocky Horror Picture Show, The, 273
Roosevelt, Eleanor, 111
Roosevelt, Theodore, 146, 198, 227
Rosa, Charles D., 180
Rose Bowl, 91, 271
Rouse Simmons disaster, 146, 236
Rowland, Pleasant, 236
Rowlands, Gena, 132
Roy Chapman Andrews Society,
    267, 269
Rusk, Jeremiah "Uncle Jerry," 54–55

S

Sabathia, CC, 96
Safe House restaurant, 155
Sagal, Bill, 27
St. Croix, 215

Salem, 101
Santiago, Kim, 258
Saturday Night Live, 143
Sauerkraut, 200, 202
Scheer's Lumberjack Show, 247
Scheinfeld, Aaron, 194
Schilling, Robert, 53
Schlitz, Joseph, 211
Schlitz beer, 211
Schrank, John, 198
Schurz, Margarethe, 15
Schwarzenegger, Arnold, 206
Sci-Fi Café, 155
Scott, Leigh, 101
Seadlund, John Henry, 119
Selig, Bud, 188
Sewage disposal, 15
Seymour, 204
Shadow of the Vampire, 103
Shalhoub, Tony, 30
Shannon, Frederick, 165
Sheboygan, 7, 45, 209, 215, 261
Shepard, Gene, 130–31
Shiocton, 200
Shipwrecks, 146, 163–65, 236
Sholes, Christopher Latham, 207–8
Shrine for Anglers, 166
Shrine of Mary, 25–26
Shriners' temple, 75
Sijan, Lance, 265
Silence of the Lambs, The, 194
Sioux Uprising, 121
Sister Bay, 155–56
Skating, 77–79, 219
Skiing, 40–41
Slavery, 52
Smith, Nelva Jean, 111
Smoky's Club, 199
Snowmobiles, 176, 270
Socialist Party, 124
Songs and ballads, 120, 179–81, 237–38
Soubrio, Francois, 25
Soule, S. W., 207–8
Spacecraft, 7, 52, 62, 243
Spahn, Warren, 96
Spark (vehicle), 270
Spies, 154, 190
Spray, Louis, 73
Sprecher, Randal, 212

Sprecher Brewing Company, 212
Spring Green, 93, 140–42, 176
Spy Who Shagged Me, The, 143
Squirrel and Chipmunk Museum, 103
Stanton, Edwin M., 229
Star Is Born, A, 206
Starr, Bart, 145
Statehood, 36
State songs and ballads, 120, 180
State symbols, 19–21
Statue of Liberty, 122–23
Steenbock, Harry, 270
Step by Step, 65
Stevens, John, 121
Stevens Point Brewery, 212
Stoll, Scott, 271
Stone Elephant, 154
Story of Alexander Graham Bell,
    The, 250
Story of My Boyhood and Youth, The
    (Muir), 137, 139, 162
Stoughton, 230
Strang, James Jesse, 16–18
Strickner, George, 25
Summerwind, 216–18
Sun Prairie, 185–86, 215
Super Bowl, 194, 236
Superior, Lake, 71, 72
Suter, Bob, 258
Suter, Gary, 258

T
Tape ball, world's largest, 84
Taylor, Jim, 184
Taylor, Victor, 50
Tegenkamp, Matt, 219
Television shows, 64–66
Television stars, 143, 206
Territory of Wisconsin, 36, 91
Texas Chain Saw Massacre, The, 194
That '70s Show, 66
Theresa, 231
3rd Rock from the Sun, 143
Thomas, Gorman, 184
Thomson, James, 271
Thorsness, Kris, 258
Thurston, "Fuzzy," 124
Timelines, 36, 121, 146, 176, 194,
    236, 271

Times Cinema, 273–74
Timid Soul, The, 171
Tohak, Bob, 209
Tomah, 215, 231
Tomahawk, 231
Tommy Boy, 143
Tornados, 146
Towne, Chari, 258
Tracy, Spencer, 250
Trading Places, 250
Trane, Reuben, 240
Trempealeau, 232
Tripoli Shrine Temple, 75
Truck in the Tree, 74
Trumpeter Meadow cheese, 233
Tunnel Bob, 242
Tunnels, 241–43
Twinkie the Loon, 184
Twin Lakes, 102
Two Rivers, 121, 167–68, 202, 236
Typewriter, 207–8

U
Uecker, Bob, 82–83
UFOs, 52, 62, 209, 243
Underground passages, 241–43
Underground Railroad, 241
Unemployment compensation, 176
University of Wisconsin. *See also*
    Football (college).
    alumni, 206, 240
    cheerleading, 239
    fight song, 179–81, 237–38
    homecomings, 157, 237–38
    Iron Cross Society, 15
    mascot, 27–29
    Statue of Liberty and, 122–23
    traditions, 237–39
    tuition (1900), 240
    tunnel system, 242
Usinger, Debra, 259–60
Usinger's Famous Sausage, 259
USS *Arizona,* 15

V
Valley of the Dolls (Susann), 206
Van Slyke, David O., 112–14
Van Valkenburgh, Franklin, 15
Veeck, Bill, 124

Vietnam War, 265
Villa Terrace, 194
Vineyard, James, 36
Viola, 231
Violent Femmes, 273
Vitamin D, 270
Voree, 16–18

W

Walker, Jonathan, 52
Walleye War, 265
Ward, Walter, 221
WARF, 270
War of 1812, 36
Warped Cast, 274
Washington Island, 213
Watertown, 37
Waukesha, 70
Waupaca, 232
Wausau, 154
Wazee Lake, 73
WDA, 133–35
Weber-Gale, Garrett, 158
Webster, H. T., 171
Weller, Peter, 206
Welles, Orson, 176, 250
Werewolves, 262
West Bay Lake, 216–18
West Salem, 215
White buffalo, 98–100
Whitewater, 229
Whittlesey, Charles, 45
Whole New Ballgame, A, 65
Widen, Larry, 274
Wilcox, Ella Wheeler, 172
Wilder, Gene, 103, 236
Wilder, Laura Ingalls, 8–9, 43, 162
Wildlife, 85–87
Williams, Eleazar, 199
Williams, Zane, 197
Winnebago, Lake, 72
Winnebago Mental Health Institute
        museum, 255
Winneconne, 229
Winter, Elmer, 194
Wisconsin (pronunciation), 230, 232
Wisconsin Alumni Research Foundation
        (WARF), 270

Wisconsin Dairy Business
        Association, 148
Wisconsin Dairymen's Association
        (WDA), 133–35
Wisconsin Dells, 111, 121, 177
Wisconsin River, 71–72
Wisconsin State Capitol, 191–93
Wisconsin Telephone Company, 213
Wisconsin Territory, 36, 91
Wise, Tony, 40–41
Witty, Chris, 79
Wolves, 86–87
Women, famous, 57, 132, 146, 190,
        236, 271
Women's corsets, 146
Women's liberation, 45
Women's rights, 106
Women's suffrage, 132, 176
Worden, Frank, 254
World Dairy Expo, 149
World Series, 194
World's Largest Brat Fest, 261
World War I, 45, 176
World War II, 15, 45, 124, 132, 177,
        178, 253
Wright, Frank Lloyd, 92–94, 140, 146,
        176, 240
Writers, 91

Y

Yanoff, Scott, 240
Young, Richard, 244
Young and the Restless, The, 66
Young Frankenstein, 103
Yount, Robin, 96

Z

Zachow, Otto, 153
Ziegler, Annette, 221
Zimmerman, Joseph, 95
Zoch, Jackie, 258

Contributing Writers

❋ ❋ ❋ ❋

Linda S. Godfrey is the author of the best sellers *Weird Wisconsin, Weird Michigan, Strange Wisconsin, The Beast of Bray Road,* and others. She has been featured on many national TV and radio shows, including *Monsterquest* and *Coast to Coast AM.* Also an artist and illustrator, she hunts monsters and investigates oddities from her home in southeast Wisconsin. Follow her online at twitter.com/lindagodfrey.

J. K. Kelley has a B.A. in history from the "other UW" in Seattle and has contributed to numerous Armchair Reader™ books. He was known as "The Badger" for his combative style in amateur hockey and baseball. Today, he resides in the desiccated sagebrush of eastern Washington with his wife Deb, his parrot Alex, Fabius the Labrador Retriever, and Leonidas the miniature Schnauzer.

Nina Konrad studied Journalism at the University of Wisconsin-Milwaukee and has spent most of her life in Wisconsin. She has white-water rafted on Wolf River, cliff-dived at the Racine Quarry, gone snowmobiling in Door County, swam the Chippewa Flowage in Hayward, rocked out to Pearl Jam at Summerfest, and cheered the Packers in zero-degree weather at legendary Lambeau Field.

Jay Rath is an award-winning humorist who has contributed to *The Onion,* Disney, MTV, National Public Radio, and Dr. Demento. He directed the world premiere of Orson Welles's *Bright Lucifer* and has written and performed in indie film.

Mike Sandrolini is a native of Peru, Illinois, and an award-winning writer, editor, and columnist whose stories have appeared in several Chicago-area newspapers and nationally published magazines. He has either contributed stories to, or has helped edit, six books. Mike is a graduate of Illinois State University.

Sue Sveum is a Madison-area author and freelance writer. A graduate of the University of Wisconsin-Madison, Sue is a Badger through and through. She has visited many nooks and crannies of Wisconsin with her husband, two children, and faithful golden retriever.

Lynda Twardowski is an award-winning writer with more than a dozen books and hundreds of magazine articles under her belt, which is ever tightening thanks to an unbridled addiction to Wisconsin cheese—squeaky and otherwise. Although she is currently a resident of Traverse City, Michigan, she often sails to the Badger State from across the Big Water to abuse her lactose intolerance, enjoy PBR in its hometown, and celebrate the home team, while donning the appropriate cheese-wedge headgear.

Amanda N. Wegner is a writer and editor in Madison, Wisconsin. With the exception of five dreadful months across the Mississippi in Minneapolis, Minnesota, Amanda is a lifelong Wisconsinite who doesn't mind finding out where all the unmarked lanes and back-country roads take her. She's also an ardent fan of cheese, beer, and bratwurst—but only with kraut.

Jennifer Plattner Wilkinson is a writer and teacher, enjoying life in her current home in Wisconsin.

Hope you enjoyed this Armchair Reader™

You'll find the rest of the crop quite exciting.
Please look for these titles wherever books are sold.

The Gigantic Reader • The Last Survivors • The Origins of Everything • The Book of Myths & Misconceptions • Weird, Scary & Unusual • The Colossal Reader • The Book of Incredible Information • The Amazing Book of History • The Extraordinary Book of Lists • Civil War • World War II • Grand Slam Baseball

Coming Attractions
Armchair Reader™ Goes Hollywood
Armchair Reader™ *USA Today* The Best Places to Go

Visit us at *www.armchairreader.com*
to learn all about our other great books from
West Side Publishing, or just to let us know
what your thoughts are about our books.
We love to hear from all our readers.

WEST SIDE PUBLISHING